DEMANDING OUR ATTENTION

DEMANDING OUR ATTENTION

The Hebrew Bible as a Source for Christian Ethics

Emily Arndt

William B. Eerdmans Publishing Company
Grand Rapids, Michigan / Cambridge, U.K.

Published 2011 by
Wm. B. Eerdmans Publishing Co.
2140 Oak Industrial Drive N.E., Grand Rapids, Michigan 49505 /
P.O. Box 163, Cambridge CB3 9PU U.K.

Printed in the United States of America

17 16 15 14 13 12 11   7 6 5 4 3 2 1

Library of Congress Cataloging-in-Publication Data

Arndt, Emily K.
   Demanding our attention: the Hebrew Bible as a source for Christian ethics /
   Emily Arndt.
       p.   cm.
   Originally presented as the author's thesis — University of Notre Dame.
   Includes bibliographical references (p.   ).
   ISBN 978-0-8028-6569-4 (pbk.: alk. paper)
       1. Isaac (Biblical patriarch) — Sacrifice. 2. Bible. O.T. — p Genesis XXII, 1-19 —
   Criticism, interpretation, etc. 3. Ethics in the Bible. 4. Christian ethics.   I. Title.

BS1238.S24A76   2011
222'.1106 — dc22

                                                                        2010040496

www.eerdmans.com

For

Virginia Marguerite
and
Langston Nathaniel

Contents

Emily Arndt: A Tribute, *by Yvonne Sherwood*   ix

Foreword, *by Jean Porter*   xii

Preface   xv

PART I: DEFINING TERRITORY

1. The Hebrew Bible as a (Re)source for Christian Ethics:
   Contemporary Challenges and Approaches   3

2. Critical Distance: The *Akedah* in the Writings
   of Ronald Green   23

3. Religious and Ethical Preconceptions: The *Akedah*
   in the Writings of Philip Quinn and Timothy Jackson   48

PART II: MAKING THE JOURNEY

4. Renewing Acquaintance: Reading the *Akedah* (Again)
   with Kierkegaard, Philip the Chancellor, and the
   Rabbis of *Genesis Rabbah*   79

5. Demands of the Text, Demands of the Other:
   Why (and How) the *Akedah* Matters for Christian Ethics   135

References   191

Index   195

Emily Arndt: A Tribute

This book, like its author, first commanded my attention in 2005. Emily Arndt had contacted me as a fellow "Genesis 22/*akedah*/sacrifice of Isaac"–obsessive and someone who, like her, was actively thinking about ways to read the Hebrew Bible "responsibly" in dialogue with contemporary politics and ethics. She had anticipated that we might have a lot to say to one another, and she was right. That meeting, which went on animatedly for over two hours, proved to be one of the most wonderful first meetings that I have ever had with a fellow academic. I came away thrilled to have met a Christian ethicist with such a deep appreciation for biblical literature and a critical sensitivity to some of the more evasive moves in my discipline and hers. I was encouraged that the ghettoization of disciplines was being perceived as problematic by academics in other rooms on the religious studies/theology corridor, just down the hall, and also a million miles, from mine.

My admiration multiplied when for the first time, on the flight home, I devoured the manuscript that has now (thanks to the work of Arndt's supervisor and friend Jean Porter and her husband Michael Smith) turned into the book you are now holding in your hand. As a self-confessed obsessive with an addiction to the kinds of sources usually excluded from studies that adhere to disciplinary boundaries, I was delighted and surprised by the array of sources that Arndt had assembled. I loved the profitably eclectic conjunction of Kierkegaard, Genesis Rabbah, and Philip the Chancellor — the third being entirely unknown to me until I read Arndt's careful dissection (based, I know, on Jean Porter's extensive work). I greatly appreciated the careful analysis of each work combined with the larger crucial narrative exploring massive conceptual differences in the perceived relationship between ethics and the biblical text. I realized that, like me, Arndt had been profoundly affected by her encounter with rabbinic reasoning. She begins the book, after all, by announcing her faith in the process of "laying texts side by side and reading them together until in the reading a conversation can be discerned" (p. 3). She uses this as the defining structure of her own work, as she puts texts normally insulated from one another in the filing cabinets of different faith traditions, disciplines, and epochs side by side.

In what is, effectively, a history of the relationship between ethics and the Bible (and an explanation of why these disciplines separated), Arndt demonstrates the major modern shift in the relationship between the Bible and ethics. As she shows through her incisive readings of Green, Quinn, and Jackson, modern readers are far more likely to begin with the primacy of ethics and insist that the Bible obey preconceived ethical norms. This renders some texts, like Genesis 22, impossible to read — even, in fact especially, in faith traditions that valorize those texts. What does it mean that religious commitment and religious identity seem to enforce, for the very best of reasons, an occlusion of some of the foundational texts of Christianity and Judaism? It seems that non-reading of the Bible is not simply an accident of increased "secularity" and indifference to religion, as we often say, rehearsing the old truisms. Non-reading is also sometimes enforced, for good reasons — indeed, the best of reasons — at the very heart of "faith." Similar occlusions and repressions take place in biblical studies, the discipline that, ostensibly, is there to study and protect and perpetuate the text. Here Genesis 22 is often explained (away) as a remnant of bad sacrificial habits, originating not in the voice of God (positive) but in cultural influence from the Canaanites (negative). Though Christian ethics and biblical studies have been separate as disciplines, they are markedly similar in this respect.

Arndt's most important contribution is to press, in beautiful and lucid prose, without flinching from lines of questioning that she finds "frightening," the twofold question: What does it mean when Christianity forces the occlusion of key texts in the Bible? and What would it mean to take the text seriously, in ethics, rather than carry out Green's mantra that *"it would be a mistake to focus on the narrative itself"* (p. 29, her emphasis)? Questions that lurk in the back of our consciousness, so that we can continue our disciplinary work unhampered, are kindly forced out into the open. Arndt insists that we need to think explicitly about the calculations and negotiations that take place in modern readings (or non-readings) of our traditional texts. In a remarkable and powerful move, she turns the story of the "sacrifice"/the *akedah* into a parable for modern reading. Our relationship to the text is as ambiguous as Abraham's love for his beloved son. "Loving it, favoring it, recognizing it as 'sacred' (a text loved by us and belonging to God) carries with it the willingness to 'sacrifice' it, 'humiliate' it. Subjecting it to our methods and critical perspectives is the counterpart of allowing the text to emerge in our world with its own value and power" (p. 190).

I love this way of putting things, as I love many aspects of this book. I will go on turning it and turning it and reflecting on its implications for my own work for many years to come. I know that I will not be the only one grateful to those who have ensured that these thoughts and others like them achieve the permanence of print — even if these printed words also inevitably convey a sense of mourning for the other books and articles that she was yet to write. I know I express the thoughts of many, including not least Emily's colleagues at the University of Georgetown, in conveying my appreciation for the quality of the work of this fine career-young academic who had already achieved so much. I have no doubt that her book will inspire and provoke Bible specialists and ethicists for many years to come.

YVONNE SHERWOOD
Professor of Bible, Religion, and Culture
University of Glasgow, Scotland

Foreword

For many centuries now, the Christian churches have almost unanimously agreed that the Hebrew writings comprising the Old Testament are canonical scriptures, mediating the revealed Word of God and therefore authoritative in matters of faith and morals. Yet it has proven difficult to say exactly what it means to take the Old Testament with full seriousness as Christian scripture, providing standards for faith and practice that stand apart from, and in some ways over against, the commitments we bring to the text. Historically, the Old Testament has all too often been read as if it were not only a preparation for the Gospel, but a set of texts whose meaning and value depend without remainder on their status as supposed prophecies and foreshadowings of Christ. Modern critical scholarship, together with a new awareness of the significance of these as shared sacred texts held in common by Jews and Christians, have rendered this kind of supersessionism suspect, even though we do still see it cropping up as an easy way to resolve tensions between Old and New Testaments. It has been largely replaced, however, by a supersessionism of another kind, which subordinates the Old Testament (and often the New Testament as well) to supposedly universal standards of reasonableness and morality. Approached in this way, the Old Testament serves as a source for general religious truths and moral laws that can be extracted from their context and justified in general theoretical terms. Those awkward passages which do not lend themselves to this kind of treatment are ignored or dismissed out of hand.

The difficulty with both these approaches, seen from a theological standpoint, is that they fail to take the status of the Old Testament as revealed text with due seriousness. That is to say, they do not recognize that these writings demand our attention on their own terms, calling on us to engage them in such a way as to take seriously their integrity and their strangeness, and challenging us to allow our own cherished theological and moral certainties to be put into question through that engagement. In this remarkable study in biblical ethics, Dr. Emily Arndt sets forth an alternative approach, focusing on an illustrative analysis of the narrative of Abraham's attempted sacrifice of Isaac in Genesis 22, commonly referred to as the *Akedah* (or "binding"). This text is particularly well suited to Arndt's purpose, precisely because it confronts us with a vision of God and humanity that runs deeply counter to our presuppositions, and for this very reason it has long been a locus for theological and philosophical discussion. In modern times, these discussions have focused on theoretical issues such as the killing of the innocent or the moral status of divine commands, and while these are important, they do not necessarily reflect the central concerns of the text itself.

In contrast, Arndt draws on recent exegetical work and literary theory in order to develop an interpretation of the *Akedah* that attempts to engage the text on its own terms through a process of informed and attentive reading. This interpretation is grounded in a close reading of the Hebrew text, together with a selective reading of the history of its interpretation. She thus brings together two approaches that are often seen as necessarily opposed, namely, the historical-critical exegesis of biblical texts, and theological reflection on those texts. She argues that these approaches do not need to be opposed; on the contrary, adequate theological appropriation of the Bible requires a foundation of serious historical-critical exegesis if we are to enter (as far as possible) into the concerns and perspectives of the text itself. In the process of developing her own reading of this text, Arndt rules out some lines of interpretation, and, more importantly, she uncovers the dynamics of the text as a narrative. On this basis, she then argues that this and similar narratives are centrally important for our moral appropriation of the Hebrew Bible because they challenge us to enter into the dynamics of the narrative itself, in such a way as to be engaged and transformed as a reader and as a discerning moral agent.

This book was originally written as a dissertation at the University of Notre Dame. Emily Arndt intended to revise it for publication, and had entered into conversation with prospective publishers, when she was stricken with breast cancer in the summer of 2007. She died on December 1, 2007, leaving behind her much-loved husband, Michael Smith, her children, Virginia and Langston, her parents, Frances and Murray Arndt, together with many close friends among her former professors, colleagues, and students. Michael and Emily's parents had expressed a wish that her dissertation could be published, and they graciously entrusted me with the tasks of locating and working with a publisher. This volume is the result. Emily would probably have revised and expanded it in the light of her later work, but I do not know what she had in mind, and I have not wanted to try to second-guess her. As it stands, this is a fully formed, sophisticated, and beautifully written book, offering an important contribution to the field of theological ethics. With the exception of minor, mostly stylistic changes, this is Emily's work as she wrote it.

Near the end of her dissertation, Emily writes movingly of her own experiences in writing the dissertation — which for her called for a kind of sacrifice of her own beloved, her own promise, in the form of the scriptural texts themselves. When I read those words a few years ago, I could not have foreseen that Emily herself would be the beloved child, the child of so much promise, whom we would be called on to sacrifice. We have lost an extraordinarily gifted scholar and teacher at the very beginning of her career; her parents have lost their only child, and her husband and young children have lost a beloved wife and mother. She has left to us all the legacy of this remarkable book, a beautifully written and important contribution to the field, and a fitting tribute to a scholarly career that was cut short all too soon.

On behalf of Emily and her family, I would like to thank Jon Pott and his colleagues at Eerdmans Publishing, for their faith in this project and their invaluable assistance in bringing it to completion. Special thanks are due to Katherine Jeffrey, whose painstaking editorial work enabled Emily to speak more clearly and forcefully in her own voice. Thanks also to Lindsey Esbensen, who prepared the indices for this book.

JEAN PORTER

Preface

This project is interdisciplinary as well as theological; it involves, thus, all the complications of terminology that go along with such endeavors. It is a study in Christian ethics and moral theology, but it is not defined by any particular method, approach, or "school" of Christian moral theology. It does, however, reflect my assumption that a Christian ethicist has a call to relate to the biblical text as an important (re)source in her work. I usually refer to the Christian Old Testament and the Jewish TANAK with the academic construction "the Hebrew Bible" unless I am discussing the work of another scholar who chooses a different designation. While the term "Hebrew Bible" is neutral as to religious meaning and avoids questions of the composition of different canons, it has the advantage of designating the text as one shared by many different interpretive communities, including scholars.

Finally there is the question of naming the story that stands at the center of this study: Genesis 22. The story told in this chapter of the Hebrew Bible is referred to by many titles or descriptions. Christians have traditionally spoken of the "sacrifice of Isaac," a description which carries strong interpretive assumptions. In Jewish traditions, the story is usually referred to as the *akedah* (sometimes transliterated *aqedah*), the Hebrew word for "binding," a designation that also carries interpretive weight. It is also frequently described as "the last (or tenth) trial of Abraham," a climactic moment in the larger Abrahamic narrative. I use all of these terms in my own study, often echoing the choices of other interpreters as I discuss them, though I show a preference for *akedah*, a title that for me captures both the strangeness and the provocation of this biblical text.

There are several people without whose guidance and support I could not have completed this project. These include the members of my graduate committee at Notre Dame: Todd Whitmore, who shares and encouraged my interest in literature, literary theory, and ethics; Maura Ryan, who pushed me from the very beginning to find and to speak in my own voice; Timothy Jackson, who has been an important conversation partner both on paper and in person; and Hindy Najman, who, among other things, gave me both the love for and the discipline of reading Hebrew, which in turn deepened my own relationship with the Hebrew Bible. And most importantly, thanks are due to my director, Jean Porter, whose support for this project even before it took firm shape, encouragement to combine concerns I held dear, and guidance — intellectual, practical, and professional — were indispensable. I would also like to thank all those friends and family who made the completion of this project possible, particularly Carla Ingrando and Anne Barnhill. My parents, Murray and Frances Arndt, will be better able than anyone else to see through this work how much I owe to them. On the other hand, I do want to note here my gratitude for their reading and their caring comments throughout the progress of this work. Finally, most of all, I thank my husband, Michael Smith, who also read, commented, and read and commented again, with unfailing patience. I thank him for this but also for his gifts that go far beyond — especially for his demanding love of the written word and his immeasurable love for me and our daughter and son.

PART I

Defining Territory

The Hebrew Bible as a (Re)source for Christian Ethics: Contemporary Challenges and Approaches

My interpretations are no doubt guided by a specific purpose. Yet this purpose assumed form only as I went along, playing as it were with my texts, and for long stretches of my way I have been guided only by the texts themselves.

Mimesis
Erich Auerbach

She might say that he was still harping on that old (yet still barely asked) question of the relationship between the Bible, responsibility, and ethics.

Derrida's Bible
Yvonne Sherwood

וַיְהִי אַחַר הַדְּבָרִים הָאֵלֶּה וְהָאֱלֹהִים נִסָּה אֶת־אַבְרָהָם
And it was after these things God tested Abraham.
Genesis 22:1

There are very few things as exciting as laying texts side by side and reading them together until in the reading a conversation can be discerned. The most ancient interpreters of biblical texts practiced this method, placing, for example, a verse from Genesis beside a verse from the Book of Psalms; they not only found in the intercourse between them worlds of possible meaning, but also detected in these worlds rigorous expectations about how we should be and behave in the world around us. There are scores of wonderful quotations that could be set at the beginning of this volume. The three I have settled on reveal, partly, my own predilections. But each of them — one from Auerbach's scholarly magnum opus on Western literature written in the early 1940s, one from the introduction to a collection of postmodern readings of biblical texts published in 2004, and one from the beginning of a story written, perhaps, almost three thousand years ago — betrays assumptions about the power of reading texts. Auerbach's vast study of Western literature revolved around the intuition (guided by the literature itself) that the great texts human beings write and the readings we make of them are deeply linked to our understanding of the world around us.[1] In the brief epilogue to this massive study, he recognizes the power of these texts not only to represent (and create) perceptions of reality but to guide the reader (in this case Auerbach himself) in his own appreciation of the relationship between literary representation and reality. His theories about that relationship are not merely *applied* to his practice of reading; they develop out of it, from the experiences of reading itself. Sixty years later, Sherwood is imagining leading a "Bible Study with a Différence." She goes on in the same passage to say that reading the Bible "with Derrida" involves

> reanimating those old Kantian and Kierkegaardian anxieties that have been so thoroughly eclipsed by The Battle Between Religion and Science that it's as if this were the only question that the Enlightenment had ever asked. . . . It seemed to her that Derrida was asking, once again, what it might mean to read the Bible *humanly,* as if it mattered, which does not always mean *humanely,* as if God and all the biblical protagonists could be expected to act as members of the bourgeois middle class.[2]

This question, posed by the leader of the "Derrida Bible Study" in Sherwood's scenario — what it might mean to read the Bible "humanly, as if it mattered," and without domesticating it to our own ethical expecta-

---

1. Erich Auerbach, *Mimesis: The Representation of Reality in Western Literature,* trans. Willard R. Trask (Princeton: Princeton University Press, 1953), 556.

2. From the "Introduction" by Yvonne Sherwood, ed., *Derrida's Bible: Reading a Page of Scripture with a Little Help from Derrida* (New York: Palgrave Macmillan, 2004), 6. Here Sherwood intentionally echoes Kierkegaard's use of "human" and "humane"; see her note 14.

tions — is another invitation to appreciate the powerful possibilities of reading. It assumes that the experience of approaching the text in this way would have repercussions in, well, human matters.

Similar assumptions would seem to have been shared by the writers and preservers of Genesis 22, though we do not know who they were or anything much about them. That they wrote and preserved this story suggests that they thought that it mattered. But reading it now, we find ourselves in the situation of Auerbach or Sherwood, of our contemporary worlds and understandings. We read it "after these things," historically, critically, and self-consciously. Unfortunately, those who deal critically and theoretically in human matters — contemporary ethicists — rarely read the biblical text, particularly the Hebrew Bible, "humanly, as if it mattered." Rarely does the contemporary ethicist find herself, in Auerbach's words, "for long stretches . . . guided only by the [biblical] texts themselves." Of course, for many ethicists, such inattention is unimportant; the Hebrew Bible only matters to them as one among many ancient literatures, which may (or may not) evoke insights into the human condition. For ethicists who identify themselves as working within ethical traditions of biblical religions, however, what it might mean to read the Bible as if it mattered, as if reading the text itself might guide our understanding of reality, takes on a significantly different weight.

This, then, is the backdrop for my study, which grapples with the role of the Hebrew Bible in contemporary Christian ethics. To remark that the Hebrew Bible is important for Christian ethics is both to state the obvious and to make a claim fraught with countless complications. Biblical scholars and ethicists have grappled with articulating and overcoming the complexities of accounting for the Hebrew Bible in Christian moral theology in a variety of ways during the last twenty-five years or so.[3] The concerns these scholars have raised and the contributions they have made are wideranging. Unfortunately, much of this methodological work has failed to make a significant impact on contemporary *ethical* scholarship — so much so that the claim that the treatment of the Hebrew Bible in contemporary Christian ethics is problematic is neither surprising nor original. While this sacred text is fundamental to Christian religious and ethical traditions, it often presents a significant stumbling block for moral theologians. A vast array of challenges and pitfalls have been outlined in various ways, some of which will be discussed later in this chapter. In introducing

---

3. There are good bibliographies of this work in all of the volumes discussed below.

my own approach to the subject it may be helpful to mention briefly three forms such challenges take.

The first problem facing contemporary Christian ethicists relates to the interdisciplinary hurdles of working with the Hebrew Bible itself. As a critical discipline, biblical scholarship involves a vast amount of expertise — in ancient languages, in ancient cultures and religions, in a variety of methodologies, contemporary theory, and so forth. Grappling in a scholarly and responsible way with biblical texts is daunting to those who do not have primary training in these fields.[4] While these difficulties confront ethicists who seek to engage the Christian New Testament as well, with the Hebrew Bible they loom much larger. The Hebrew Bible is longer, more ancient, contains an even greater number of diverse perspectives and subjects, as well as significantly more genres and apparent purposes, all of which are subject to various interpretive methods producing what can seem an infinite number of readings. The historical, literary, sociological complexities of this text have become for contemporary ethicists both the reasons and the means to distance themselves and their moral theology from this source.

Secondly, Christian ethical interpreters of the Hebrew Bible are faced in particular ways with the challenges of relating to this sacred text in a pluralistic context. The contemporary ethicist inhabits a world that is self-consciously diverse and considers such diversity valuable — not merely a human condition but also a human good. Negotiating between the Hebrew Bible and other sources of ethical reflection, including perceptions of the world around us, often becomes complicated to the point of (unintentional) repudiation. Added to these challenges is the fact that the Hebrew Bible is a source that Christian ethicists share, more or less, with others, past and present. This fact has a variety of repercussions, the most profound of which faced by the Christian ethicist is her need to eschew the tendency towards supersessionist interpretation, a tendency deeply imbedded in the Christian tradition. Ethical reflection on history and contemporary situations and critical biblical scholarship both de-

---

4. As we will see, biblical scholars have similar challenges in talking about ethics but have been more daring thus far in attempting to try their hands with the language and concerns of that field. Perhaps the expertise needed seems less daunting — no ancient languages, no responsibility to several millennia of various cultures, and an underlying assumption that "ethics" is something everyone can (and must) do. Of course, this project assumes that reading the Hebrew Bible (well) is *also* something Christian ethicists can (and must) do.

mand that we consciously avoid reading the Hebrew Bible through the lens of the New Testament.

Finally, the contemporary ethicist reading the Hebrew Bible is confronted by the problem of relating to an ancient and strange text as a twenty-first-century person. How can a text produced in (and producing) worlds so removed from our own be a crucial source for how we are to act and be now? How can we read it as if it really matters (to us and to our world)?

Such challenges go a long way to explain why many scholars of Christian ethics avoid working with the Hebrew Bible or at least avoid delving into the myriad methodological concerns that go along with doing so. However, this experience of reading and the concerns this experience generates must be granted more prominence in moral theology if the Hebrew Bible is to be maintained as important, even authoritative, for the moral lives of those who hold it to be a sacred text and thus authoritative (in some way) for contemporary Christian ethical scholarship. Otherwise, the text is likely to pass out of critical hands and fall solely into the hands of those who read both it and themselves uncritically; Christian moral theology as a critical endeavor would thus lose a crucial relationship, a crucial source. While biblical reading certainly involves personal and communal engagement and interpretive moments, exegetical work that takes advantage of the contributions of biblical scholars, modern and postmodern, can and should make an important contribution to the ethical appropriation of these texts. But beyond this, Christians *as* Christians have a basic imperative to be attentive readers, rereaders, and retellers of the biblical story. The Christian ethicist must consider what it means to our moral lives to be this kind of reader.

During the last two and a half decades there has been growing scholarly interest in both ethics and the Hebrew Bible. Much of this scholarship is brilliant and courageous, but very little of it has been performed by or even engaged by scholars whose primary field is ethics. One set of contributions comes from those whose background and methods are, for lack of a better description, traditional biblical criticism, both historical and literary.[5] A fine example of this kind of scholarship is found in the work of John Barton, particularly in his recent volume of collected essays, *Understanding Old Testament Ethics: Approaches and Exploration* (2003), and a series of lectures written for a general audience, *Ethics and the Old Testa-*

---

5. The designation "traditional biblical criticism" is not meant to imply either a commendation or a dismissal of certain kinds of approaches to the text.

ment (1998). These two books represent Barton's ongoing interest in ethics and interpretation of the Hebrew Bible. Barton identifies many of the same difficulties in talking about the Old Testament and ethics that have already been mentioned here, remarking on the violence and strangeness of the narratives, pointing out that the texts are bound to specific times and places, that they contain a wide array of ethical positions, perspectives, and inconsistencies, and that they utilize categories for understanding reality that differ from those of contemporary readers.[6] Nonetheless, he argues that what he calls "Old Testament ethics" is a more "coherent system than modern western people are apt to assume." Barton is not claiming a unity, a single "ethic" that is expressed in all texts of the Hebrew Bible, but he does want to suggest that this complex text is more than "just a jumble of isolated precepts with no underlying rationale."[7] While warning against "explaining away" any of the text, Barton believes that even though law codes and more explicit ethical norms are certainly culture-bound, the "social vision" of how to live well expressed more broadly in the biblical texts is helpful today. He argues that many of the evident contradictions within biblical texts fit into this vision — that they are, in fact, "opposite responses to a shared ethical agenda" or framework. And, while this framework is expressed in vocabulary different from our own, the "underlying concerns are not dead," but are, rather, found not only in Jewish traditions but in Western ways of thinking about reality more broadly.[8]

In his work on Old Testament ethics, Barton examines the relationship between natural law and divine commands (positive law) in "Old Testament ethics" and claims that natural law has a pervasive presence in an ethics proceeding from order and reason in the biblical text.[9] He also grapples with questions about the motivations for ethical behavior presented in biblical narrative. In the Hebrew Bible he identifies three kinds of motivations for obeying God's law (whether implicit or explicit, whether posi-

---

6. John Barton, *Ethics and the Old Testament,* The 1997 Diocese of British Columbia John Albert Hall Lectures (Harrisburg: Trinity Press International, 1998), 5-6.

7. Barton, *Ethics,* 18; and his *Understanding Old Testament Ethics: Approaches and Explorations* (Louisville: Westminster John Knox Press, 2003), 46.

8. Barton, *Ethics,* 14.

9. Barton, *Ethics,* Chapter 4: "Divine Commands or Natural Law?" His argument here includes the claim that there is not a distance between these bases of ethics in the biblical text as is usually presumed in both Protestant and Catholic ethics. He also makes the point that one of the results of fixing the biblical canon was to transform the natural law it contained into "revelation" or positive law.

tive law or natural law): looking forward to blessing or punishment; looking back in gratitude and fear to "who you were"; and appealing to encounters with God in the present through obeying God's law.[10] Additionally, Barton provides particular studies of "Old Testaments ethics," both through (ethical) analysis of specific texts such as the prophetic books of Amos, Isaiah, and Daniel,[11] and through discussing specific topics like ecology, sexuality, and property.[12] He also gives some consideration to whether or not virtue ethics is a helpful way of thinking about ethics in the Hebrew Bible. In doing so he argues that looking for an explicit virtue ethic is misleading because "what the Bible thinks about is not moral progress but *conversion*."[13] On the other hand, he argues that the intention of biblical storytellers was not to provide a narrative presentation of moral obligations, but to invite empathetic connection with the characters; in this way the reader learns "from them about the difficulties and merits of living a moral life or the problems of failing to do so."[14]

While strongly commending the study of the Old Testament for ethics, he identifies three significant stumbling blocks for modern readers: that biblical narratives are "often far from morally edifying"; that the "laconic" narrative style found in the Hebrew Bible makes it difficult to decide what is being commended and what deplored; and that describing the moral world of biblical narrative is complicated by questions of intention: does the narrative purport to describe a real world or an imagined one, and, if the latter, are the stories to be taken as normative for the real world or merely as presenting a mythological past?[15] Despite these obstacles, however, Barton claims not only that certain biblical narratives provide nuanced and powerful presentations of what it means to be a moral agent, but also that the writers of these stories realized that human ethical inquiry needs to be

> anchored in specific cases, and that it is only through the richness of storytelling that we come to understanding what it is to be human and to make informed choices in a world which is only partly predictable.[16]

10. Barton, *Ethics*, Chapter 5: "Why Should We Be Moral?"
11. Barton, *Understanding*, Chapters 6, 7, and 8.
12. Barton, *Ethics*, Chapter 3: "Three Ethical Issues."
13. Barton, *Understanding*, 68.
14. Barton, *Understanding*, 72.
15. Barton, *Understanding*, 3.
16. Barton, *Understanding*, 11.

Thus the Hebrew Bible, with its refusal to generalize, its attention to particularities instead of systems, especially in narratives, provides a useful way of reflecting on the moral complexities of the world.[17] Ethical insight comes from the experience of *reading* these narratives (as it does from literature more generally), "*not* from trying to extract a 'message' from it."[18] In his discussions of biblical narratives and ethics, Barton draws heavily on the work of literary scholar and moral philosopher Martha Nussbaum, especially in his emphasis on characters and particulars and on the significant role of past writers as important conversation partners for us. Additionally, Barton is drawn to Nussbaum's work because, while she articulates ways in which ancient stories afford a powerful aid for contemporary ethical reflection, she does not remove ancient texts from their historical moorings. Barton hopes that this way of reading will help "redraw" the lines between traditional historical work and more recent "aesthetic" approaches to biblical texts.

While engaging some of the categories and concerns of contemporary ethical and philosophical study, Barton's way of addressing ethics and the Hebrew Bible is rooted in traditional biblical criticism. One place this is most clearly revealed is in his discussion of the future of Old Testament ethics. Like other historical critics,[19] Barton encourages more descriptive work. He wants other biblical scholars to take up the task of giving a historical account of the ethical beliefs and practices of ancient Israel and, in doing so, to ask sociological questions about whose ethics are being described — avoiding attempts to systematize. He also calls for more work on the ethical vision propounded in Old Testament prophetic texts, acknowledging that this requires attention to what he calls "implicit" ethics versus explicit norms.[20] These suggestions are, to use Barton's own word, descriptive, and seem specifically directed to other practitioners of traditional biblical criticism rather than to scholars grappling with contemporary ethics, though he would claim that this historical work is an important asset for contemporary ethicists. His historical/literary interests shape his view of the text: he explicitly and carefully avoids making any appeal to the Old Testament in terms of its role as scripture for Jews or Christians. He wants to make the case that the Hebrew Bible is "at least" as relevant to ethics as other "great ancient texts" which "survive because they have been found in successive generations to il-

17. Barton, *Ethics,* 18.

18. Barton, *Understanding,* 63.

19. Most specifically Eckart Otto, *Theologische Ethik des Alten Testaments* (Stuttgart: Kohlhammer, 1994).

20. Barton, *Understanding,* 173.

luminate the human condition."[21] The "at least" argument is persuasive in some ways, but it avoids complex and crucial issues surrounding the ethical authority of the biblical texts, and it indicates a defensive posture in critical scholarship's attempt to engage the Hebrew Bible ethically.

Yet Barton's work provides provocative glimpses at ways of engaging the relationship between the Hebrew Bible and contemporary Christian ethics. His biblical scholarship opens up the power of the text, particularly of the narrative and prophetic books, and his ethical interest in narrative draws attention to the experience of reading. Barton occasionally reflects on "how we use or should use the Bible, irrespective of what it may originally have meant." He identifies two ways the Bible is "used" in ethics: first, and most simply, as a source of norms (ethically interpreting narrative is in this case a task of extracting law); and second, and less simply, as a source of ethical edification whereby the experience of story allows readers to imagine moral possibilities. While warning against possible hazards in the second approach, he entertains the possibility that "the biblical text works in some way on what we might call the subconscious mind, helping to shape and train it."[22]

There are several other biblical scholars whose work has made important contributions to the field of ethics and the Hebrew Bible;[23] one recent volume, especially, warrants mention here: Gordon Wenham's *Story as Torah: Reading the Old Testament Ethically* (2000). Wenham envisions his task — the task he calls "reading the Old Testament ethically" — as investigating the "ethical norms and values embodied in the stories of the Old Testament."[24] In this book Wenham adapts the methods of both historical criticism and literary criticism to create a version of rhetorical criticism he applies to the books of Genesis and Judges in order to discover the ethical agendas of the writers of biblical narrative. "What interests us," he writes, "is that stance of the biblical writers to the deeds they describe. Writers, whether of fact or fiction, write with a view to influencing their

---

21. Barton, *Ethics*, 7.

22. Barton, *Understanding*, 73-74.

23. Some important book-length examples are Eckart Otto, *Theologische Ethik*; Cyril Rodd, *Glimpses of a Strange Land: Studies in Old Testament Ethics* (Edinburgh: T&T Clark, 2001); and John Rogerson, *Theory and Practice in Old Testament Ethics,* ed. Daniel Carroll (London: T&T Clark, 2004). In addition, articles and proceedings from several conferences on this topic have been published in recent years.

24. Gordon Wenham, *Story as Torah: Reading the Old Testament Ethically* (Grand Rapids: Baker Academic, 2000), 5.

readers to think or act in a certain way."[25] Like Barton, he acknowledges that there are several challenges faced in reading biblical narrative ethically — particularly in clarifying the ethical perspective of the authors. He observes that those who study Old Testament ethics have tended to stay away from narratives, "except on an *ad hoc* basis to interpret individual stories" and have limited themselves to historical questions only.[26]

Wenham's commitment to historical criticism is set over against what he characterizes as "postmodern approaches to Scripture which stress that the reader creates the meaning."[27] Without historical awareness, he argues, "texts are liable to serious misinterpretation, especially in the realm of ethics."[28] Since his main interest lies in the ethics of the narratives of the Hebrew Bible, he adds to historical-critical methods the insights of literary theory and ethics, drawing on the work of literary critic Wayne Booth, as well as that of Martha Nussbaum. He describes Booth's view of reading as a conversation between reader and text, a conversation dictated by the writer but sustained by the reader who chooses whether or not to keep reading. Participating in this conversation demands that the reader "submit[s] at least partially to the interest and value of the author."[29] Another pertinent insight he draws from Booth about reading narrative (though it does not finally factor into his own argument in significant ways) is that "the images we derive from narrative become part of us, so that it becomes difficult to distinguish who we were before we read from who we have become through reading stories."[30] And again, like John Barton, Wenham is drawn to Nussbaum's emphasis on the concrete and particular ethical responses presented in stories versus general rules or norms.[31] In biblical narrative, he observes, the world is presented as a complex reality. Beyond this, however, Wenham seeks to identify the ethical ideals to which he believes the original or implied author of the narrative is attempting to persuade his first or implied readers to aspire.[32] He pro-

---

25. Wenham, *Story*, 6.

26. Wenham, *Story*, 1.

27. Wenham, *Story*, 1.

28. Wenham, *Story*, 5.

29. Wenham, *Story*, 11.

30. Wenham, *Story*, 12.

31. Wenham, *Story*, 14.

32. Wenham emphasizes the idea of the implied writer and reader of the biblical text, as we cannot know much about the authors and first readers of the Bible beyond what the text itself tells us.

poses, then, to read and analyze biblical books, using the insights of literary criticism to illuminate the relationship between story and ethics, while considering this relationship as it pertained historically — that is, between the written text and its original readers.

After discussing his proposed methodology, Wenham turns his attention to the study of two biblical books, Genesis and Judges. In an attempt to avoid what he identifies as a dominant tendency in Old Testament ethics to see parts of the Bible in isolation, he presents each book as a narrative whole (which means giving ultimate hermeneutical authority to the complete canonical books in preference to the voices within them). His study of Genesis follows the common division of that book into stories of primeval history and stories of the patriarchs. Wenham analyzes structure, key words, themes (particularly that of divine promises), and the setting of the story in the history of Israel. While suggesting that there are "multiple thrusts to the book of Genesis," he also discusses the task of establishing "the main thrust of the book."[33] His study of the book of Judges proceeds in the same way, though the specific words and themes differ. He follows these book studies with a chapter on "Ethical Ideals and Legal Requirements,"[34] in which he continues to argue that readers should respect the "standard [the implied writer] expected his implied readers to bring with them when they read the text," and that they should avoid approaches that "read against the grain," whether they derive from historical-critical (source-critical) dissection of the text or from contemporary prejudices.[35] Wenham again makes the case for studying biblical narrative ethically, proposing that in these narratives an ethical idealism, particularly a "call to imitate God," can be discerned. He ends his study with a look at the way the New Testament uses Old Testament narratives for ethics, identifying in New Testament readings of these texts strong tendencies to supersessionism (though he himself does not use this word). Drawing attention to the work on ethics and the New Testament by Richard Hays, he quotes Hays's dictum: "If irreconcilable tensions exist between the moral vision of the New Testament and that of particular Old Testament texts, the New Testament vision trumps the Old Testament."[36]

33. Wenham, *Story,* 41, 43.

34. Much of this chapter is a reworking of an article published in 1997: "The Gap Between Law and Ethics," *Journal of Jewish Studies* 48 (1997): 17-29.

35. Wenham, *Story,* 75, 77. Here again one sees Wenham's preference for the authority of the final editors of biblical books as the ultimate source of ethical reflection.

36. Richard B. Hays, *The Moral Vision of the New Testament* (Edinburgh: T&T Clark, 1997), 336; quoted by Wenham, *Story,* 147.

Wenham takes issue with this approach but he does so on the grounds that the two Testaments are not "deeply opposed" and that the New Testament does not contradict the Old.[37] Thus, according to Wenham's reading, it is the ultimate ethical harmony of the entire Christian biblical canon that provides the reason that the Hebrew Bible cannot be superseded by the New Testament. "Difficult" texts within that canon, should, according to Wenham, be read as they fit the implied author's (final redactors'?) moral vision as a whole.

By casting the "study of narrative ethics" as "essentially an attempt to elucidate the writer's outlook" (and when accounting for the reader, doing so mostly in terms of the original "implied readers"), Wenham makes "reading Old Testament narrative ethically" a historical project. His contribution is in recognizing narrative as a source for grasping the ethics embodied in this ancient text. His movement from general ideals (like imitation of God) and the "multiple thrusts" of the narrative books he examines to specific ethical issues seems somewhat disconnected. For example, he does not make clear why ancient attitudes towards monogamy and other sexual ethics he discerns in the biblical narrative should have bearing in the contemporary world. He envisions "individual Christians and the Church" as "afflicted by sin and violence" so that they "need the laws and narratives of the Old Testament to remind them of the creator's ideals and how to handle situations which fall short of these ideals."[38] Thus, not only are the perspectives of the Old Testament and New Testament unopposed, but contemporary experience is assumed to be like the experience of those depicted in the Hebrew Bible, whose original situation, according to Wenham, was the occasion for its norms and stories. The relevance of Old Testament narrative for contemporary readers is, in Wenham's view, dependent on commonalities between now and the past and harmony within the biblical text. Finally, Wenham can only claim that reading such stories "may" be a source for contemporary moral life, ethical insight, and hope.[39]

In an important way, however, Christian ethicists have to start from the other side — that is, they have to begin with the acknowledgment that

---

37. Here Wenham reveals his own tendency to smooth away possible ethical contradictions in biblical texts by asserting *ethical* unity — unity within biblical books (Genesis or Judges) or unity between the Hebrew Bible and Christian New Testament. Wenham assumes that the canonical status of the texts means there must be this overarching unity; rather than adopting a supersessionist stance he thus asserts (against Hays) a strong textual consensus.

38. Wenham, *Story*, 154.

39. Wenham, *Story*, 155.

the Hebrew Bible is authoritative in their ethical tradition and then negotiate how this authority functions. While scholarly interest in the Bible and ethics has grown during the last several decades, very little of this work has been done by ethicists, and much of that has focused on the Christian New Testament. An exception is the joint effort of ethicist Larry L. Rasmussen and Old Testament scholar Bruce Birch. In the late 1970s they published *Bible and Ethics in the Christian Life*; they then revised and expanded it in a new edition in the late 1980s.[40] In this book, Birch and Rasmussen attempt to articulate and clarify the complex relationship between the biblical text and contemporary Christian life. Their work can be described as methodological rather than constructive in purpose, though it does present at length a particular way of understanding what the Christian moral life is. In fact, for Birch and Rasmussen, this is the first major part of their endeavor, taking up seven of the ten chapters of the book, after establishing their starting point that "Christian ethics is not a synonym for biblical ethics, yet the Bible is a shaping force for Christian moral life."[41] They argue that it is necessary to "clarify" what Christian ethics and moral life are before asking "how does Scripture address them?"[42] It is outside the scope of these remarks to provide an exposition and analysis of Birch and Rasmussen's picture of Christian ethics, but within their discussion some noteworthy ideas about the Bible are presented. After mapping out "the four dimensions" of the moral life and claiming that these are presented and promoted by the biblical text, they go on to recognize that "the Bible emphasizes some dimensions of the Christian life which our chart does not."[43] Here they go on specifically to discuss the theological dimension of setting the moral life within a theological reality, the "God-story." They emphasize the importance of the Bible as *canon* in Christian ethics and so avoid limiting themselves to the New Testament as is often the case in Christian ethics. They make the point that "the biblical canon canonizes pluralism."[44] "Story" is another important emphasis of their work. Having defined Christian ethics in terms of community and for-

40. Bruce C. Birch and Larry L. Rasmussen, *Bible and Ethics in the Christian Life*, revised and expanded edition (Minneapolis: Augsburg, 1989). Bruce Birch has written several other essays and books about the Hebrew Bible and Christian ethics. I have chosen to discuss this work in particular since it provides a good example of starting from the perspective of Christian ethics, and since in it Birch enlists an ethicist as co-author.

41. Birch and Rasmussen, *Bible and Ethics*, 15.

42. Birch and Rasmussen, *Bible and Ethics*, 16.

43. Birch and Rasmussen, *Bible and Ethics*, 64.

44. Birch and Rasmussen, *Bible and Ethics*, 105.

mation, the authors show how the narrative as a form takes on significance as a way to order human experience and tie together human past, present, and future.[45] To relate to a narrative is particularly formative, because the moral life of the individual takes a narrative shape.

Finally, after a long discussion of the character of Christian ethics, Birch and Rasmussen provide two important chapters dealing with how the Bible is authoritative and how it can be a resource in Christian ethics. While explicitly rejecting the notion that the Bible can be authoritative in contemporary Christian ethics "at the point of making ethical decisions for us" and acknowledging that it is not the only source of insight, Birch and Rasmussen recognize that "Christian ethics . . . is not free to regard the Bible as only one among a myriad of historic and modern cultural factors to be taken into account."[46] It has the authority of "primacy rather than self-sufficiency" as a necessary source of influence in Christian ethics. Quoting James Barr, Birch and Rasmussen argue that authority is a kind of relationship, and part of this relationship is submission to the text.[47] They reject views of this authority which encourage the elevation of any one portion of Scripture "as more inspired" than others — their case in point being the tendency in Christian ethics to regard the New Testament as having preeminence over the Hebrew Bible. In what they call the "collapse of biblical authority," Birch and Rasmussen describe two causes: the development of historical-critical methods in biblical study and the hermeneutics of suspicion (though this is not their terminology) arising from theologies of marginalized peoples.[48] Thus, there needs to be room for "modeling process" as well as appropriating content in Christian ethical understanding of biblical authority. Following this discussion, Birch and Rasmussen offer proposals for "making biblical resources available." Here their perspective shares much in common with my own concerns in this volume:

> Christian ethicists often acknowledge the Bible in chapters on biblical foundations, but its influence is meager within the pages of discussion

---

45. Birch and Rasmussen, *Bible and Ethics,* 105. Here they are specifically discussing what they call the "Jesus-story," a kind of meta-narrative for Christian ethics but one they do not mean to limit to the New Testament; they see the Hebrew Bible as a canonical part of this story.

46. Birch and Rasmussen, *Bible and Ethics,* 141.

47. Birch and Rasmussen, *Bible and Ethics,* 153, 143 (I am paraphrasing their quotation from James Barr, note 3).

48. Birch and Rasmussen, *Bible and Ethics,* 146-7.

that follow. . . . It seems ironic that in a time when critical scholarship has clarified so much in our understanding of the Scriptures that the Bible actually seems less available as a resource for the Christian moral life than in previous generations.[49]

The authors speculate that this might be the case because biblical study is a demanding enterprise — especially for those acclimatized to a culture of immediate gratification and to contemporary ethical situations that would seem to demand urgent resolution.[50] They call for more exegetical work on the part of ethicists, but argue that this task must move beyond description, to asking "how a passage, fully and critically understood, lays its claim on the contemporary community of faith."[51] They seem to be arguing that contemporary Christian ethics and the Bible need to be in conversation, a conversation in which the voices of the biblical text are "fully audible."[52] Yet at the same time (and this seems somewhat contradictory), Birch and Rasmussen acknowledge that "in some instances, our clear understanding of the text becomes a source of problems and impediments to our theological appropriation." Their own language about establishing — "fully" and with "clarity" — what the text means may seem at times overconfident. Nonetheless, the argument for critical scholarship in ethical appropriation is important.

Birch and Rasmussen make two other points towards the end of this volume worth recounting here. First: the idea of canon is a powerful force in the relationship between Bible and ethics. The complex tensions in the biblical canon, with its multitude of voices which must all be accounted for in a Christian ethics, is not unlike the "tensions . . . present in the contemporary ethical situation" that need to be faced as well.[53] This analogy between the experience of relating to the biblical canon and of negotiating contemporary ethical situations will come up again towards the end of this volume. Second: "if the Bible acts to shape basic identity . . . [then] this is not a function which can be left until a moral dilemma presents itself for decision. This use of the Bible requires long-term nurturing of the community of faith."[54] Birch and Rasmussen point to the need for an ongoing

49. Birch and Rasmussen, *Bible and Ethics*, 159.
50. Birch and Rasmussen, *Bible and Ethics*, 159.
51. Birch and Rasmussen, *Bible and Ethics*, 170.
52. Birch and Rasmussen, *Bible and Ethics*, 170.
53. Birch and Rasmussen, *Bible and Ethics*, 176.
54. Birch and Rasmussen, *Bible and Ethics*, 181.

relationship between the Bible and ethics, particularly for those reflecting on ethics for Christian traditions. While limiting themselves to brief considerations of the biblical text itself and displaying considerable naiveté about the complete accessibility of biblical texts to contemporary readers (assuming that critical scholarship ultimately will provide full and clear understanding), Birch and Rasmussen succeed in evoking the missing methodological counterpart to the studies of the Bible and ethics emanating from biblical scholars — the necessary role of the biblical text (and specifically of the Hebrew Bible) in contemporary Christian ethics.

Two other sources of reflection on the relationship between contemporary Christian ethics and reading the Hebrew Bible warrant recognition at this point. The first of these is a group of scholars specifically interested in character ethics in biblically-rooted communities.

With few exceptions, there is a tendency in the work published so far to focus on texts that seem to explicitly address character and community formation — the Wisdom books and the prophets.[55] In recent years such a group has formed within the Society of Biblical Literature of biblical scholars, ethicists, and theologians interested in examining the "*formative*, as well as normative, impact that Scripture qua Scripture makes upon reading communities."[56] A collection of essays arising from this conversation is now published in book form and addresses methodological, exegetical, and practical issues. This appears to be a growing area of scholarly interest — asking how the reading of the Hebrew Bible affects its readers morally (this group shares Birch and Rasmussen's emphasis on community in that relationship). One of the most illuminating essays in the collection is Carol A. Newsom's "Narrative Ethics, Character, and the Prose Tale of Job."[57] Newsom, who is a trained Hebrew Bible scholar, not an ethicist, utilizes the theoretical work of Nussbaum and Booth, which she characterizes as focusing on the role of moral imagination, and draws additional attention to the performative elements of engaging narrative ethics, those that move beyond cognition. Having laid out various ideas about how the reading of a text affects (morally) its reader, she explores the nar-

---

55. The key exceptions to this include attention to complex narratives — narrative that also interested Barton and Wenham; for example: Richard Bowman's "The Complexity of Character and the Ethics of Complexity: The Case of King David." See Brown, *Character and Scripture*, 73-97.

56. William P. Brown, ed., *Character and Scripture: Moral Formation, Community, and Biblical Interpretation* (Grand Rapids: Eerdmans, 2002), xi, xiii.

57. Brown, *Character and Scripture*, 121-34.

rative framework of the book of Job, producing a provocative and disturbing presentation of the possibilities of that experience. The interesting resonances between those who are interested in how character is formed, particularly in religious traditions or communities that claim a scriptural or authoritative role for the Bible, and those interested in reading as a process, as an experience, and/or a relationship between reader and text, is likely to continue to generate important contributions to our understandings of the role of the Hebrew Bible in contemporary Christian ethics.

The other set of scholars making important contributions to ethical reflection in light of the Hebrew Bible are biblical scholars, philosophers, and religious and cultural studies scholars directly engaging the challenges of postmodern critical theory. This chapter began with a quotation from Yvonne Sherwood's introduction to a collection of essays that fits this description, *Derrida's Bible (Reading a Page of Scripture with a Little Help from Derrida)*.[58] In these ventures can be found some of the most extraordinary and exciting readings of the Hebrew Bible. Perhaps the vivid attention typically given in postmodern approaches to the relationship between the reader (here and now) and the text, and the acute awareness of ethical repercussions in this relationship, provide a space where contemporary ethics and this ancient text can be in authentic conversation. Not surprisingly, what tends to be missing from these discussions is consideration of the particular role of the biblical text for Christian ethicists; for their own part, Christian ethicists tend to avoid critical theory almost as assiduously as they avoid critical study of the Hebrew Bible.

While reflecting diverse training and purposes, the work of the various scholars discussed in this chapter shares assumptions about the ethical power of texts "in the reading" of them. And yet, though so much important work has been done on this topic as it relates to the Bible, it remains the case that when the Hebrew Bible is adduced within a work of Christian ethics, it is typically examined (albeit sometimes in a sophisticated manner) for the sake of discovering or supporting a theological or ethical proposition or set of propositions. Although contemporary ethical interpreters do not necessarily limit their consideration to particular law codes or commands contained in the Hebrew Bible, to explicit ethical formulations, or even to expressly ethical texts in Wisdom literature, prophetic books, or complex ethical narratives, they nonetheless continue, by and large, to treat the Hebrew Bible in a somewhat limited, one-dimensional,

---

58. See note 2, above, for publication data.

and often dismissive way. They tend to use the categories determined by their moral and philosophical training as ways to distance themselves from the biblical text and, therefore in effect, to stop themselves from reading well.

These tendencies are especially pronounced in contemporary ethical treatments of a particular biblical text of perennial interest to moral theologians — Genesis 22, the story of the aborted sacrifice of Isaac by his father, Abraham, in accordance with God's commands. This story illuminates in particularly dramatic ways the challenges of reading the Hebrew Bible in contemporary Christian ethics. It presents a host of exegetical issues. It is a text not only shared by several different religious communities but also viewed by each of them as central to their distinct identity: for example, Christian interpretation of this narrative of sacrifice has a long supersessionistic history as prefiguring the Jesus story. It is, however, a story that often strikes contemporary readers not only as disconnected from their own lived experiences and ethical questions but also as profoundly ancient, strange, and violent. For these reasons, and others, this account of God asking Abraham to sacrifice his beloved son has generated, and continues to generate, significant ethical discussion. It provides, thus, a particularly apt locus for wrestling with the challenges of Christian ethical interpretation of the Hebrew Bible, and for addressing methodological considerations.

Several textual characteristics of the *akedah* also make it suitable as a kind of case study. It is generally accepted that verses 1-19 of this chapter form a coherent unit (though 15-18 probably were not part of the original story). The story of this tenth trial of Abraham, while obviously part of a larger narrative about the patriarch, as well as of the whole Hebrew Bible, also has a certain narrative independence: the story has its own beginning and end, its own climax, its own drama and resolution. It simplifies matters that the Hebrew or Masoretic Text of this chapter does not vary greatly from the version in the Greek Septuagint. Although close reading of the text will certainly show that there are many philological, narrative, and compositional issues to consider, this generally straightforward chapter is free of some of the complexities of longer, more fragmented, or textually variant portions of the Bible.

But the most significant appeal of this text for a consideration of the relationship between the Hebrew Bible and Christian ethical inquiry lies in the challenge at the heart of the story itself, in which it appears that the declared requirement of God and the very basic demands of morality conflict. This apparent contradiction is what makes Genesis 22 the subject of continual attention from religious ethicists. Interestingly, this story has generally been avoided by scholars whose primary field is Hebrew Bible but who are secondarily interested in ethics. Most likely this is because, from the perspective of historical criticism, the *akedah* is not a text about "ethics" as such. To be sure, it is not a story about laws, social norms, or everyday behavior. Nor does it offer moral edification in the manner of the great narratives of Joseph or Daniel. Gordon Wenham scarcely mentions the *akedah* in his discussion of the book of Genesis and narrative ethics. When he does, he treats it as a paradigmatic example of biblical sacrifice.[59] Nor is the story typically taken up by scholars interested in character and community formation. On the other hand, in *Derrida's Bible* the story is given central attention in three essays. Perhaps in their willingness to embrace critical reading theory, these postmodern scholars are more ready to negotiate the difficult relationship between this story and the ethical life of a contemporary reader (and/or perhaps they, like Christian ethicists, are natural inheritors of Kierkegaard's famous interest in Genesis 22).

In recounting the methodological problems that arise in discussing ethics and the Hebrew Bible, Robert R. Wilson writes, "perhaps the enormity of the problems will have the unexpected benefit of forcing biblical scholars to cooperate more closely with their colleagues in theology and ethics."[60] This volume intends to offer a mirroring prospect — that the complexity of the problems demands that ethicists work more closely with scholars in biblical studies and other critical disciplines.

What follows, then, is a kind of case study, or perhaps more properly, a journey through the world of ethical readings of the *akedah*/"sacrifice" of Isaac. It begins, in Chapters Two and Three, "at home," exploring contemporary treatments of the text in ethical work, attempting to observe in these actual examples the pitfalls and possibilities of ethical reading of the Hebrew Bible. Then, in Chapter Four, we depart from the contemporary ethical world, moving backwards through time, beginning with *Fear and Trembling*, Søren Kierkegaard's influential meditation on the *akedah*, continuing back to a medieval discussion by Philip the Chancellor, and finally

---

59. Elsewhere, this is how he has shaped his own study of the text: "The Akedah: A Paradigm of Sacrifice," in *Pomegranates and Golden Bells: Studies in Honor of Jacob Milgrom*, ed. David P. Wright, David N. Freedman, and Avi Hurvitz (Winona Lake: Eisenbrauns, 1995), 93-102.

60. Robert R. Wilson, "Sources and Methods in the Study of Ancient Israelite Ethics," *Semeia* 66 (1995): 62.

exploring a selection from the midrash of ancient rabbis in *Genesis Rabbah*. These historical close readings supplement the contemporary discussions, offer interesting interpretive insights, and perhaps most importantly, demonstrate alternative ways of relating to the biblical text through its reading. Finally, the journey returns to the text itself in Chapter Five, as I attempt to see the *akedah* afresh, through my own eyes and through the lenses of my own training, contemporary Christian ethics, and various critical perspectives.

CHAPTER TWO

Critical Distance: The *Akedah* in the Writings of Ronald Green

The examination of contemporary material in this chapter and the chapter that follows focuses on the readings of the *akedah* in the ethical work of Ronald Green, Philip Quinn, and Timothy Jackson. The goal is not to reject the interpretations of these scholars in any comprehensive way. Each embodies a sophisticated attempt to grapple with the challenges raised by the story of Genesis 22; each makes important contributions to the development of a theory that the process of reading the Hebrew Bible is a morally relevant experience. And to varying degrees each contributes to this study by offering specific worthy insights about Genesis 22 and a more general appreciation of the ethical significance of reading sacred texts well. This scholarship warrants attention precisely because it has had a significant influence in the field of Christian ethics and moral philosophy.

However, analysis of the treatment of the Hebrew Bible in the context of the ethical projects of Green, Quinn, and Jackson will demonstrate three different ways that scholars invested in the concerns of Christian ethics, in effect, stop reading — stop attending to the concerns of the biblical text itself. Ethicist and comparative theorist Ronald Green puts a great distance between himself and the narrative of the near-sacrifice of Isaac by situating himself outside the reading process and viewing the Jewish and Christian traditions of interpretation as evidence of a general structure of religious reasoning and as comprehensible without reference to the primary text itself. Philosopher Philip Quinn argues for a better grasp of the tragic dilemma faced by Abraham, but avoids engaging the biblical text directly; moreover, he argues that we must dismiss the "actuality" of the story in order to maintain a sense of God's moral perfection. Christian ethicist Timothy Jackson uses Christian theological categories foreign to the *akedah* and its larger narrative context as his chief interpretive key, conforming the story to his project of presenting and defending a notion of *agape* as the overarching framework of Christian ethics. In addition to demonstrating the fundamental ways ethicists tend to undercut their ability to read the Hebrew Bible attentively, these chapters will show more specifically that treatments of the Hebrew Bible in Christian ethics often lack any significant engagement of biblical exegesis or scholarship, or, if they acknowledge and include these resources to a certain extent, this inclusion does not seem to have any real bearing on their ultimate ethical claims. The examination of these three notable ethical considerations of Genesis 22 will also provide the foundation for a subsequent argument of this volume: that in addition to better engaging exegetical resources, ethicists can offer conclusions that are both more critically cautious and more morally ambitious than has typically been the case. The primary text may place certain limitations on the interpretations of the story — and thus prompt a certain (appropriate) critical caution. At the same time, our prior theological, philosophical, and ethical commitments may limit our ability to read the Hebrew Bible well. This twofold challenge makes a self-critical and self-aware stance all the more crucial as we approach the *akedah* narrative. It is the profoundly problematic and unsettling nature of the story of the near-sacrifice of Isaac that highlights these challenges, and prompts us to reflect on what it means to be an engaged reader of this ancient and alien text. Indeed, it forces us to come back to the *akedah* again and again, reading, rereading, and retelling.

It is especially fitting to begin this journey by examining the work of Ronald Green since the long and complex history of the moral interpretation of Genesis 22 is also a focus of his case study. Green's treatment of the *akedah* is important to this project for several reasons. On the one hand, Green provides a valuable overview of traditional Jewish and Christian interpretations of the story of Isaac's near-sacrifice that provides both a context and a point of departure for my own consideration of similar historical readings in Chapter Four, below. On the other hand, in his treatment of Genesis 22, Green demonstrates a remarkable tendency to distance himself from the primary biblical text, justifying this estrangement through the stated aims of his ethical inquiry; he thus provides an important counterexample to the "engaged" reading that this volume regards as crucial. Finally, Green's scholarship touches ultimately upon the relationship between reading, religion, and moral formation in an important, if oversimplified, way.

Ronald Green's treatment of Genesis 22 was published in its most complete form as part of his book *Religion and Moral Reason: A New Method for Comparative Study.*[1] Green himself is an interesting figure in the field of Christian ethics. He describes himself as a "Jewish Christian ethicist" because, while he comes from a Jewish family and background, he studied, teaches, and writes in the field of moral philosophy and Christian ethics.[2] His Jewish background, as he recounts it, was shaped more by broadly construed cultural and philosophical influences than by religiously devout practice. The Christian part of his self-description derives not only from his academic training and professional associations (he is the only Jewish scholar to have held the position of president of the Society of Christian Ethics and in recent years he has taken a leading role in the founding of the Society of Jewish Ethics), but also from his engagement of many central themes of Christian ethics in his own research. However, it is important to note that much of Green's work argues for a broader kind of religious ethics — for an understanding of religion itself as primarily driven by the rational impulse of human beings to make moral sense of their existence.

This is the impetus behind *Religion and Moral Reason.* Here Green develops a method of comparative study of religions by identifying what he describes as the "deep structure of moral reasoning." His book has two aims, both of which spring from his conviction that religions are primarily (though not merely) animated by a rational drive to make sense of nonrational and seemingly antirational aspects of human existence. In an earlier book, *Religious Reason: The Rational and Moral Basis of Religious Belief* (1978), Green introduced his paradigm of a process he calls religious reasoning, using it to explain central beliefs and practices of many major world religions. In *Religion and Moral Reason,* he attempts to show that this structure of moral reasoning can be identified in widely diverse religious beliefs and practices, including traditional African religions, the historical ethical monotheism of China, traditional Judaism, and Christianity. More generally, it seems that Green is attempting to make the case that there exists, at least at the structural level, a common religious ethics. His

---

1. Ronald Green, *Religion and Moral Reason: A New Method for Comparative Study* (New York: Oxford University Press, 1988).

2. For this self-description and the biographical material to follow, see the beginning of Ronald Green's essay "Christian Ethics: A Jewish Perspective," in *The Cambridge Companion to Christian Ethics,* ed. Robin Gill (Cambridge: Cambridge University Press, 2001), 138-53.

intended audience is comprised principally of two groups: students and scholars of comparative religion who he believes have overlooked the universal "deep structure of moral reasoning," and moral philosophers whom he characterizes as often ignoring or rejecting the "rationality" of religious reasoning.[3]

The deep structure of religious moral reasoning that Green identifies has three elements, each progressively more morally sophisticated. The first is the establishment and encouragement of what Green simply calls the "moral point of view," the development of a sense of impartiality and of social mores that enable a commitment to something transcending one's own needs. The second is the justification or rationale for the moral point of view, particularly when it may come into conflict with one's own needs. This is the purpose, Green argues, that concepts of retribution and reward play in religious traditions. When the two dimensions of rationality — morality, which is outwardly directed, and prudence, which is self-directed (as Green has defined them) — come into conflict with each other, religion steps in as "human reason's effort to resolve its own internal dispute and to make possible coherent rational choice."[4] The third element of the structure of moral reason comes into play when the second (and in turn the first) seems to break down under the pressure exerted when human beings are confronted with the sometimes radical demands of morality. Green argues that religious reasoning must facilitate moral commitment by preventing us from being paralyzed by such situations. Thus in any given set of religious beliefs we will find that the ultimate judgment of our worth is not constrained by the standard by which we must judge ourselves. Since such a conviction makes moral reasoning possible, the belief in a "higher reality 'beyond morality' serves to fulfill and complete, not undermine, moral striving" and is ultimately rational itself.[5] Through identifying this three-part structure of religious moral reasoning, Green believes he can demonstrate that religious thinking is coherent and rational and that "religions are morally inclined at their deepest levels."[6]

Demonstration of this conviction is the main project of *Religion and Moral Reason,* and it is as evidence of this claim that Green's treatment of Genesis 22 appears. Two chapters of *Religion and Moral Reason* are devoted

---

3. Green makes explicit these audiences in the conclusion of *Religion and Moral Reason,* 228. He also refers generally to "students of religion."

4. Green, *Religion and Moral Reason,* 15.

5. Green, *Religion and Moral Reason,* 21.

6. Green, *Religion and Moral Reason,* 23.

to a history of interpretation of Genesis 22, in which Green identifies the "deep structure of moral reasoning" in traditional Judaism and in Christianity. While analyzing the overall success or failure of Ronald Green's larger argument is not the task of this book, his general view of the nature of religious moral reasoning has at least three consequences relevant to this project. First, it is clear that, for Green, a text considered by a particular religion to be sacred is not significantly different from any other religious or ethically oriented text. Green acknowledges, as we will see in his discussion of Genesis 22, that such a text might be regarded as unique by a particular religious group. However, the way such texts function morally can be understood in a general sense to be not very different from the way, for example, the recitation of epic poetry functions. Green argues that such narratives (religious stories or epic poetry or even a John Wayne film) can be understood as appealing to our "deepest moral yearnings."[7] Thus, Green can justify concentrating on shared mythological and moral patterns in the stories of religious founders or other religious literature without acknowledging the complex issues surrounding what it may mean in a particular religious context to designate a text as sacred, or how such a designation may influence the moral life of its readers.

Second, Green makes some rather broad or general claims about the interpretation of Genesis 22 in both Jewish and Christian thought — arguably oversimplifying these complex religious traditions. This tendency is apparent in two central features of these chapters: his claim that the Jewish and Christian faiths are both "essentially divine command traditions," and his restriction of his analysis of the respective traditions to a selection of (typically pre-modern) sources. In characterizing both religions as "essentially divine command traditions" in which any other way of understanding the world ethically is "dwarfed by the authority and importance of revelation,"[8] Green provides no adequate explanation of what he means by "revelation" or what each tradition understands the term to imply, though it seems he is applying the concept of revelation exclusively to the biblical text or, even more specifically, to moral laws contained within the biblical text. To be fair, Green clearly assumes a more sophisticated and complex understanding of "divine command tradition" than is usually indicated by this label; after all, such traditions must be primarily motivated by moral rationality in order to fit the overall criteria of his project. However, with-

7. Green, *Religion and Moral Reason*, 195.
8. Green, *Religion and Moral Reason*, 78.

out including any meaningful definition of revelation, the characterization seems too vague to be theoretically useful. With respect to sources, Green draws his characterization of Jewish and Christian understanding of the binding/sacrifice of Isaac story from a rather small sample. In describing "the Jewish view" of this story, Green depends almost exclusively on a selection of ancient rabbinic commentaries, justifying this decision with the blanket designation of "traditional" Judaism. While this might not be problematic in itself, in the context of Green's project, this delimitation creates two major problems. He presumes an agreement and consistency of purpose among these ancient commentaries that he fails to prove exists. Green goes so far as to state that "where the understanding of Genesis 22 is concerned . . . Jewish thinkers over the ages speak with almost one voice on the central religious and ethical meaning of this text."[9] Then he goes on to compare this "traditional Jewish" understanding of Genesis 22 to a generalized "Christian view" that, while it includes a broader historical survey of commentaries, culminates in and is most significantly identified with Søren Kierkegaard's nineteenth-century interpretation in *Fear and Trembling*. However interesting and fruitful the dialogue he constructs, his equation of Judaism with a selective and collapsed reading of ancient commentaries on Genesis 22 and Christianity with his own interpretation of Kierkegaardian thought is obviously problematic. Both larger religious traditions are simplified in order to make them manageable subjects for a comparative study, and much of their religious and moral vitality is neglected in the process.

The third and final consequence of Green's treatment of Genesis 22 that needs to be acknowledged is that, though he makes certain claims about the biblical text itself, he relies completely for evidence to support those claims on historical interpretations of the *akedah*. He offers no exegesis of his own, and all the commentaries he relies upon (Jewish and Christian) predate modern historical and literary criticism; he thus fails to justify interpretation of the biblical text that both he and most contemporary scholars of religion take for granted.[10] Green defends his focus on traditional sources, arguing that the opinions of more recent biblical scholars regarding the meaning of the original text vary too widely. He also, even

9. Green, *Religion and Moral Reason*, 86.

10. Green does provide a slightly more careful look at the biblical text (occasionally comparing Genesis 22 to what the commentaries claim about it) in an earlier article "Abraham, Isaac, and the Jewish Tradition: An Ethical Reappraisal," *Journal of Religious Ethics* 10 (1982): 1-21.

more fundamentally, argues that *it would be a mistake to focus on the narrative itself*:

> Whatever the original meaning, I believe it is a mistake in trying to come to terms with the rational and moral intentionality of a religious tradition to focus primarily on early narratives of this sort. Even a tradition as powerfully shaped by moral concerns as biblical faith contains within its earliest strata isolated texts or teachings that defy rational or moral explanation. In seeking to understand a tradition, therefore, the meaning of this earliest material is far less important than what is subsequently done with it. A tradition reveals its deepest impulses not in single texts, but in the ongoing ways these texts are interpreted and handled.[11]

While Green's claims about the importance of examining the ways a tradition understands a narrative like the *akedah* are well-justified, neglect of the text itself hinders our ability to appreciate the historical commentaries and exegesis,[12] which depend upon a deep familiarity with the text, and prevents us from acknowledging the limits the primary text itself puts on any interpretation of it — limits which might not be recognized in every individual commentary but which remain part of a vital biblical tradition. Furthermore, to dismiss the importance of the range of "opinions of biblical scholars" is to risk being naively unaware of how our own interpretations of such a narrative are actually shaped by these opinions. In thus making a historical object of the "ongoing" ways pre-modern commentators struggled with a difficult text, we disconnect these interpretations from our own religious-ethical explorations.

It is noteworthy that Green describes the primary text as sometimes defying rational or moral explanations. In the case of Genesis 22 such a perception has certainly affected the way the text has been interpreted by some readers throughout its history. Green's own approach to the story of the binding/sacrifice of Isaac is shaped by his view of "Revelation and Reason in Biblical Faith," his title for his chapters on Traditional Judaism and on Christianity — and consistent with his failure to consider what it means to designate a text as sacred and how revelation is understood by vi-

---

11. Green, *Religion and Moral Reason*, 83.

12. For a forceful argument that study of the text is necessary for understanding the (ancient) commentaries on it see James Kugel, *In Potiphar's House: The Interpretive Life of Biblical Texts* (Cambridge, MA: Harvard University Press, 1990).

tal and diverse religious and moral traditions. In his overall objective of establishing the existence of a general religious moral reasoning, Green assumes a posture of critical detachment from the text, setting himself outside the traditions of interpretation he is presenting.

I have argued that one of the reasons the *akedah* is a worthwhile subject for an investigation of the Hebrew Bible in Christian ethical inquiry is that it is one of the paradigmatic presentations of apparent possible contradiction between religious faith and rational ethics. Green, likewise, turns to Jewish and Christian interpretations of the *akedah* in *Religion and Moral Reason* because it is the "hard case" against which to test his theory about the deep structure of moral reasoning being the primary drive behind religious traditions. Since he identifies both Judaism and Christianity as essentially divine command traditions he is concerned that, as such, they might be viewed as challenging his claim that "religion finds its human basis in moral reasoning" because they appear to subordinate human reason to God's command. However, he goes on to argue that such a commitment to the primacy of revealed morality is actually the "natural outcome" of the moral reasoning process as he has identified it.[13] Green believes that people are able to adjudicate the conflict between the outwardly focused claims of morality and the inwardly focused needs and desires of the individual by attributing moral norms and ethical codes to a god whose authority and moral position are outside those of any individual human being's. Such an understanding of how God's authority functions must presume, as Green notes, that God's will itself is moral and rational.

It is with this view of the relationship between moral rationality and divine command ethics that Green commences his examination of Genesis 22:

> Here is the divine command at its starkest, requiring the slaughter of an innocent child. . . . Genesis 22 is at the heart of biblical religion. Abraham's willingness to sacrifice his son on Mount Moriah is not only frequently commented on by Jewish and Christian writers, but it is consistently regarded as the archetypical expression of faith. Genesis 22, therefore, is the hard case against which any claim that revealed religion has an essentially rational basis must be measured.[14]

13. Green, *Religion and Moral Reason*, 78-79.
14. Green, *Religion and Moral Reason*, 83.

Green therefore proposes to examine within these religious traditions' interpretations of the narrative the content and nature of God's command itself. If, in these interpretations, God's command is understood as anti-rational or anti-moral, this would afford damaging counter-evidence to Green's claims about the deep structure of religious moral reasoning. However, if the content of God's command is understood to be morally justifiable, then, according to Green, the "gap between reason and revelation disappears."[15]

Green structures his first chapter on this "hard case" as a compilation of traditional Jewish midrash drawn specifically to show that what he describes as the Jewish point of view is utterly opposed to any non-rational and non-moral reading of the story. Green compares Jewish interpretations to his reading of Kierkegaard's *Fear and Trembling*, which he takes to be the most prevalent contemporary (Christian) understanding of the text. "It is this uncompromising, antirational interpretation of Genesis 22 that has shaped our modern approach to the biblical text itself."[16] In structuring his argument this way, with Kierkegaard as a foil, he hopes to show that traditional Judaism, specifically traditional Jewish understanding of this "hard case" of biblical narrative, exhibits his deep structure of moral reasoning.

Green identifies several key elements in Jewish commentary on the *akedah* that he believes exhibit strong agreement about the religious and ethical meaning of the text (and which oppose the "anti-rational" assumptions of Kierkegaard's reading as he presents it here). Concerning the drastic nature of God's trial of Abraham, Green argues that the "Jewish position here is almost unvarying" in that the purpose of such trials is understood not to show something about the tested one to God but to demonstrate (or re-demonstrate) his or her righteousness to the rest of the world.[17] Such a trial is therefore not cruel or arbitrary but has an important and rationally explainable moral purpose. In addition, Green maintains that the content of the trial is not as ethically inconceivable to the rabbis as it is in the Kierkegaardian reading, which presupposes that Abraham's most fundamental ethical obligation is to the well-being of his son. Rather, Green notes that the traditional commentaries give "ongoing testi-

---

15. Green, *Religion and Moral Reason*, 84.

16. Green, *Religion and Moral Reason*, 86. An earlier version of this chapter appeared as "Abraham, Isaac, and the Jewish Tradition."

17. Green, *Religion and Moral Reason*, 87-88.

mony to the moral limits of natural relationships" and that this trial and the earlier command that Abraham leave his father and his homeland (Genesis 12:1-3) "symbolize the transcendence of God's moral will over the most important natural relationships."[18]

Another element of the traditional Jewish interpretations examined by Green is the question of Isaac's own participation in carrying out God's command. He notes that both the biblical and rabbinic writers view children as legal, physical, and emotional extensions of their father rather than independent (or equivalent) centers of moral obligation. In addition to this general presumption of the lack of moral distance between parents and children, Green draws our attention to ancient rabbinic discussions of God saying to Abraham, after the events of this narrative, that now it is known that he wouldn't have even withheld his own life if it had been asked of him. Green argues that this shows that the command to sacrifice one's son is equivalent to a form of self-sacrifice.[19] Another set of rabbinic strategies to make this story more morally rational that Green brings to our attention takes a very different tack regarding Isaac's role in the sacrifice. Instead of claiming that the child is an extension of his father and thereby absolving God of having commanded Abraham to do something immoral to another person, some commentators assert that Isaac is a full participant in the sacrifice. They understand the use of the Hebrew word that means "lad" or young man to indicate that Isaac is not a small child but rather a man of as much as thirty-six years of age whose participation must have been voluntary. The repeated use of the word "together" in the narrative is taken to support this interpretation.[20] Both of these ways of describing Isaac's role in the sacrifice do appear to be attempts to minimize or even remove any problematic moral content from God's command to Abraham to sacrifice his son. On the other hand, Green does not address the fact that these are fundamentally contradictory claims (Isaac is Abraham's child and thus merely an extension of himself; Isaac is a young man who knowingly and voluntarily participates in sacrificing himself) that exist together within authoritative Jewish interpretation. It is worth asking whether their coexistence might require nuancing of Green's claims about the nature of the moral reasoning of this biblical religious tradition.

The other elements of Jewish commentary on the *akedah* that Green

18. Green, *Religion and Moral Reason*, 89.
19. Green, *Religion and Moral Reason*, 91-92.
20. Green, *Religion and Moral Reason*, 92.

explores include Abraham's evasion of Isaac's question about the whereabouts of the animal for the sacrifice, the issue of death and resurrection, the establishment of proper sacrifice, and the blessing of future generations through Abraham's obedience. The first of these topics, Abraham's silence, is important for Green's purposes because of the use Kierkegaard makes of this episode in what Green continues to refer to as an anti-rational and non-moral reading of the story. For Kierkegaard, Abraham must be silent (or evasive) because there is no intelligible answer he can give to his son when he is asked where the ram is for the sacrifice. Green notes that the rabbinic commentaries do not comment on this so he draws instead on the writings of Philo of Alexandria. However, while Philo does comment on Abraham's so-called silence, he is referring not to the patriarch's avoidance of his son's question about the ram but rather to the private way in which Abraham goes about obeying God's command — failing to announce his intentions, taking only two servants, and leaving them behind when the sacrificial site is reached. According to Philo, this behavior shows that Abraham is not seeking praise from any witnesses for his absolute obedience in doing such a difficult thing. Green then concludes that

> Clearly, Philo does not present here an antimoral interpretation of Abraham's solitary silence. His point is not that Abraham is silent because of the ethically unjustifiable nature of his act, but rather that this silence proves the absolute purity of Abraham's intention.[21]

Since the "silence" discussed by Kierkegaard and the "silence" discussed by Philo are two different things, it seems unclear how Green's use of Philo answers the particular challenge to a morally rational reading of Abraham's evasion of Isaac's question. It is also worth noting that in Green's presentation of Philo, the silent way Abraham fulfills God's command seems at odds with the argument that God tries Abraham in order to demonstrate or make known his righteousness. Again, such variations and even apparent contradictions in interpretation within "traditional Judaism" are ignored in Green's exposition.

When Green turns his attention to interpretation of the moment when God stops Abraham from sacrificing Isaac and the ram is substituted, his examination of traditional Judaism becomes even more superficial and he continues to ignore the significance for his project of the exis-

21. Green, *Religion and Moral Reason*, 95.

tence of divergent interpretations. In this case, the dissimilarities lie in the fact that on one hand some rabbinic commentators are "troubled . . . no less than the modern reader" by the real possibility that Isaac might die.[22] And yet other commentators "repeatedly affirm, for example, that from the outset God had no intention of asking the sacrifice of Isaac and was always prepared to provide the ram in his place."[23] Aside from this persistent problematic neglect of such variety and difference within a tradition Green defines as univocal from the outset, his discussions of death, resurrection, and sacrifice do very little work in furthering his thesis. His claim regarding God's staying of Abraham's hand is that the doctrine of resurrection is tied to the third facet of his deep structure of religious reasoning in that it "affirms that present suffering is not the ultimate fate of the just."[24] However, he gives very little attention to the complications, and perhaps even the inappropriateness, of equating this episode with such a doctrine.[25] Green's discussion of the substitution of the ram is very brief; the commentaries he treats here do most of the work in supporting his claim that these traditional writings were motivated by a desire to read the *akedah* as a thoroughly rational and moral story. These include the rabbinic speculation that the ram was ownerless, thus absolving Abraham of stealing someone else's property, and a midrash in which the ram volunteers itself for the sacrifice. These rabbinic elaborations on Genesis 22 are clearly interpretive attempts to "ensure that an ethically intentioned narrative not be blemished in any way."[26]

Green finally turns to portrayal of the relationship of this event to the future blessings of God's people. He argues that in traditional Judaism, at least as much attention was given to the outcome of this narrative — the blessings of future generations — as was given the difficult and painful events themselves. Abraham's (and Isaac's) sacrifice functions as a "vicari-

22. Green, *Religion and Moral Reason*, 96.

23. Green, *Religion and Moral Reason*, 98.

24. Green, *Religion and Moral Reason*, 97.

25. He refers us only to Shalom Spiegel's *The Last Trial*, which asks whether speculation about whether or not Isaac actually dies under the sacrificial knife and then has his life returned when God calls off the trial precedes Christian thought or is influenced by it. See Green, *Religion and Moral Reason*, 96. An important study of biblical stories of son-sacrifice is Jon Levenson's *Death and Resurrection of the Beloved Son: The Transformation of Child Sacrifice in Judaism and Christianity* (New Haven: Yale University Press, 1993). See Chapter 5 for an extended discussion of this work.

26. Green, *Religion and Moral Reason*, 97.

ous sacrifice for future generations" thus making this primarily a narrative about the forgiveness of sin.[27] It is this theme in the rabbinic interpretations of the *akedah* that Green claims most powerfully illustrates the deep structure of moral reasoning in this religious tradition, specifically the third element of that structure — God's willingness to overturn or somehow go beyond God's own established moral order so that human beings do not despair, "to make possible human moral renewal."[28] That is, such interpretations of the blessings of future generations through Abraham at the end of this trial function for Green (and, according to him, for traditional Judaism) to make of this narrative a completely moral and rational tale, and the God of Abraham a completely moral and rational God (in our terms). Perhaps what is most noteworthy in this presentation of the theme of blessings is Green's claim that traditional sources (in this case liturgical ones) make an analogy between God's transcendence of God's own established moral order by saving Isaac after commanding his sacrifice and Abraham's resistance of the impulse to remind God of his previous promises (to provide him numerous descendants through Isaac and to bless future generations through him) when the command is first given.[29] While this analogy between divine and human behavior, as Green describes it, is provocative, it remains unclear how such a comparison supports the idea that the content of the command to sacrifice Isaac is morally reasonable.

In the course of presenting these interpretations of Genesis 22 as evidence that traditional Judaism is a religious faith fundamentally driven by moral rationality, Green seems to strip them of much of their distinctive richness, and to gloss over the challenges to what is usually considered reasonable in the commentaries as well as in the narrative itself. While he shows to some extent the "ways rational and moral considerations mold a tradition ostensibly based on revelation and the divine command,"[30] he

27. Green, *Religion and Moral Reason*, 99.

28. Green, *Religion and Moral Reason*, 101. While Green notices rabbinic attention to the end of Genesis 22 and sees it as supporting his third element of religious reason, he forgoes any discussion of the midrash about Sarah's death in Genesis 23, which does not leave this story with such a "just and reasonable" ending. For a more comprehensive discussion of Sarah's role in the ancient commentaries on this story see Yvonne Sherwood's "Binding-Unbinding: Divided Responses of Judaism, Christianity, and Islam to the 'Sacrifice' of Abraham's Beloved Son," *Journal of the American Academy of Religion* 72 (2004): 821-61. For specific discussion of Sarah in *Genesis Rabbah*, see below, Chapter 4.

29. Green, *Religion and Moral Reason*, 100.

30. Green, *Religion and Moral Reason*, 101.

fails to recognize important and ethically relevant complexities in the text he has chosen and its interpretive tradition. The first and most fundamental problem with Green's use of pre-modern sources on Genesis 22 as evidence to support his claims about religious reasoning is that he neglects to address the issue of genre, the ways these sources — ancient rabbinic midrash, liturgical texts, and other Jewish commentaries — read and present their material, and the way they are themselves understood and read in the religious tradition to which they belong. Green avoids dealing with the character and authoritative status of the Midrash (and other textual sources) he uses to illustrate what he calls "traditional Judaism." But surely all of these issues would seem to be relevant to the way they show forth "the rational and moral considerations that mold a tradition." For example, *Genesis Rabbah* is a closed and authoritative body of writings that understands itself and Judaism in particular ways and is studied within its traditions in particular ways (not as just another text). It is written in a distinctive style[31] and the manner in which it is traditionally read and studied is similarly distinctive. In both cases this reflects a certain understanding of the status, content, and centrality of the biblical text.

Another related problem with Green's treatment of these traditional interpretations is his claim that they are basically univocal. Even among the excerpts selected by Green himself, there are significant differences in the strategies used to interpret problematic aspects of the *akedah* narrative. It is possible that such differences do not necessarily upset Green's purpose of showing that these commentators have moral and rational intentions, but the diversity of ways in which the commentaries embody such intentions is itself at least as important as the possibly common goals they have in doing so.[32] Together, these two aspects of Green's examination of interpretation of Genesis 22 in traditional Judaism — neglect of the religious and moral role and status of the commentaries which he

---

31. Though I think it is important to acknowledge the particular character of *Genesis Rabbah*, for instance, it is equally important to be skeptical of attempts to define or characterize the "hermeneutics of midrash," and so forth, as such characterizations usually lead to other forms of oversimplification of these texts. For discussion of this issue, see David Stern, *Midrash and Theory: Ancient Jewish Exegesis and Contemporary Literary Theory*, in the Rethinking Theory Series (Evanston: Northwestern University Press, 1996), Chapter 1: "Midrash and Hermeneutics."

32. For an analysis that reveals richer, more diverse, and potentially critical possibilities in ancient Jewish interpretations of Genesis 22, see Yvonne Sherwood's "Binding-Unbinding."

draws from, and underestimation of the diversity within these sources — would seem to deplete both the religious tradition and the sacred narrative of much of their vitality, complexity, and profundity. Traditional Judaism becomes merely the subject of a historical comparative project, with the *akedah* appearing as the textual artifact (once removed) of a historical religion.

Green concludes this chapter in the following way:

> Perhaps the most astonishing piece of evidence for Judaism's commitment to reason and morality is the fact that although Genesis 22 was interpreted in many ways within this tradition, the text itself was never conceived to present a moral problem but was always regarded as one of the most important biblical illustrations of God's righteousness.[33]

Here he finally acknowledges the diversity within the tradition that he has glossed over throughout the chapter. His point is that traditional Judaism presupposes that moral reason and revelation agree and thus the interpreters of this "hard case" narrative never question the moral content of God's command to Abraham and the justification of subsequent events of the story. While this supposition about God is often fundamental to Jewish or Christian religious ethics, by ignoring the issues surrounding the character and authority of rabbinic midrash, the style in which it was written and the way in which it is studied, Green misses the point that it may be precisely *because* this narrative is evidently challenging to moral reason that it is such an important occasion for ongoing study and argument in biblical religions.

Having devoted a chapter to exploring traditional Judaism, Green turns to Christian interpretations of Genesis 22. He describes a broader diversity of opinion in Christian commentary regarding the relationship between revelation and moral reason, but ultimately finds that these interpretations of the story of the near-sacrifice of Isaac support his thesis of the existence of a deep structure of moral reasoning driving religious traditions and theological speculation. In this chapter Green organizes the commentaries he discusses historically rather than thematically, and, in this broader historical overview, he is more willing to acknowledge that "we have to locate and understand treatments of Genesis 22 within the

---

33. Green, *Religion and Moral Reason*, 102.

context of the discussions where they occur"[34] than was evident in his discussion of Judaism. On the other hand, his approach is shaped by the same desire to contrast many of these interpretations to (his reading of) the Kierkegaardian "non-rational, anti-moral view" of the sacrifice of Isaac.

Green begins by characterizing most Christian interpretations of this challenging narrative as shaped by the belief that it was a prefigurement of the Christ event. As such, the themes of vicarious atonement and divine mercy become central to Christian readings of Genesis 22. As in his discussion of these themes in traditional Judaism, Green argues that Christian interpretations see this story as one of divine mercy through the suspension of the usual moral order and, as such, provide evidence of the third element of the deep structure of moral reasoning in biblical religious traditions — the conviction that there is a higher reality beyond the usual limits and failures of human morality that renews and completes our moral striving.

Green's historical overview of Christian interpretations begins with New Testament references to Genesis 22. The first that he addresses, James 2:21-23, shows how Christian thinkers tend to use discussions of the binding of Isaac as occasions for "exploring other theological concerns."[35] In this particular case, the theological concern is the relationship between faith and works — or, more specifically, the writer's conviction that faith is completed by works. Green draws our attention to the fact that the writer of this New Testament epistle does not raise questions regarding the moral content of God's command, but rather concentrates on how through his works (obedient action toward God) Abraham perfects his faith. The moral issues surrounding the command given to Abraham and his justification in obeying it are more directly addressed in another New Testament letter, Hebrews 11:17-19, which interprets Genesis 22 as a resurrection text. Green claims that this kind of interpretation addresses the moral issues of the story because the doctrine of resurrection is understood to justify God's command: Abraham's belief in the resurrection of his son ultimately validates his obedience, and the outcome of the episode (the "raising" or sparing of Isaac) reveals God's righteousness in that God's promises to the patriarch are upheld and God's will towards his faithful is shown not to be arbitrary. According to Green, this interpretation seems to view faith as a "*moral trust* in God [Green's emphasis]"

34. Green, *Religion and Moral Reason*, 104.
35. Green, *Religion and Moral Reason*, 105.

rather than merely volitional action.[36] This view is held up in opposition to Kierkegaard's view of the narrative.

To represent the interpretations of the early Christian church, Green briefly examines readings of Genesis 22 by Origen and Augustine. Origen applies his allegorical method of interpretation to this text, seeing it in almost exclusively Christological terms and identifying its central theme as that of personal sacrifice and martyrdom. Morally speaking, he concentrates on the trial of Abraham's faith rather than the reasonableness of the divine command. Green goes on to identify other specific moral issues central to Origen's reading of the story: the importance of trusting God (for which Abraham serves as a great exemplar) and a concern to demonstrate Abraham's truthfulness throughout the narrative. Green sees Origen's reading as depicting "an intensely moralized faith" that is again very distant from Kierkegaard.[37] Augustine also reads the story figuratively, seeing Abraham, Isaac, and the ram in Christological terms. The central theological concern that Green identifies in Augustine's reading is the provision of a moral justification of God's conduct which he achieves by claiming that the trial is set for Abraham's own good — to make his righteousness known to himself and to others. Green's purpose in depicting these various early Christian readings of Genesis 22 from the New Testament and from the early church is to show that they all manifest moral concerns and are based on a fundamental presumption that revelation is in agreement with moral reason. He understands each of these treatments of Genesis 22 to support his overall thesis in a straightforward way.

Until the emergence of medieval theological speculation, embodied for Green in Thomas Aquinas, he finds that Christian interpretations of the *akedah* continue to repeat the themes found in the earliest readings. But as medieval Christian thinkers attempted to combine a form of philosophical rationalism (influenced by the rediscovery of classical Greek philosophy) with their biblically revealed faith, Green asserts that "we find evidence for the first time in the history of Western religious thought of moral discomfort over the Genesis episode."[38] This "very qualified" discomfort was, for Aquinas, due to the "surface" of the story and *not* to any actual reality of injustice or moral irrationality in God. Aquinas's brief mention of Genesis 22 appears in his discussion of law, which Green char-

---

36. Green, *Religion and Moral Reason*, 106.
37. Green, *Religion and Moral Reason*, 108.
38. Green, *Religion and Moral Reason*, 109.

acterizes as a whole as giving a central importance to human moral reasoning without limiting God's power or freedom. Through Aquinas's view of law, particularly the presentation of natural law as part of eternal or divine law, it is clear that for Aquinas moral reason and biblical faith are entirely consistent but, as Green points out, the structure of this position poses a new problem, for the two can now be seen in some way as distinguishable sources of moral teachings.[39] It is precisely to address the question of whether these sources can conflict that Aquinas brings up the Genesis 22 story (as one of three biblical examples). Aquinas offers the explanation that the lives of all people are forfeit to God on account of Adam's sin and thus God's command to have Isaac's life taken is merely his reasonable right. According to Green, what is noteworthy about this treatment of Genesis 22 is that Aquinas does not make use of earlier commentaries' attempts to justify God's command, nor does his reading include any denial that God intended the sacrifice to be completed. Green identifies Aquinas's treatment of Genesis 22 as a watershed event for the reading of this biblical text because he believes it to be the "first explicit effort to harmonize revelation and moral reason."[40] Aquinas's discussion may thus be in some ways the source for less traditional views of the relationship between moral reason and biblical revelation but, Green reminds us, Aquinas himself was firmly embedded in the understanding of this relationship which preceded him and which was characterized by a fundamental confidence that these two sources of morality are one.[41]

This confidence was "fractured" by the emergence of nominalist divine command ethics which was deeply critical of rationalism. Green draws his example of this turn in Christian thought and how it affected the reading of Genesis 22 from the work of John Duns Scotus where he finds the argument being made that if God commands killing (as in the case of Abraham) then such an act becomes meritorious.[42] Green sees the concern that lies behind such a conclusion as actually supporting his own theory regarding the deep structure of moral reasoning in religious belief. He argues that a nominalist divine command theorist like Scotus is willing to sacrifice aspects of the first two elements of his deep structure by compromising God's "morality" in order to better preserve and strengthen the

39. Green, *Religion and Moral Reason,* 110-11.

40. Green, *Religion and Moral Reason,* 113.

41. For further discussion of this as Green's representative medieval reading see Chapter 4.

42. Green, *Religion and Moral Reason,* 114-15.

third element — God's ability to suspend the moral order in order to preserve us from despair brought on by the difficulty and paradox of our moral existence.[43] Green argues that the way in which these writers attempt to do this is part of a unique heritage traceable back through a Pauline doctrine of justification by faith, which includes an underlying assertion of God's freedom from the constraints of human morality. The kind of reading Scotus gives to the Genesis 22 episode reflects at a fundamental level a particular understanding of human sinfulness and our complete dependence on God's forgiveness.

When Green turns to Reformation readings of the story, specifically the commentaries of Luther and Calvin, he sees their indebtedness to the prior nominalist tradition but characterizes these readings (and the view of the relationship between reason and revelation of which they are examples) as embedded in a more mainstream view of faith and morality consistent with traditional views of God's just and moral character. In addition to drawing upon some of the rabbinic traditions about God's full knowledge of the outcome of the trial and Isaac's full participation in the sacrifice, both Luther and Calvin utilize the story as a source of evidence supporting certain Reformation views. Thus: grace precedes good works, as is shown in the fact that Abraham is chosen by God prior to being tried; the doctrine of *sola scriptura* is upheld by Abraham's obedience to God's word alone, not to human rules; preeminently, the story reinforces the theme that God is faithful to God's promises.[44] Green identifies this last theme as central to Luther's entire interpretation of Genesis 22 "since faith is the ability to rely on the fact that God keeps the promise of redemption he had made in Jesus Christ."[45] Luther treats the story of the binding of Isaac as the story of the father of faith (Abraham); it is precisely because the command to sacrifice his son appears contrary to our moral reasoning that Abraham's act takes on significance, for he depends completely on God's word, not on his own human sense of moral contradiction and despair. Reformation thinkers also argue that Abraham was able to continue to rely on God's word in the face of such a command because of his belief in the resurrection of the dead.

The conflict between reason and faith that appears to be part of Ref-

43. Green, *Religion and Moral Reason*, 116.

44. Green, *Religion and Moral Reason*, 119-20. Green seems to draw most of these themes particularly from Luther's *Lectures on Genesis*, but suggests they apply more generally to Reformation interpretations of Genesis 22.

45. Green, *Religion and Moral Reason*, 120.

ormation readings of Genesis 22 does not seem to concern Green. Again, he sets these interpretations against his reading of Kierkegaard's *Fear and Trembling,* arguing that the Reformers saw reason as inadequate to grasp the true moral content of God's command but, by faith, presumed it to be consistent with God's righteous character, whereas Kierkegaard allowed reason to judge that killing Isaac was morally wrong but still asserted that faith demands obedience to God's command, whatever its moral content.[46] While there are clearly important differences between these two positions, it is unclear why Reformation readings of Genesis 22, as Green elaborates them, do not undermine his overall thesis, since human moral reasoning is considered to be so limited by these theologians. Green claims that the Reformation readings, which amount to claims that moral righteousness triumphs even if our experience of the world leads us to believe otherwise, are evidence of the third element of his deep structure. However, he fails to deal with how his thesis is affected by the suggestion, in his presentation of Reformation thought, that not only is our ability to live a moral life called into question but also our very ability to reason out what such a life might be.

Green ends his survey of Christian interpretations of Genesis 22 with several pages dedicated to *Fear and Trembling.* He wants to argue that Kierkegaard's reading of the Genesis story was wholly "novel" and "eccentric" and yet incredibly influential to Christian thought coming after it. If Green can demonstrate this then he thinks that "we can better understand the recurrent impulse within Christianity to view religious morality as sharply opposed to ordinary moral reasoning,"[47] an impulse which seems to threaten his thesis. First, Green describes several of the generally accepted reasons scholars believe Kierkegaard interpreted Genesis 22 in the way he did. These included a wish to challenge the apathy of his contemporary Christians who appeared to take their religious life for granted and to counteract a popular understanding that Christianity could be reduced to a set of moral teachings. Green goes on to argue, however, that despite its apparent rejection of rational morality, ultimately *Fear and Trembling* is actually "a very traditional work of Pauline-Lutheran theology."[48] He iden-

---

46. Green, *Religion and Moral Reason,* 121.

47. Green, *Religion and Moral Reason,* 122.

48. Green, *Religion and Moral Reason,* 123. This reading of Kierkegaard is described and defended to a greater extent in Ronald Green, "Deciphering *Fear and Trembling's* Secret Message," *Religious Studies* 22 (1986): 95-111; and more recently in his essay "Enough Is Enough! *Fear and Trembling* Is Not About Ethics," *Journal of Religious Ethics* 21 (1993): 191-209.

tifies the central theme of the book to be the belief that sin can be overcome through the grace of God.[49] This was Kierkegaard's way of criticizing a form of moral rationalism that Green associates with Immanuel Kant[50] that does not take the problem of sin seriously enough. *Fear and Trembling* and Kierkegaard's idea of a religious "teleological suspension of the ethical" become, in Green's view, strong evidence in favor of the third element of his deep structure of moral reasoning. Even in the face of condemnation according to the most significant sphere of human moral reasoning, a figure like Abraham can become the "father of faith" through God's grace.

In the history of Christian (and traditional Jewish) interpretation of Genesis 22, Green reiterates, this story is typically understood as "proof" of God's perfect justice and righteousness. When, on occasion, it has been read as supporting an extreme divine command ethics (*Fear and Trembling* being the most significant example), this has reflected deep moral concern for how humanity can be preserved from the paradox and despair that result from moral striving rather than for the purpose of establishing normative moral principles. In interpretations of Genesis 22 in both traditional Judaism and Christianity, Green claims to have uncovered "the spontaneous instincts . . . [that] conformed in every way to the program of religious rationality and its deep structure."[51] He believes this insight to be important in the field of Christian ethics (and more generally, religious ethics) because it identifies "religion's essential moral foundation."[52] Grasping the existence of this foundation is especially important, Green goes on to argue, in comprehending Jewish and Christian views of the relationship between revelation and reason.

In several ways, Green's claims that human beings have an impulse to apply reason to religious morality, and that this inclination can be seen throughout the interpretive history of the *akedah,* are illuminating. However, setting aside the issue of whether or not this insight is useful in the study of religious ethics or comparative studies, my own central concern with Green's utilization of the binding of Isaac story still remains: Is his treatment of Genesis 22, as a religious ethicist, adequate and accurate, satisfying and responsive, to the challenges of this biblical story in the moral

49. Green, *Religion and Moral Reason,* 125.

50. One of Green's significant contributions to the scholarship surrounding *Fear and Trembling* is his identification of Kant (in addition to Hegel, more usually cited) as Kierkegaard's target.

51. Green, *Religion and Moral Reason,* 128.

52. Green, *Religion and Moral Reason,* 128.

lives of those who read it? As was noted earlier, Green's dismissal of the primary text is problematic even though he argues he is only concerned with the way the text has been interpreted and not with any scholarship regarding its "original meaning" or intent. Biblical scholar James Kugel has argued persuasively that one ought "to read all ancient retellings, translations, sermons, prayers, and even commentaries with Bible in hand."[53] Kugel's concern is that any deviation from the biblical story can become a significant part of its interpretive history. But even more generally, presenting this material in a way that removes it from the biblical text itself ultimately fails to do justice to the very commentaries and interpretations which Green is examining, since they themselves presuppose, at the very least, considerable familiarity with the Bible. As another scholar of midrash and theory puts it: "Only by seeing how deeply the tradition reads its sources will we be able to learn to read the tradition deeply for ourselves."[54] To attempt to read interpretations apart from serious consideration of the primary text is to risk misunderstanding the commentaries themselves and their role in their respective religious traditions. A related set of concerns is generated by Green's inadequate reflection on the role of the text itself and the status of the commentaries he discusses for the religious tradition in which they are read. The conviction, in the religious traditions Green is discussing, that the biblical text is sacred and revelatory affects the way it is read and interpreted within those communities. Green is, of course, aware of this in that this tendency is relevant to his consideration of how the religious traditions attempt to make rational sense of the *akedah* (rather than abandoning it or dismissing it as apparently irrational or anti-moral). However, Green's analysis of the role of the near-sacrifice of Isaac for Judaism and Christianity does not entertain the possibility that this story might be read and function differently from a non-sacred religious or moral text.

In his treatment of Genesis 22 in *Religion and Moral Reason* Green ultimately fails to account for the truly unsettling nature of this story. Nor does he consider that the complex history of its interpretation may signal that the narrative is morally and religiously challenging enough to resist any given interpretation. In the history of Christian interpretation, even as

---

53. *In Potiphar's House*, 6.

54. David Stern, *Midrash and Theory*, 12. He credits this concern in part to the work of Geoffrey Hartman in his note 26 ("Who Is an Educated Jew?" *Tel Aviv Review* 2 [1989/90]: 186).

Green outlines it, we never arrive at a reasonable and satisfying, agreed-upon reading. In a body of closed and authoritative Jewish commentaries like *Genesis Rabbah,* interpretation of Genesis 22 is far less univocal than Green suggests. And what of Kierkegaard? In exploring the underlying message of *Fear and Trembling* Green appears to ignore Kierkegaard's own presentation of the experience of reading this text and his experimentation with multiple readings within the four versions of the story offered early in the book.[55]

Much of what is neglected and what is attended to in Green's examination of Genesis 22 is plainly shaped by his stated purpose in *Religion and Moral Reason.* The task of examining religious interpretive traditions as a means of uncovering a basic structure of moral reasoning puts a formidable critical distance between Green and the biblical story of Abraham and the near-sacrifice of Isaac. His analysis is removed in the first instance by the generality of his religious ethical theory, which puts him outside and beyond the interpreters he discusses and fails to take account of the sacredness or authoritative status of the Bible for many of its interpreters. The further remove comes from Green's insistence that these interpretations be presented and analyzed without reference to the biblical text itself. In his critical detachment from the narrative and its commentators, in his treatments of Jewish and Christian traditions of interpretation of Genesis 22 as evidence for a deep structure of moral reasoning, Green has in effect stopped being a reader of the text.

On the other hand, Green's work represents a worthy contribution to ongoing ethical inquiry, not least in its assumption of the ethical importance of the act of interpreting Genesis 22 in biblical religious traditions. His presentation of traditional Jewish and Christian readings of the *akedah,* whatever its shortfalls, will be a significant resource and point of departure for further consideration of historical commentaries. *Religion and Moral Reason* offers insights valuable to this volume in ways that go beyond the two chapters centered on Genesis 22. Green's concern to identify the basic structure of religious moral reasoning leads to an illuminating account of the relationship between religious faith and moral reasoning, a relationship that will always be part of ethical interest in Genesis 22.

Moreover, throughout *Religion and Moral Reason* Green takes seriously the relationship between reading and storytelling (versus rule giving)

---

55. These "versions" as well as other readings of *Fear and Trembling* (including my own) will be discussed in Chapters 3 and 4 below.

and moral development and ethical practice in religious communities. It is unfortunate that his failure to take sufficiently seriously the *akedah* story at the heart of his examination of biblical faiths and moral reason weakens his argument in the chapters on Judaism and Christianity (which constitute half of his comparative evidence). Elsewhere in the book Green actually does a better job of relating religious reading and rereading to our moral lives and development than he offers in those two important chapters. For example, he concludes *Religion and Moral Reason* with an involved and ethically-attentive reading of an ancient religious epic from Indian literature, Vâlmîki's *Râmâyaòa*. In this chapter he discusses how such stories appeal to us, influence us, and develop in us the "art of moral judgment."[56]

> They see the righteous undergo hardship and suffering, including the rejection and scorn by the society they benefit. They witness the temporary flourishing and prosperity of the wicked, along with the unbearable pride this brings. And in the end, they see moral retribution upheld. In a more or less violent finale the weakness and impotence of the wicked are exposed and the power of the righteous is dramatically displayed. [57]

Perhaps it is because the *akedah* would not fit easily into Green's particular characterization of such stories and the ways in which they provide occasions for our moral development that he fails to give the binding of Isaac narrative the kind of consideration he gives to other texts. Genesis 22 defies normal expectations of how a "story with a moral" functions, especially according to the above description. It does not seem that the biblical story is simply an occasion for the reader to realize that her actions impact the lives of others, or that it simply expresses the lesson that a "morally acceptable decision is marked by care in reasoning and by the exercise of judgment."[58] Nonetheless, it is a story centrally important to members of biblical faith traditions and it is of perennial interest to thinkers and scholars who consider themselves to be religious ethicists. Green makes an important point when he observes that

> because moral judgment involves this difficult process of reasoning, and not simply the rules it produces. . . , it is a skill that must be taught,

---

56. Green, *Religion and Moral Reason*, 196.
57. Green, *Religion and Moral Reason*, 195.
58. Green, *Religion and Moral Reason*, 206.

learned, exercised, and retaught. Hence, the surprisingly great emphasis in texts like the Râmâyaòa on episodes that allow listeners or readers to participate in the exercise of moral judgment.[59]

To which one might add that it is precisely because of the morally formative possibilities in the process of reading that one of the most important and enduring characteristics of vivid narrative lies in its very ability to unsettle our confidence in our own moral reasoning, or in Green's words, to "defy rational or moral explanation."[60] Such a story keeps us reading.

59. Green, *Religion and Moral Reason*, 224.
60. Green, *Religion and Moral Reason*, 83.

CHAPTER THREE

Religious and Ethical Preconceptions: The *Akedah* in the Writings of Philip Quinn and Timothy Jackson

The kind of critical detachment imposed upon the reading of a specific biblical narrative by the concerns of a larger critical project — such as one finds in Ronald Green's *Religion and Moral Reason* — is not the only impediment to reading the *akedah* well as a contemporary Christian ethicist. Treatments of the binding of Isaac narrative by Philip Quinn and Timothy Jackson demonstrate another way that a specific approach can shape and even impede one's engagement of the biblical text: bringing religious and ethical categories extrinsic to the narrative itself and giving these categories a weight or role that exceeds that of the text itself. Unlike Green, Quinn and Jackson present their own interpretations of the story, while drawing on other important readings, especially that of *Fear and Trembling*. Like Green, both offer valuable insights about Genesis 22 while also illustrating the special challenges contemporary ethicists face when engaging the Hebrew Bible.

Philip Quinn

In an article published in *The Journal of Literature and Theology* in 1990, Philip Quinn turns our attention explicitly to questions about how we should read Genesis 22 — with "careful and imaginative" attention. Quinn argues that Abraham is involved in what he terms a "tragic dilemma," a situation where he is caught between two conflicting requirements, separately fulfillable but impossible to combine. Quinn begins with a concept of "moral dilemma" from contemporary discussions of moral philosophy, but amends it in two ways to fit his designation of "tragic" dilemma."[1] The first is to acknowledge that the dilemma need not be between two ethical requirements only. This allows Quinn to accommodate the Kierkegaardian assertion that the divine command to kill Isaac has its source outside the ethical or moral realm. Quinn's second modification draws upon the work of Martha Nussbaum; with her he insists that "in a tragic dilemma violating either requirement is wrong even though the agent cannot avoid violating one or the other of them."[2] This holds even if one requirement is "weaker" than the other. This modification is necessary to one of the central points of Quinn's essay, that in the story of the binding of Isaac, Abraham cannot but do wrong: the divine command to sacrifice Isaac cannot be disobeyed but neither does it "override" the moral obligation not to kill an innocent child. In a dilemma like this, it is precisely the agent's inability to escape wrongdoing and guilt that characterizes the situation as tragic.

Quinn points out that in *Fear and Trembling*, Kierkegaard, like other traditional interpreters of Genesis 22, does not believe Abraham "does wrong" in obeying God's command to sacrifice his son. Commentators who hold to the "received view in moral theory" that there cannot be tragic dilemmas (unless the agent has performed some kind of prior wrongdoing) are constrained in what they can say about Genesis 22.[3] Kierkegaard develops his idea of the teleological suspension of the ethical in order to view the situation as something other than a tragic dilemma. He reasons that the requirement imposed on Abraham to sacrifice his son comes from outside the realm of ethics and that this religious requirement is so important that it overrides or "suspends" the ethical duty not to kill an innocent child. Quinn, harkening back to an argument he made in a previous essay, insists that overriding either requirement in this story "misses what is deepest and most poignant about [it]."[4] Here, he pushes

---

1. Philip Quinn, "Agamemnon and Abraham: The Tragic Dilemma of Kierkegaard's Knight of Faith," *The Journal of Literature and Theology* 41 (1990): 182-3. Quinn's summary of "contemporary discussions of moral dilemmas" and this definition are drawn almost exclusively from the work of Walter Sinnott-Armstrong, *Moral Dilemmas* (Oxford: Basil Blackwell, 1988).

2. Quinn, "Agamemnon and Abraham," 183.

3. Quinn, "Agamemnon and Abraham," 187.

4. Quinn, "Agamemnon and Abraham," 191. Quinn is quoting his "Moral Obligation, Religious Demand, and Practical Conflict," in *Rationality, Religious Belief, and Moral Commitment*, ed. Robert Audi and William J. Wainwright (Ithaca and London: Cornell University Press, 1986), 207.

the point still further by arguing that "it would be *wrong* for Abraham to kill Isaac and also *wrong* for him to disobey the divine command."[5] The story, Quinn says, is more accurately read as a truly tragic dilemma; he believes that the only way to perceive the (dark) depths of the binding of Isaac is to recognize it as a narrative in which Abraham cannot but do wrong.

According to Quinn, one of the reasons Kierkegaard does not capture this tragic side of the Genesis 22 story is that he compares Abraham's situation, rather superficially, to that of Agamemnon.[6] Kierkegaard's Agamemnon, taken from Euripides' *Iphigenia in Aulis,* is presented as a paradigmatic ethical hero who chooses a higher or more universal expression of the ethical (the good of his nation) over a less comprehensive, more particular, and thus weaker expression of the ethical (his wish not to sacrifice his daughter). In Kierkegaard's reading of Agamemnon, there is no "tragic dilemma," as Quinn has defined it (though Kierkegaard refers to Agamemnon as the tragic hero), because the ethical obligation Agamemnon has to his daughter is eclipsed by the more universal obligation to his nation; the more specific familial relation is thus reduced to a wish or a sentiment. As a tragic hero, then, this Agamemnon sacrifices his wish or sentiment for his daughter's well-being to a greater ethical obligation.[7] Kierkegaard uses this reading of Agamemnon to provide a contrast to Abraham, whose choice to sacrifice his son is *not* an expression of a greater, more comprehensive ethical obligation but a requirement set for him from a source outside the ethical realm.[8] Because Kierkegaard does not read Agamemnon as being caught in a situation of tragic dilemma, Quinn argues, he does not read Abraham as being in one either.

> So the Kierkegaardian knight of faith is like the Kierkegaardian tragic hero at a very deep level. Both have a guilt-free option; neither does wrong in consenting to kill his child. As I see it, what makes the two of them brothers under the skin is that, in both cases, the requirement or duty not to kill an innocent child is overridden. Where their situations differ is in the source of the overriding requirement or duty.[9]

5. Quinn, "Agamemnon and Abraham," 191, my emphases.
6. Quinn, "Agamemnon and Abraham," 191.
7. Quinn, "Agamemnon and Abraham," 185.
8. Quinn, "Agamemnon and Abraham," 185.
9. Quinn, "Agamemnon and Abraham," 190.

Kierkegaard's point in making the comparison between the two heroes is to show that, for Abraham, obeying God's command has no more comprehensive *ethical* purpose. But underlying this main purpose, his reading assumes that neither hero is guilty of wrongdoing when he accepts the divine command to sacrifice his child.

Quinn suggests that to see Agamemnon as merely an ethical hero who meets his greater ethical obligation at great personal cost is inadequate, and ignores the very thing — his inability not to do wrong in the situation in which he finds himself — that makes his story tragic. Quinn prefers a reading of the Agamemnon story that "takes full measure of its terrifying depths";[10] he finds such a reading in the work of Martha Nussbaum. Unlike Kierkegaard, Nussbaum takes her Agamemnon from Aeschylus rather than Euripides, describing him as caught between differing divine commands that leave him in a tragic dilemma. In order to meet the requirements of both Zeus and Artemis, Agamemnon must sacrifice his daughter, but the ethical requirement not to kill his daughter is *not* overridden in Nussbaum's reading (even though she allows that it is clear that Agamemnon must do so). Quinn qualifies Nussbaum's reading of this story in only one respect — whereas she describes the situation as a moral conflict, Quinn, like Kierkegaard, would like to leave room for a source of obligation outside the realm of morality or ethics:

> Though the requirement not to kill an innocent child clearly is a moral requirement, the requirement to obey the commands of a god may, in some cases at least, be distinctively religious rather than moral.[11]

With this reservation noted, Quinn agrees with Nussbaum that the Agamemnon story fits the definition of a tragic dilemma.

Quinn then argues that Nussbaum's reading of Aeschylus's Agamemnon, rather than Kierkegaard's reading of Euripides' Agamemnon, should shape the way we understand Abraham. Kierkegaard's reading fails to "plumb the tragic depths of the conflicts they [Agamemnon and Abraham] confront."[12] In other words, by comparing Abraham to an Agamemnon whose heroism is characterized by a difficult choice to sacrifice a personal relationship but who is not considered to be guilty of doing something terribly wrong by doing so, Kierkegaard portrays the tension

10. Quinn, "Agamemnon and Abraham," 191.
11. Quinn, "Agamemnon and Abraham," 184.
12. Quinn, "Agamemnon and Abraham," 181.

between God's command and the ethical duty not to kill Isaac (as an innocent child, or as Abraham's son) in Genesis 22 as too easily resolved.
Kierkegaard uses the story of Agamemnon to show how Abraham's situation is different — comparing a situation where two conflicting requirements come from within the realm of ethics to a case where two conflicting requirements come from different sources (one ethical, one religious).
However, by contrasting the two situations, Kierkegaard presumes an important similarity between them in that they are both resolvable (regardless of how difficult the resolution may be to the hero). This presumption
is not problematic for Kierkegaard, who continues to take the traditional
view of the impossibility of true dilemma if no antecedent wrong has been
committed. It is, however, problematic to a reader like Quinn, who believes
that the true challenge of the story of the binding of Isaac lies not in getting Abraham off the hook but rather in presenting the reader with the
possibility of a fully tragic dilemma where an agent is caught between ethical and religious demands and cannot escape wrongdoing because in
meeting one he must violate the other.

For Quinn, a "careful and imaginative" reading of Genesis 22 reveals
that such a tragic dilemma exists in the *akedah*. But this reading also presents a theological problem for Quinn; it challenges the conception of God
as morally perfect:

> Consider the following argument: (1) Suppose God commands Abra-
> ham to kill Isaac; (2) If God commands Abraham to kill Isaac, then
> God commands Abraham to do something wrong; (3) If God com-
> mands Abraham to do something wrong, then God himself does
> wrong; (4) If God himself does wrong, then God is not morally per-
> fect; and so (5) God is not morally perfect.[13]

Divine moral imperfection, Quinn allows, is not problematic for the interpretation of Agamemnon's story since it is part of the traditional understanding the ancient Greeks had of their gods. However, "the god of the
monotheistic religions is supposed to be morally perfect, and so traditional theists cannot . . . accept the conclusion of this argument."[14] Quinn
resolves this tension by starting with the premise of God's moral perfection and rejecting the "actuality" of the *akedah*:

13. Quinn, "Agamemnon and Abraham," 191.
14. Quinn, "Agamemnon and Abraham," 192.

We can reverse the argument. Since God is morally perfect, we may say, God does not command Abraham to kill Isaac. The story of Abraham illustrates a possibility not an actuality. So there is a way out of the difficulty whose cost is denying the scriptural literalist's claim that the narrative of Genesis 22 is in all details sober historical truth. It is a price I am willing to pay.[15]

Quinn ultimately claims that the story of the near sacrifice of Isaac is "emblematic of a horrible possibility for religious tragedy,"[16] though it is a little difficult to see how Quinn can characterize it as even a "possibility" following his line of thought. By rejecting the "actuality" of the story because it is incompatible with a rational grasp of the moral perfection of God, Quinn appears to be saying that such a tragic dilemma *is* impossible, and thus finally siding with the received view, rejecting the existence of a true tragic dilemma. This final rejection occurs even though Quinn believes that "careful and imaginative" reading tells us that the Bible presents just such a story. Quinn's main ethical motivation is to argue that the "normal human duty not to kill one's own child" cannot be "suspended or overridden in the presence of a divine command to the contrary."[17] This is for him the "possibility" illustrated by the story. If such a situation could occur, guilt would be unavoidable since some moral requirements are indefeasible. But it becomes difficult to take this point to heart if it is clear that such a situation cannot really occur.

Regardless of confusing distinctions among actuality, possibility, and impossibility, Quinn's solution to the tension between the "tragic dilemma" of Genesis 22 and religious and philosophical commitment to the reasonableness and moral perfection of God has greater costs than he is willing to acknowledge. First of all, when he writes that the "cost is denying the scriptural literalist's claim that the narrative of Genesis 22 is in all details sober historical truth," he makes it sound as if his reasoning leads to the rejection of some incidental "detail" of the biblical account. However, as Quinn himself argues throughout his essay, the dilemma is central to any but a superficial reading of the *akedah*.

More importantly, any claim that "God does not command Abraham to kill Isaac" represents a radical challenge to the veracity of a central biblical text. The argument does not seem to be limited to the idea that we can-

---

15. Quinn, "Agamemnon and Abraham," 192.
16. Quinn, "Agamemnon and Abraham," 192.
17. Quinn, "Agamemnon and Abraham," 192.

not read the Hebrew Bible as we would a modern historical text. Rather, it constitutes a denial that the fundamental action of the story is, can be, or even should be, entertained as true. The story then becomes merely a lesson in moral reasoning: we read it as an occasion to argue whether or not divine command overrides basic human moral obligations. Rejecting the real possibility that God might command Abraham to kill his son, based on an argument that follows from the premise that God is morally perfect, allows our modern moral premises and reasoning to be the ultimate judge of the moral import of this, and, by implication every biblical text. This may not always be problematic, but Genesis 22 is not merely a culturally or historically bound ethical text, one that embodies ideas about human actions and morality that no longer seem appropriate. Nor in the case of Genesis 22, are we merely sacrificing the "scriptural literalist's claim" about the historical truth of the Bible story. If we take Quinn's theological premise as a means of simply rejecting the "actuality" of the story, we are no longer even forced to "plumb the tragic depths of the conflict" Abraham confronts. Through this kind of reasoning about God's moral perfection, we are protected from acknowledging those depths in any meaningful way. By denying that God makes this command, Quinn essentially removes the tragic from this tragedy and offers a too-easy "resolution" of Genesis 22.

Quinn's "Agamemnon and Abraham" nonetheless provides several important insights that can contribute to the project of exploring the relationship between reading the Hebrew Bible and living moral lives. In his suggestion that Nussbaum's reading of Agamemnon, rather than Kierkegaard's, should inform our reading of Abraham in Genesis 22, Quinn illustrates the way that our reading of one narrative can shape the way we read another (even if that other narrative involves a biblical figure and we are reading from the perspective of faith). Quinn shows how, when Kierkegaard draws on a particular reading of Agamemnon to make a point about the sources of the requirements that Abraham faces, the philosopher ends up oversimplifying another, perhaps more central, aspect of the story. Since Kierkegaard reads Agamemnon as a hero who, while he must make a terrible choice, is not caught up in a "tragic dilemma" where he will be guilty of wrongdoing even if he meets the stronger or more comprehensive ethical requirement, he tends to read the same assumptions into the biblical story. But if we read the biblical story with a more complex and tragic Agamemnon in mind (the character from Aeschylus rather than Euripides), we can more fully grasp the tragic and dark overtones of Genesis 22. Thus, it is not simply that our moral preconceptions shape the way we read biblical texts, but that they shape our reading of other complex and morally relevant stories which in turn shape our reading of the Bible. As we see in Quinn's essay, such inter-textual comparisons can be both enlightening and constraining.

Quinn offers another worthy insight about the reading of biblical narrative: that the narrative in its complexity and importance demands a particular kind of reader and a particular kind of reading. In the course of making the case that the Abraham and Isaac story should be categorized as a tragic dilemma, Quinn tells us that "in the end, my argument has to appeal to the reader's response to careful and imaginative reflections on the story itself."[18] This (possibly offhand) statement is ultimately very important. Most fundamentally, Quinn insists that our understanding of the moral role this story may have for us begins with consideration of the story itself (though, like Ronald Green, he gives very little attention to the actual biblical text), but never takes place in a vacuum. Rather, various reflections on Genesis 22, including the connections that we make between this story and other narratives, various traditional interpretations of the *akedah,* and our assumptions about the divine nature and the possibility of moral dilemma, in many ways mediate this story to us and become part of the reading, very broadly understood, to which we respond. The only criteria Quinn offers for judging the significance of these reflections is found in the adjectives "careful and imaginative." An invested reader must bring all her critical and creative reading skills to bear not only on the biblical narrative itself but on these other reflections that shape her response to the story. She must be self-aware about the limitations these reflections may impose. In this essay, Quinn applies this kind of "careful and imaginative" critique to Kierkegaard by arguing that the philosopher was constrained by the particular characterization of Agamemnon he employed in his reading of Abraham. Of course, perfect self-awareness is not attainable. And so, Quinn's own reading is ultimately limited by his explicit commitment to a notion of humanly perceivable divine moral perfection, in such a way that he is forced to undo all the work he has done in showing the reader the truly tragic character of this narrative.

Finally, both Quinn's exposition of the theological problem of divine moral perfection and his response to it illuminate one of the most conceptually difficult challenges of this project. How does any reading of the *akedah* in contemporary Christian ethics hold together a moral religious

18. Quinn, "Agamemnon and Abraham," 191.

tradition in which rationality is a key characteristic and a sacred text (one of the sources of that religious ethical tradition) that offers complex challenges to that very rationality? At the very least, it must be admitted that the *akedah* is not an easily resolvable story. But to attempt to resolve it with a suggestion that Genesis 22 merely gives us an "illustration" of a tragic dilemma that would never actually occur seems far from satisfactory. Perhaps it would be more fruitful to attend to the process and morally formative experience of "careful and imaginative" reading than to attempt to identify the best interpretation or to take a definitive position on the status of the *akedah* as a moral resource. From the perspective of Christian ethical inquiry, such an emphasis on the process and experience of reading a biblical narrative means that we must also be especially concerned that the theological and ethical categories we bring to our reading do not prevent us from reading well or taking its "dark depths" to heart.

Timothy Jackson

If Quinn's concern about (humanly perceivable) divine moral perfection causes his reading of Genesis 22 to pull up short and bars him from really engaging the implications of the text, Timothy Jackson's reflections on the story of the near-sacrifice of Isaac, while rich and evocative, are ultimately hampered by the preeminence he gives to Christian categories in his attempt to make moral sense of the *akedah*.

Of the scholars examined so far, Jackson is the only one whose primary field, by training and profession, is Christian ethics. Jackson's treatment of Genesis 22 was first published in an article in *The Annual of the Society of Christian Ethics*,[19] but found a larger audience as the sixth chapter ("Is Isaac Our Neighbor?") of his book *Love Disconsoled: Meditations on Christian Charity*.[20] This book is a series of essays that, taken together, form a presentation and defense of Jackson's case for the priority and challenge of "strong" *agape*, or charity, in Christian ethics. The chapter on the sacrifice of Isaac holds the penultimate place in this treatise, immediately following the chapter in which Jackson argues that Christian charity offers

19. Timothy Jackson, "Is Isaac Kierkegaard's Neighbor: *Fear and Trembling* in Light of William Blake and *Works of Love, Annual of the Society of Christian Ethics* 17 (1997): 97-119.

20. Timothy Jackson, *Love Disconsoled: Meditations on Christian Charity*, Cambridge Studies in Religious and Critical Thought Series (Cambridge: Cambridge University Press, 1999).

no assurance of comfort or consolation, that "the greater the love, in fact, the more it will be disconsoled and disconsoling." Jackson's final chapter, "Love on the Cross," presents his understanding of how Christ's Passion embodies perfect "disconsoled" love that suffers unto death in sinless obedience.

More than either Green's or Quinn's, Jackson's treatment of Genesis 22 represents the way the Hebrew Bible is typically used in Christian ethics, in that the story of the near-sacrifice of Isaac becomes a central occasion to discuss an overarching proposal about the shape of a Christian moral theology. While more complex than a mere reduction of narrative to norms, Jackson reads the *akedah* as a means of exploring and developing his particular thesis about the primary role of agapic love in relations between people when these are lived out within a Christian theological perspective. This *agape* love has three features, as Jackson defines it: "(1) unconditional commitment to the good of others, (2) equal regard for the well-being of others, and (3) passionate service open to self-sacrifice for the sake of others." While Jackson's articulation of these characteristics of *agape,* his "vocabulary," is drawn from the work of ethicists Paul Ramsey and Gene Outka, he claims that all three characteristics are scripturally based, though not necessarily in the form of commands or norms. They are, he says, demonstrated in the Bible as aspects of the way God loves us. We are called to express the same kind of love through the command "love one another as I have loved you" (John 15:12).[21] Jackson's reading of Genesis 22 centers around the question of how this story can be interpreted in light of his understanding of *agape,* and an ensuing argument that this kind of charitable love is the way of God and the ethical obligation of humanity.

The interpretation of Genesis 22 offered by Jackson is a sophisticated attempt to show that the love commands ("love God" and "love your neighbor as yourself, and as God has loved you") do not and cannot conflict. Jackson asks "How, more generally, can we square Genesis 22, Matthew 22, and John 15?" Like Ronald Green and Philip Quinn, he delves deeply into critical appraisals of other interpretations of the *akedah.* (It is evident from his notes that Jackson is in fact familiar with the work of both Green and Quinn, although he does not engage their treatments of the binding of Isaac in any significant way.) He begins his discussion with an analysis of "traditional" readings of Genesis 22 (such as that of Aquinas) that emphasize the obedience owed to God and the idea that, since the

21. Jackson, *Love Disconsoled,* 13.

fall, every human life is forfeit. He argues that such readings are as pious in their theocentricity but also problematic in three ways: they deny the goodness and inherent value of creation (especially of human beings); they emphasize, even value, power over morality; and, most importantly to Jackson, they "evacuate God's own *agape* of any meaningful content."[22] In this way Jackson brings the critique of "traditional" readings of Genesis 22 back around to his central concern — the definition and primacy of agapic love in Christian ethics. Instead of this traditional kind of reading, Jackson proposes an interpretation of Genesis 22 that understands the command issued by God as "ironic" rather than "literal," arguing that we must accept that God issued such a command (or else do significant damage to the biblical text) and yet recognize that he did not intend for Abraham to carry out the sacrifice. Instead, receiving this terrible command was meant to be a transformative experience; it was meant to teach Abraham to be unwilling to sacrifice Isaac. In order to construct a reading of the *akedah* that expresses his idea of *agape,* Jackson (again, like Green and Quinn) relies heavily on his reading of Kierkegaard's *Fear and Trembling* but significantly augments this reliance with a serious consideration of Kierkegaard's later thought, especially as expressed in *Works of Love.* For Jackson, *Fear and Trembling* represents precisely the kind of interpretation of Genesis 22 that he explicitly rejects — one in which the two love commands conflict. Unlike either Green or Quinn, Jackson carefully distinguishes the reading given by Johannes de Silentio, Kierkegaard's pseudonym in *Fear and Trembling,* from the reading Kierkegaard defends in his own name, in *Works of Love.* In addition to this nuanced reliance on Kierkegaard, Jackson also draws heavily on his own analysis of William Blake's interpretation of Genesis 22, especially in his painting *Abraham and Isaac.* While Jackson himself claims that this chapter/essay is *not* a full articulation of his reading of Genesis 22 but more of a "gesture towards it by noting the shortcoming of its competitors,"[23] he does far more than critique other readings here; this characterization seems overly modest.

The two aspects of William Blake's painting of the *akedah* story that most interest Jackson are Abraham's anguished expression and Isaac's tugging the ram into his father's view. The portrayal of Isaac as actively engaged in convincing his father that the ram would be the better sacrifice appeals to Jackson because he is wary of any reading that views Isaac, the

---

22. Jackson, *Love Disconsoled,* 181.
23. Jackson, *Love Disconsoled,* 178.

intended sacrificial victim, as quietly and willingly submitting to his own death — particularly once he is aware that a ram has been provided as an alternative. He finds Blake's notion of Isaac drawing Abraham's (and our own) attention to the ram a fruitful addition to the story.[24] Jackson sees in this portrayal of an Isaac who is showing interest in protecting his own life "the *limits* put on self-sacrifice" by *agape* which "might demand self-sacrifice but has no room for self-hatred."[25] In this action of Isaac, Jackson reads a clarification of the third feature of charitable love (passionate service open to self-sacrifice for the sake of others), demonstrating how it ought never to be confused with self-destructive impulses. Jackson's concern with Isaac's self-sacrifice can be compared to the related concern apparent in Green's presentation of the traditional Jewish material, noting that the ancient rabbis had a very different set of concerns. One way *they* found to make moral sense of this story was by suggesting that Isaac was a young man rather than small child and, more importantly, that he was a full participant in the sacrifice. In their reading, Abraham and Isaac went "together" to make the offering to God.

Blake's interpretation of Genesis 22 appeals to Jackson in other ways. More complex and more central to his own reading than the notion that Isaac attempted to protect his own life is his interest in Blake's portrayal of Abraham suffering from terrible anguish even after the ram has been provided to substitute for his son as the sacrificial offering.[26] In Jackson's articulation of Blake's interpretation, the possibility of sacrificing Isaac functions as a temptation for Abraham that he must overcome. The temptation lies in the understanding that as Abraham's firstborn, Isaac is his "best" sacrifice, and to his "ancient cultic instincts" the sacrifice of his son is the

---

24. One can hypothesize that it is Isaac's earlier concern about their lack of a sacrificial animal (v. 7) that makes this representation possible. See related concerns in Jackson, *Love Disconsoled*, 192, n. 26.

25. Jackson, *Love Disconsoled*, 186-7.

26. Jackson does not comment on the collapse of time that goes on in Blake's visual depiction of this narrative. Because Blake is representing several aspects of the story in one image, he is able to ignore the sequence of events as they are presented in narrative form and can thus manipulate the chronology while appealing to all our concerns about the story. As readers of this story, we are familiar with reflections on an Abraham suffering hypothesized anguish as he holds the sacrificial knife, just as we are familiar with Isaac's early concern about the whereabouts of the ram for the sacrifice and the later appearance of just such an animal. However, in Blake's rendition, all these elements of the story are "told" simultaneously. Perhaps this damage to the sequencing of the story is another explanation for why such an option was not entertained in the rabbinic material.

ultimate way to secure the future of his household, his descendants, and ultimately, the future nation, Israel. Jackson notes that this is not a purely etiological reading of the story, simply explaining the move away from human sacrifice to animal sacrifice in an ancient society. Rather it is the more complex depiction of Abraham's need to give up his understanding of his own power as patriarch. As Jackson describes it:

> A sacrifice is called for in the name of finer love, but it is a *self*-sacrifice: Abraham must die to his own ancient cultic instincts rather than kill Isaac. Abraham must sacrifice sacrifice in order fully to realize himself as a creature of conscience.[27]

In Blake's painting we are shown an Abraham who is anguished because he is torn between his prior understanding of the world, of power, and ethical order, in which he could most likely secure the future of all those who depend on him through his sacrifice of his most cherished possession — his only son Isaac — and a new possibility, a new ethical horizon in which he must relinquish such power. Again it is striking to compare Jackson's understanding of Abraham's self-sacrifice, grounded in the Blakean presentation, to that of the ancient rabbis. As was shown in Green's overview, the rabbinic material sees the self-sacrifice of Abraham very differently. By being willing to give up his son, who he understands to be a legal, physical, and emotional extension of himself, as well as his only and beloved, Abraham is showing his willingness to sacrifice himself. He is showing that he wouldn't withhold even his own life from God. In this kind of reading, Abraham's love and value for Isaac is equivalent to or greater than his love and attachment to anything else, including himself.

This traditional midrash seems more attentive to this story in light of larger narratives about this already chosen, blessed, and tried patriarch. Jackson, however, is interested in Genesis 22 as the story of Abraham's ethical transformation. He tells us that he "read[s] the story as most fundamentally a parable about love and justice, about how love may transform a limited or non-existent conception of justice into something higher."[28] To read the story this way it is necessary, as Jackson acknowledges, to assume that human sacrifice was not only not strange or surprising to ancient Israelites, but was "acceptable." Or as he puts it, that "the sacrifice of Isaac would, in short, do justice as the Hebrews at that time understood it" be-

---

27. Jackson, *Love Disconsoled*, 185.
28. Jackson, *Love Disconsoled*, 188.

cause it embodied the hierarchical order of things. To corroborate this view of sacrifice as acceptable to the ancient Israelites Jackson cites David P. Wright's article "Molech," in *Harper's Bible Dictionary*, but it is worth noting that the Hebrew word for a cultic child sacrifice *(mlk)* is not actually used in Genesis 22. The story uses the word for "as a burnt offering" *(le'ola)*, which clearly indicates the sacrifice of Abraham's son, Isaac, but without, perhaps, directly indicating a cult of child sacrifice.[29] While Jackson rejects Blake's (psychological) interpretation that the command itself originates in Abraham's own cultic instincts and sense of ethical order as doing too much damage to the biblical text, he accepts that Abraham must have such instincts, that the idea of sacrificing Isaac is a temptation for the patriarch. Jackson mines what he finds useful in the Blakean reading — the idea of the *akedah* being a story of transformation of Abraham to a new sense of ethical order — while demonstrating, through his rejection of Blake's view that the command to sacrifice Isaac did not come from God, that his own interpretation is in keeping with the biblical text itself. He also draws on Blake to express his conviction that "Love" does not try Abraham but rather that the "trial" is the temptation of Abraham by his prior cultic context. In Jackson's more orthodox hands this "Love" is the God who created human beings in the divine image and who neither wants this sacrifice nor even "knowingly elicit[s] the intention" of it.[30] Jackson suggests, instead, that while the command did come from God, it was "ironically" and not "literally" intended. The command was made in order to push Abraham towards this new ethical horizon, to engineer Abraham's self-overcoming.[31]

The characterization of God's command to Abraham as "ironic" but real is the most critical part of Jackson's reading of Genesis 22. To better reveal the importance of seeing such a command as truly originating with God, Jackson turns to Kierkegaard's pseudonym, Johannes de Silentio. Jackson notes that the reading presented in *Fear and Trembling* shares a few key insights with the Blakean reading. Both interpreters view the situation presented in Genesis 22 as problematic for Abraham because of the way he understands himself and his world. This leads both to highlight the

29. Jackson, *Love Disconsoled*, 190. There are other historical complications as well. A more complex treatment of this issue can be found in Jon Levenson's *The Death and Resurrection of the Beloved Son: The Transformation of Child Sacrifice in Judaism and Christianity* (New Haven: Yale University Press, 1993).

30. Jackson, *Love Disconsoled*, 192.

31. Jackson, *Love Disconsoled*, 198.

idea that the solution is a choice of the will, not a matter of gathering more information about what is happening, and that Abraham is alone in making his choice (without the support of his received understanding of the world). Finally, both are interested in examining ways the story might be presenting the "limits of ethics."[32] But for Johannes de Silentio, the command to sacrifice Isaac comes from God himself, not from Abraham's psyche or his cultic and ancient worldview. This understanding of the divine origin of the command is perhaps the central insight that Jackson shares with de Silentio in opposition to Blake. He also affirms de Silentio's insistence that "the paradox of faith is that the singular is higher than the universal, that the individual's duty to God trumps any and all social mores." On the other hand, against de Silentio, Jackson emphatically denies that God intended for Abraham to murder his son or even to elicit such an intention from him.

Jackson characterizes Johannes de Silentio as representing a perspective outside of Christian faith that can only see this as a story where God and ethics contradict one another. He argues that Kierkegaard's other work, particularly *Works of Love*, expresses a "religious point of view" which holds that "what is forbidden by Christian ethics must also be forbidden by Christian faith, because God is author of both."[33] With his own understanding of the overarching character and the ethical primacy of strong *agape* in hand, and the resulting commitment to the compatibility of love of neighbor and love of God which always functions as his touchstone, Jackson gives a final rejection of the reading that God meant any harm to come to Abraham or Isaac. He argues that without the insights of faith Johannes de Silentio is unable to read Genesis 22 as a story of "paradigm shift . . . in which the definition of justice itself changes in light of a better appreciation of God's love."[34] Without the insights of faith, Abraham's choice can only seem absurd since the "better appreciation" Jackson speaks of is dependent on a leap, an act of will, that is above, but not *against*, reason.

With the insights of faith, however, the command given to Abraham by God can be understood as an occasion for Abraham to experience and demonstrate pity and love for Isaac, and to sacrifice his own power over his son. Jackson is arguing that a person (such as Abraham) can be deceived

32. Jackson, *Love Disconsoled*, 192.
33. Jackson, *Love Disconsoled*, 193.
34. Jackson, *Love Disconsoled*, 195.

for the sake of being educated to a more complex and fuller understanding of truth, claiming that Kierkegaard opens us to this prospect through his own notion of *"via media"* ("how divine love engineers individuals' inwardness nonrationally and theonomously"[35]) and through "preserv[ing] a distinction between an apparently harmful command and a really harmful one."[36] The purpose of this referencing of Kierkegaard appears to be to make the case that the reading given in *Fear and Trembling,* that God's command demanded a "teleological suspension of the ethical," is not only a non-Christian reading of Genesis 22, but not Kierkegaard's own reading as a "mature believer." Irrespective of these references to Kierkegaard, however, the interpretation presented in "Is Isaac Our Neighbor?" is Jackson's own. It is Jackson who carefully ascribes his notion of strong *agape* (as well as Kierkegaard's understanding of "neighbor") to the *akedah* in order to present this narrative as one of God transforming Abraham's ethical horizon by commanding him (with ironic, not literal intent) to sacrifice his son Isaac and thus "schooling" the patriarch "in a more egalitarian, even a selfless, love."[37] Clearly, this is an important and provocative claim, seen from the standpoint of Christian ethics. However, it is not Jackson's particular interpretation that is most relevant to the concerns of the present volume. Rather, it is the way in which he approaches the binding of Isaac narrative and the methods of interpretation he uses as a Christian ethicist reading the Hebrew Bible that warrant further consideration.

Jackson situates his own reflections of Genesis 22 in the long and complex history of the story's interpretation. He does this selectively, making choices that illuminate his own reading, as exemplified in his concentration on William Blake's painting of *Abraham and Isaac,* and Kierkegaard's reflections on the *akedah* in *Fear and Trembling* and *Works of Love.* This is one of the notable strengths of Jackson's contribution: he sees his own reading as part of a long tradition of interpretation that has formed his understanding of Genesis 22, and afforded a resource for both critique and retrieval. His exposition and analysis of key (at least for him) readings within this tradition is distinguished not only by the care he employs but by the way he sees each reading as part of the author's larger ethical and theological purpose.

But what of Jackson's use of historical-critical biblical scholarship? At

35. Jackson, *Love Disconsoled,* 197.
36. Jackson, *Love Disconsoled,* 198.
37. Jackson, *Love Disconsoled,* 199.

certain points throughout his essay, particularly when analyzing other interpretations, Jackson turns to biblical commentaries and a more historical-critical view of the purpose of the text in its original context. This may be illustrated in his brief discussion of the practice of human sacrifice, acceptance of which in ancient Israel is a basic assumption of his argument about the transformation of Abraham. He defends this assumption with recourse to sources such as *Harper's Bible Dictionary* and *The New Standard Jewish Encyclopedia*. Elsewhere, as he explores the different ways to interpret Abraham's distress (as expressed in Blake's painting and de Silentio's treatise), he draws on the resources of biblical scholarship in observing that this command is problematic for Abraham precisely because it would seem to contradict God's earlier promise of blessings to flow to future generations in and through Isaac. It is this exegetical insight that prompts Jackson to characterize Abraham's wish to secure stability for Israel through the killing of Isaac as "paradoxical."[38] The subject of the divine promise does not ultimately enter into Jackson's own final reading of the narrative, however, but is used only to illuminate the shortcomings of others' interpretations. In general, Jackson's application of the insights of biblical scholarship to his own argument is rather selective and inconsistent.

Respect for the biblical text itself is an important criterion for Jackson as he evaluates other interpretations. This is most notable in his identification of the main shortcoming of William Blake's presentation of the *akedah* as the "real violence" it does to biblical text when it denies that the command to sacrifice Isaac comes from God, and instead radically reimagines the source of the idea for this sacrifice to be Abraham's self-involved commitment to a primitive cultic religion. Again, there is some selectivity in Jackson's critique, as it does not seem to worry him that Blake also ignores the chronological sequence of events in the biblical story (Jackson himself is inclined similarly to ignore the chronology of Genesis 22). Another instance of Jackson using the biblical text itself as a measure of the strength of its interpretations is his discussion of the possibility that faith in resurrection or immortality plays a part in the binding of Isaac story. When identifying the problems such a reading presents, he notes that "first, resurrection is nowhere explicitly mentioned in Genesis 22."[39] He goes on to dismiss some interpreters' (including possibly Kierkegaard's) contention that Abraham must believe in some form of resurrec-

---

38. Jackson, *Love Disconsoled*, 194.
39. Jackson, *Love Disconsoled*, 196.

tion since he tells his servants that both he and Isaac will come back after they have made their sacrifice. Jackson points out that in the biblical narrative "in fact we do not see Isaac return with his father."[40] Jackson also rejects the resurrection argument on theological and ethical grounds: "Even if Isaac had been sacrificed then reanimated, this would not change the fact that Abraham has to be willing directly to kill the innocent."[41] Since he finds the idea that God occasioned this intention in Abraham as at least as problematic as the idea that God desired the sacrifice itself, Jackson rejects any interpretation that claims faith in resurrection as a means of resolving Abraham's dilemma. It is interesting that while Jackson carefully identifies these two problems with the resurrection-reading (that such a belief is not explicitly expressed in Genesis 22 and that it would not, in any case, make God's command any less abhorrent), he seems unconcerned that reading back into this text a much later and predominantly (though not exclusively) Christian understanding of resurrection would be, at the very least, anachronistic and, at most, supersessionistic. The concept of "resurrection" does not play a significant role in the Hebrew Bible, and the possible references to it are, as the *Anchor Bible Dictionary* points out, "rare, obscure with regard to their precise meaning, and late."[42] Like Green in his presentation of traditional Jewish interpretation, Jackson fails to acknowledge the vast differences between Jewish speculation about the reanimation of Isaac and the Christian doctrine of resurrection. The foreignness of the concept of resurrection to this ancient biblical text is an important consideration but one that Jackson neglects in his reading of the *akedah* as an occasion for discussing his *Christian* theological ethics.

Overall, then, Jackson can be said to draw on biblical scholarship and to attend to the details of the biblical text in a manner that supports his interpretive claims while largely ignoring scholarly insights or textual details that might challenge those claims. A close look at his understanding of what is (not) "withheld" by Abraham in the *akedah* narrative, the crux of his reading, is telling in this regard. In order to support his reading that God does not intend Abraham to sacrifice Isaac, Jackson must make sense of verses 12 and 16-17, where the angel of the Lord tells Abraham not to lay a hand on Isaac while saying "now I know that you fear God, since you

40. Jackson, *Love Disconsoled,* 196.

41. Jackson, *Love Disconsoled,* 196.

42. Robert Martin-Achard, trans. Terrance Prendergast, "Resurrection (OT)," *Anchor Bible Dictionary* 5, ed. David Noel Freedman (New York: Doubleday, 1992), 680.

have not withheld your son, your only son from me" and where God gives
Abraham his blessing since he has "done this, and not withheld" his son.
Jackson argues that "Abraham's not withholding Isaac from God is a different act from his not withholding him from the angel, from the surrounding Israelite community, or from Abraham himself."[43] In Jackson's
reading, God blesses Abraham precisely because the patriarch comes to see
Isaac as "a vulnerable child of God, worthy of respect and protection" and
is unwilling to slaughter him: he "withholds" him from being sacrificed as
"the (earthly or heavenly) father's personal property."[44] For Jackson it is
this distinction about what Isaac is (not) withheld *from* that defines the
story as one of Abraham's transformation from a lesser or non-existent
sense of justice to one "transformed" by agapic love.

The influence of Blake's interpretation of Genesis 22 is obvious in
this portion of Jackson's reading, but, unlike Blake and with Johannes de
Silentio, Jackson is unwilling to characterize the words of either the angel
or God as internal to Abraham's psychology or "cultic instincts." While
Jackson conforms God's speech (quoted by the angel) to his reading with
his suggestion about the way the "this" in "done this, and not withheld"
should be understood, he admits that the earlier speech of the angel appears to praise Abraham for a willingness to offer Isaac as a burnt sacrifice.
How then to resolve what the commendation means? Jackson argues that
"it is crucial to note that it is not the Lord Himself speaking here."[45] Considering its importance to Jackson's thesis, this distinction between the angel and God seems a point at which some investigation of biblical scholarship would be appropriate. There are several other biblical passages that
indicate, at first glance, a similar kind of ambiguity about whether an angelic messenger is distinct from Yahweh or not[46] by having the angel
switch back and forth between speaking of the Lord in third person and
then speaking for the Lord in first person. In response to this ambiguity,
there are multiple interpretive suggestions in biblical scholarship about
how the relation between God and a "messenger/angel of Yahweh" *(mal'âk
yhwh)* should be understood. Carol A. Newsom argues convincingly that
the most likely explanation is that such passages express "a tension or paradox: Yahweh's authority and presence in these encounters is to be af-

---

43. Jackson, *Love Disconsoled*, 199.
44. Jackson, *Love Disconsoled*, 199.
45. Jackson, *Love Disconsoled*, 199.
46. For example, Genesis 16:7-13, 21:11-12, 31:11-13; Exodus 3:2-6; Judges 6:11-24.

firmed, but yet it is not possible for human beings to have an unmediated encounter with God."[47] Regardless of whether or not this is the best explanation for such passages, no prominent biblical scholarship suggests that the messengers of Yahweh have separate or distinct purposes from that of Yahweh, as Jackson's reading would seem to demand.

What is most interesting about Jackson's discussion of verses 12, 16, and 17 is that while he seems to move *away from* attentiveness to biblical scholarship (or at least to demonstrate only selective willingness to incorporate such scholarship), he also, at least ostensibly, moves *toward* the text — focusing acute attention upon small textual details — in shaping a reading of this story in the context of ethical inquiry. His project of interpreting the command to sacrifice Isaac as from God but ironically intended revolves, finally, around his attentiveness to one small pronoun — the "this" in verse 16. There are many interpretive questions that can be addressed to Jackson's understanding of this small word. First, does it make narrative sense to read the sparing of Isaac that occurs between the angel's speech in verse 12 and the speech in verse 16 as the "this" referred to in the second instance? Second, it is difficult to accept the claim that in this story Abraham's "not withholding Isaac from God is a different act from his not withholding him from the angel, from the surrounding Israelite community, and from Abraham himself"?[48] While Jackson's suggestion is thought-provoking, it seems to defy the clear sense of the text to assume that what occurs between these speeches is Abraham suddenly "feeling pity" and becoming "unwilling to kill";[49] it would seem, rather, that he is simply released from a terrible command and presented with an acceptable substitute for the sacrifice. There is simply no textual basis for seeing the withholding that the angel refers to in verse 12 and the withholding in God's speech (delivered again through the angel) in verse 16 as referring to different acts and distinct objects. However one finally evaluates the strength of Jackson's particular reading, however, it is instructive that his ethical concerns prompt him to deeply engage the biblical text, such that one small word becomes centrally important.

Another facet of Jackson's treatment of the *akedah* that warrants our attention is the set of assumptions he incorporates about Abraham, specifically about who the patriarch is before the "upbuilding" of this trial. We

47. Newsom, "Angels," *Anchor Bible Dictionary* 1, 250.
48. Jackson, *Love Disconsoled*, 199.
49. Jackson, *Love Disconsoled*, 192.

see in his characterization an implicit suggestion that Genesis 22 cannot make ethical or theological sense without the lens of the Christian gospel. This is not problematic to Jackson himself, who places his reading of the *akedah* in the context of an ethical meditation on love, specifically as revealed in the sacrifice of Christ on the cross. But as it pertains to a broad methodological consideration of how Christian ethicists read the Hebrew Bible and to more specific consideration of the meaning of the complex and powerful stories of sacrifice of beloved sons in the Bible, this tendency is deeply troubling and needs to be critically examined.[50]

In Jackson's reading of Genesis 22, the transformation of Abraham through the ironic command by God to sacrifice Isaac is discussed in isolation from Abraham's life more broadly considered. Jackson does not allude to the fact that this is the story of the tenth and final "trial" of Abraham, nor does he offer any examination of whether or not the ethical character of Abraham is recognizably different, somehow transformed, after the events on Mount Moriah. Jackson's reading of this story depends on a view of a pre-*akedah* Abraham who has a very limited concept of justice, one in which justice is an expression of power, and utterly unmingled with love. He also is a man for whom the act of child-sacrifice is acceptable, one who is "tempted" by this act as a way to secure the future of his line. It is worth noting, in this context, that Jackson's argument about the acceptability of child sacrifice is made on cultural-historical grounds and does not reflect consideration of Abraham's prior actions regarding Hagar and Ishmael, which would be perhaps a more fruitful and biblically interesting way to explore this aspect of Abraham's ethical bearing.

The ethical transformation of Jackson's Abraham, with his limited concept of justice, is read in explicitly Christian terms. "The cross, intersection of the vertical and horizontal axes of love, is the key to solving

50. In a wonderful paragraph at the end of his preface to *Death and Resurrection of the Beloved Son*, Jon Levenson writes: "Radically transformed but never uprooted, the sacrifice of the first-born son constitutes a strange and usually overlooked bond between Judaism and Christianity and thus a major but unexplored focus for the Jewish-Christian dialogue. . . . Jesus' identity as sacrificial victim, the son handed over to death by his loving father or the lamb who takes away the sins of the world. . . , ostensibly so alien to Judaism, was itself construed from Jewish reflection on the beloved sons of the Hebrew Bible. . . . The bond between Jewry and the Church that the beloved son constitutes is, however, enormously problematic. For the longstanding claim of the Church that it *supersedes* the Jews in large measure continues the old narrative pattern in which a late-born son dislodges his first-born brothers, with varying degrees of success. Nowhere does Christianity betray its indebtedness to Judaism more than in its supersessionism."

Abraham's paradox: *to show mercy to the vulnerable creature is to obey the righteous Creator.*[51] Jackson does seem to temper his supersessionistic statement with an indication that he sees this way of love to be the biblical way, represented in both the Hebrew Bible and the Christian New Testament, observing in one note that "faith moving a father freely to spare his son is the paragon of Jewish religion."[52] Yet his attempts to describe *agape* more broadly as a testamentally-inclusive biblical love are ultimately betrayed in the language he chooses. In the same note, Jackson goes on to describe Abraham as foreshadowing "the triumph of Gospel over Law" and talks about the law of sacrifice of the firstborn being transformed ultimately into the "new law."[53] The fact that such readings of Genesis 22 are common, dating back to the New Testament itself, does not mean that they are not problematic. Such traditional ways of identifying and characterizing essential moral differences between an "Old Testament Judaism" and a "New Testament Christianity" are grossly oversimplified, biblically and historically problematic, and ultimately dangerous.

The only slightly problematic issue, as far as Jackson is concerned, with his treatment of the *akedah* under the rubric of Isaac as "a neighbor for whom an Incarnate Redeemer died" is that of anachronism. This underestimation of the issue of supersessionism is consistent with Jackson's failure to question the appropriateness of applying the concept of resurrection to the world of the *akedah*. When interpretations of the New Testament are anachronistically and nonchalantly read into the Hebrew Bible in order to make Christian ethical claims, Christian readers not only risk making false and sometimes dangerous connections between the ethical implications of the two Testaments, they also risk diminishing their ability to be attentive readers of the Hebrew Bible, superimposing their understanding of Christian moral theology on the text and its interpretation. Jackson's Abraham is moved by his faith to freely spare his son and sacrifice his own understanding of the world; he is moved to "sacrifice sacrifice." Jackson has turned the story on its head and made it (by making the nature of God's command) palatable to our moral sensibilities. Just as Quinn rejects the "historicity" or "actuality" of the story on the grounds of theological propositions about the nature of God, Jackson posits an "ironic" command and an Abraham who refuses to sacrifice Isaac; the

51. Jackson, *Love Disconsoled*, 200.
52. Jackson, *Love Disconsoled*, 191, note 25.
53. Jackson, *Love Disconsoled*, 191, note 25.

akedah thus illustrates his theme of love transforming justice. The cross (re)solves the paradox of Abraham. Genesis 22 is read with much greater attention to its distant context (a Christian understanding of sacrifice) than to the immediate story of the father of God's people, his previous trials, past behavior, and future role. Any interpretation that employs Christian categories as the central criteria for interpreting the Hebrew Bible will have the shadow of supersessionism hanging over it. This dark legacy has to be taken seriously, not only because of lessons learned in the history of Jewish-Christian relations, but because it so readily becomes a way for Christians to stop reading, to stop attending carefully to the biblical text itself. When we claim that we have available to us the definitive reading of biblical narratives like Genesis 22, our relationship with the text is essentially petrified.

That Jackson's reading of the *akedah* is hampered by his desire to make the text theologically and ethically palatable is apparent in other ways. He rejects E. A. Speiser's characterization of God's command as an "unreal and gruesome mandate to be canceled out at the proper time" with one brief rhetorical question: Can a righteous God really issue such a "call for the direct killing of an innocent"?[54] And yet it is unclear how an "unreal" command that is to be canceled at the proper time is significantly different from an ironic one. While admitting that the "tactic" that God uses in Genesis 22 is a brutal one, Jackson's argument seems to be that this brutality is acceptable under the rubric of (disconsoled) love because it is an "intelligible" way of moving Abraham out of "an abominable ritual."[55] Jackson understands this brutal schooling through an ironic command to be one of the illusive, indirect, or "difficult to understand" ways that God relates to us, about which Kierkegaard also wrote. And yet, this seems a very large step to take. Can we really equate ironic with indirect, deceptive (regardless of intent) with merely elusive and difficult to understand, or being given a contrary command with being moved non-rationally or theonomously?[56]

Bracketing the issue of supersessionism, Jackson's selectivity with respect to sources should not, in and of itself, be disparaged: it is always part of the interpretive moment. It warrants attention not so much because it

54. Jackson, *Love Disconsoled*, 191.

55. Jackson, *Love Disconsoled*, 198.

56. Jackson, *Love Disconsoled*, 179, 197. I am also concerned that this chapter might short-change the notion of the "absurd" in Kierkegaard's *Fear and Trembling* but the reference to this concept is brief and the interpretation of Kierkegaard beyond our scope.

represents a flaw or failure in Jackson's treatment of Genesis 22 but because it demonstrates the way Genesis 22 defies interpretation. When it is read in light of one particular (set of) theological or ethical proposition(s), some aspects of the story are heightened even as others are neglected or misrepresented. When Jackson examines the work of other interpreters, especially Blake and Kierkegaard, his treatment is exciting and self-aware. His ability to critique, retrieve, and extend a complex interpretive tradition could be thought of as the academic or scholarly version of listening, telling, and retelling this sacred story. However, his treatment of the *akedah* fails to acknowledge its own limitations or the possible distortions that might result from placing this Hebrew narrative within an argument about the priority of agapic love in Christian ethics.

Jackson ultimately makes sense of Genesis 22 by characterizing Abraham as fundamentally morally flawed prior to the events of the *akedah* rather than seeing him as a chosen and already much-tried figure. Even the Abraham of Quinn's reading, who cannot but do wrong, is more morally sophisticated and sympathetic than Jackson's Abraham, whose pre-Moriah sense of justice is untempered by love. Such a characterization is certainly antithetical to rabbinic readings that see Abraham in the context of his own life narrative as the recipient of blessings and trials from God. For Jackson, the concept of strong *agape* is a more definitive key to interpreting the *akedah* than the character of Abraham or the larger narrative context of the story (when Jackson does consider a larger narrative context it is typically the narratively distant story of the gospel). Jackson argues that Abraham must "sacrifice sacrifice" but his own interpretation of Genesis 22 in effect sacrifices Abraham to his notion of strong *agape*. Again, the fact that Jackson's moral theology affects his reading is not, in itself, problematic. There are always moments when a reader's commitments influence the reading process, causing her to notice some things and to neglect others. And Jackson makes a strong case that his understanding of divine and human love transforming justice is drawn from the Bible itself. But in insisting on conforming Genesis 22 to explicitly Christian ethical categories, his ability to read attentively is diminished and his interpretation suffers. Thus it becomes impossible for Jackson, such an interested and interesting reader himself, to recognize the morally formative role of the process of reading (rereading, and retelling) of the story of the *akedah* even though such a role is implied in the form of his own work.

To summarize: philosopher Philip Quinn and Christian ethicist Timothy Jackson both fail the biblical narrative of the near-sacrifice of

Isaac at the very point in their scholarship where they are considering it most fully. In addition to a general disregard for the primary text and any form of biblical exegesis, Quinn's commitment to the premise of the rationally accessible moral perfection of God causes him to resist any profound engagement of the tragic depths presented in this difficult story. Jackson, who is more attentive to Genesis 22 itself and (selected) insights from biblical scholarship, insists on seeing this story as an early moment in the transformation of Old Testament justice or law to New Testament love, thereby compromising the character of Abraham and, more broadly, the moral complexity and significance of the Hebrew Bible. The problems found in Quinn's and Jackson's treatments of the *akedah* stem from their particular theological commitments whereas, as we saw in Chapter Two, religious ethicist Ronald Green imposes a critical distance between himself and Genesis 22 when he presents its interpretive history as merely an example of a universal religious moral phenomenon. The resulting neglect of Genesis 22 is similar, though: all three scholars justify the ways they approach the primary biblical text through the terms of their ethical projects; in varying degrees each fails to recognize the importance of consideration of the primary text as a necessary step in understanding and assessing its interpretations; and all tend to oversimplify the interpretive traditions. The concerns of the *akedah* narrative itself as these may be revealed through close reading and through drawing on biblical scholarship are not central to the ethical reflection of these scholars. Even in Jackson's chapter, the themes drawn from his selective attention to biblical exegesis and historical critical scholarship are only peripherally related to his main conclusions about the story. The Hebrew Bible is not actually treated as a "crucial" primary resource for Christian ethical reflection, regardless of the various theoretical pretensions that suggest otherwise.

Just as these scholars tend to sacrifice the biblical narrative to their ethical projects, in key ways all three avoid granting any morally relevant authority or revelatory status to the Hebrew Bible, sacrificing its authoritative and revelatory role in Christian moral reflection to their theoretical categories. Ronald Green treats both the biblical text and interpretations of it as historical artifacts that illustrate a deep structure of religious reasoning. Philip Quinn "solves" the challenge of Genesis 22 by suggesting that we merely need to give up scriptural literalism and see the *akedah* as only an illustration of a terrible situation that is not actually possible if God is morally perfect (as we rationally conceive such perfection). Timothy Jackson makes sense of the narrative by conforming it to Christian theological categories and thoroughly removing it from its immediate narrative and theological contexts as part of the story of Abraham and the larger story of Israel's relationship with God.

Any explicit awareness of the role of reading the *akedah* as, itself, a morally important act is absent from these discussions of Genesis 22, in part because of the lack of attention to the peculiar status and authority of the Hebrew Bible for religious ethics. Jackson never alludes to any such role for the reading of the binding of Isaac, though the critical retrievals of other readings as well as his interest as an ethicist in stories more generally implies this possibility.[57] Quinn claims that understanding his argument about Genesis 22 demands "careful and imaginative" reading of the biblical narrative, but he does not connect this care and imagining directly to our moral lives. Green, perhaps, comes closest to attributing a morally formative role to the process and experience of reading Genesis 22 when he sees the tradition of interpretations as the working out of the "deep structure of moral reasoning," but his complete omission of consideration of the narrative itself diminishes the value of this insight. Thus in Green, Quinn, and Jackson, we have examples of ethical works that center on Genesis 22 but that fail to engage the primary text attentively, give no particular consideration to the status of the Hebrew Bible as a source of moral inquiry, and offer no reflection on what it means to be readers of the *akedah*.

On the other hand, all three of these scholars are interested in Genesis 22 because they understand it to be, in Ronald Green's words, the "hard case" for a religious ethicist reading the biblical text — a story where the command of God apparently contradicts a very basic demand of human morality. Each takes this ethical challenge seriously and rejects overly simplistic resolutions. Each is compelled to acknowledge that this complex, difficult and important story demands a certain kind of reader. Green is interested in the history of its interpretation precisely because this history is filled with readers who take its challenge to heart. Quinn says such readers must be "careful and imaginative," willing to traverse the tragic situation with Abraham and Isaac. Jackson's essay illustrates both alertness to details in the biblical text (to the point where one pronoun takes on great importance) and thoughtful analysis of the interpretations of others.

57. See, for example, chapter 2 of Jackson's *Love Disconsoled* which is an extended consideration of short stories by Hemingway and Fitzgerald, "Back to the Garden or Into the Night," 32-53.

In addition to recognizing that the *akedah* demands careful and imaginative reading, Green, Quinn, and Jackson are all aware that this reading does not take place in a vacuum and that the traditions of interpretation that we have inherited are part of how we now read the story itself. While all three are heavily indebted to Kierkegaard, the broad scope of Genesis 22 interpretation is certainly presented by Green and acknowledged by the others. Jackson, in his careful exposition and analysis of William Blake's painting and Kierkegaard's reflections, situates his own unique reading within a particular tradition, drawing upon the readings of others while critically diverging from them. Quinn illuminates not only the way we are influenced by various interpretations of *this* story, but the way we incorporate readings of other related stories and characters — especially in his argument that Kierkegaard derived his understanding of Abraham from the "wrong Agamemnon." And all three scholars model the way our theological and philosophical categories shape our reading — in both positive and negative ways. At best, the categories we bring with us can prompt us to draw closer to the biblical text, involving ourselves with the narrative so intimately that each word becomes precious (like Jackson's "this" in Genesis 22:16) and we become sensible of the *akedah*'s "dark depths," to use Quinn's phrase. At worst, our categories become a barrier, prompting us to resist that very intimacy with the text that would allow it to speak to us.

One of the principal concerns of this book is the need for more critical self-awareness in our reading of the Hebrew Bible for Christian ethics. This entails the dual obligation to pay attention to the concerns of the text itself — which means having recourse to biblical scholarship and careful exegesis, as well as the history of interpretation — and to be mindful of the categories and expectations we bring to it from our own line of ethical inquiry — which means not so much searching for a definitive reading or bolstering our own claims but questioning who we are and what we are doing when we read, particularly when we read the Hebrew Bible.

Consideration of reading, rereading, and retelling the *akedah* as morally relevant acts, as morally formative experiences, will move us beyond what can be observed in the scholarship of Green, Quinn, and Jackson. As we allow ourselves to be truly present to the sacred text, narratives like the near-sacrifice of Isaac will become for us crucial occasions of personal and communal ethical reflection and formation. Developing a better understanding of the relationship between reading and ethics will not only allow us to explore the moral possibilities inherent in the process and experience of reading, particularly of reading Sacred Scripture, but will also constrain the propositional conclusions we draw from the text, encourage us to be more humble about the categories we use to try to domesticate un-domesticatable stories, and ultimately push us towards becoming better practitioners of biblical reading — self-aware scholars who read carefully, draw upon biblical research, listen to other interpretations, and then return to the text afresh, again and again.

PART II

MAKING THE JOURNEY

Renewing Acquaintance: Reading the *Akedah* (Again) with Kierkegaard, Philip the Chancellor, and the Rabbis of *Genesis Rabbah*

The contemporary scholarly readings so far adduced have clearly influenced my own central thesis in this volume — that how and what we *experience* when we read Genesis 22 is relevant, perhaps even crucial, to the importance of the *akedah* for Christian ethics. But this thesis is also inspired by and dependent on other resources, including other readings of Genesis 22. So far I have discussed the history of interpretation of the *akedah* only insofar as it has appeared in the work of other contemporary ethicists. But, as we move closer to the primary text itself, which we will ponder at length in Chapter Five, it would seem pertinent to spend more time with some of the notable figures from the rich interpretive tradition of Genesis 22.

My consideration of readings from the history of interpretation, like that of Ronald Green, ranges across a broad chronology and set of religious traditions, but, unlike Green, I do not intend to identify a common interpretive approach or idea (or form of religious reasoning) but rather to explore a variety of concerns surrounding the act of reading, rereading, and retelling this story. More in the manner of Jackson's "Is Isaac Our Neighbor?" I will focus on examining a small set of readings, drawing particular attention to ideas and approaches especially relevant to my reflections on the role of reading the *akedah* in Christian ethics.

The three studies that follow are presented in reverse historical order, beginning with some reflections on Kierkegaard's *Fear and Trembling*, then moving back to examine an example of medieval theological reflection by Philip the Chancellor, and finally turning to the midrash of ancient rabbis in the *Genesis Rabbah*. The presentation of these studies in the history of Genesis 22 interpretation has a threefold purpose. First, even such a selective sampling will demonstrate, once again, that the interpretive history of this text is exceptionally rich and diverse and itself open to a wide array of responses. Analysis and retrieval of these historical sources (like interpretation of the biblical text itself) are shaped by the reader's own context and presuppositions. Second, in various ways, these very different sources provide insights into what it means to be attentive and engaged readers (rereaders and retellers) of the story of Abraham's near sacrifice of his son. Third, these short studies will begin to illuminate some ways that the "form" of the literary choices made in our approaches to the biblical text (in)form our readings and thus in turn our moral lives.

Kierkegaard

The significance of Kierkegaard for contemporary (particularly American Protestant) Christian ethics is undisputed, and his *Fear and Trembling* has become an important (if not *the* important) text through which to reflect on the story of Abraham's last trial in contemporary Christian scholarship. So influential is his treatment, in fact, that it is not uncommon for a contemporary treatment to collapse the biblical story and Kierkegaard's version(s) of it, arguing as if the Abraham of Genesis and the Abraham of *Fear and Trembling* are, for all intents and purposes, identical.[1] In other words, many contemporary Christian ethics assume that Kierkegaard's Johannes de Silentio interprets this biblical story completely and perfectly (for us). My ultimate interests here are in the reading of Genesis 22 and not Kierkegaard, so obviously I find this collapse problematic.[2] Perhaps Kierkegaard would be concerned about it as well. While he does not make specific reference to the task of understanding Abraham in his brief epi-

1. A good example of such a collapse can be found in Jung Lee's essay "Abraham in a Different Voice," *Religious Studies* 36 (December 2000): 377-400. This article also contains a helpful review and comparison of Green and Jackson.

2. One feminist philosopher, Alison Leigh Brown, when writing about Kierkegaard, differentiates between the account of Abraham's last trial in Genesis and de Silentio's versions of the story in terms of their canonical status. The implicit feminist critique of canon and tacit privileging of de Silentio's story(-ies) are important reminders that while most of this study presumes that the Genesis (canonical) "version" has unique status and authority as a text (certainly a historically accurate assumption in Christian ethics), the authority of the canonical biblical text and its "versions" of the religious stories that shape our traditions are for some a matter of intense debate. See "God, Anxiety, and Female Divinity," in *Kierkegaard in Post/Modernity*, ed. Martin J. Matustik and Merold Westphal (Bloomington: Indiana University Press, 1995), 70-71.

logue to *Fear and Trembling*, Kierkegaard does tell us that "however much one generation learns from another, it can never learn from its predecessor the genuinely human factor."[3] By the "human factor" Kierkegaard goes on to write that he means passion or love, "in which the one generation also fully understands the other and understands itself."[4] Here his purpose is certainly to reject an aspect of Hegelian idealism, but throughout the book he also uses his reading of Genesis 22 to raise other objections to practitioners of contemporary philosophy. Just as "love" is impossible to "learn," so is faith. "Love, after all, has its priests in the poets, and occasionally one hears a voice that knows how to keep it in shape; but about faith one hears not a word."[5] Kierkegaard's de Silentio reads Abraham's story as a trial or temptation that cannot be mediated because of its singularity, a love for God that is particular, and a faith (in Isaac's return) that is absurd. It is a story about that which cannot truly be taught, learned, or understood through abstract reflections and rational accounts. Thus, according to this reading, it is a story that involves, at the very least, that genuine human factor, and so any previous interpretation (including, for us, his very own) cannot become a replacement for or even a necessary supplement for our experience of reading Abraham's trial (though from his work we may learn other things, including the weaknesses of other readings). This being said, the attention and attachment to Kierkegaard's reading of the *akedah* in contemporary Christian ethics attest to the remarkably provocative form and content of *Fear and Trembling*. It is neither the competence nor the aim of this study to represent the various debates about the interpretation of this work in contemporary Christian ethics or philosophy. Our purpose, rather, is to consider what it might mean to be (good) readers of the *biblical* text; that is a task concerning which Kierkegaard offers many insights.[6]

3. Though *Fear and Trembling* is attributed by Kierkegaard to the pseudonymous author Johannes de Silentio, this attribution, as Merold Westphal points out, "has been more honored in the breach than in the observance" (*Kierkegaard in Post/Modernity*, xii). For a good discussion of how to understand Kierkegaard's use of pseudonyms, see Mark C. Taylor, *Kierkegaard's Pseudonymous Authorship: A Study of Time and the Self* (Princeton: Princeton University Press, 1975), as well as Kevin Newmark's "Between Hegel and Kierkegaard," *Søren Kierkegaard*, ed. Harold Bloom (New York: Chelsea House, 1989), which argues that Kierkegaard's use of pseudonyms is not a clever trick to make a point, but rather "an admission of not being able to limit identity to one particular locus, or voice" (226).

4. Søren Kierkegaard, *Fear and Trembling: A Dialectical Lyric by Johannes de Silentio*, trans. Alastair Hannay (London: Penguin, 1985), 145.

5. *Fear and Trembling*, 63.

6. A fully developed study of Kierkegaard's theory of reading would require an analy-

Like any reader, Kierkegaard brings to the text his own preoccupations: his concern with Hegelian and Kantian philosophy, his Pauline-Lutheran theology, and his unique history — including his own and his father's melancholy and the personal occasion for the writing of this book, his broken engagement to Regine Olsen. Often in *Fear and Trembling*, Kierkegaard's pseudonymous author alludes to contemporary cultural forces (and the way his concerns are shaped both within and against those forces) with the sardonic phrase "our age." This heightened sense of the character of the present age is significant for Kierkegaard's treatise on Abraham's great trial, which is meant to expose not only the weaknesses of other readings of the *akedah* but the shortcomings of contemporary philosophy. If understanding faith is an immeasurable struggle (even more so than understanding love, which, we recall, has at least its poet-priests), then understanding a faith like Abraham's must be a task far more formidable than understanding a philosophy like Hegel's. To think otherwise, to think that it is "hard to understand Hegel, when understanding Abraham, why that's a bagatelle" is one of the principal failings that concerns Johannes de Silentio about his contemporaries. Philosophy, he says, he does easily,

> but when I have to think about Abraham I am virtually annihilated. I am all the time aware of that monstrous paradox that is the content of Abraham's life, I am constantly repulsed, and my thought, for all its passion, is unable to enter into it, cannot come one hairbreadth further. I strain every muscle to catch sight of it, but the same instant I become paralysed.[7]

Of course, this paralysis both belies and foreshadows a particular reading of Genesis 22, one that shows Abraham as the knight of faith whose experience cannot be mediated because it is outside the universal, particular to him and his singular relationship to God, and whose trial demands the teleological suspension of the ethical (again putting him outside the universal). But, on Kierkegaard's own account, there cannot be an interpretation that makes Abraham's story understandable. His reading and discussions

---

sis of all of his published works, not just *Fear and Trembling,* as well as an account of the variety of modern and postmodern philosophers and critical theorists who engage Kierkegaard in their work. For those interested in pursuing this topic, *Kierkegaard in Post/Modernity* provides a good introduction.

7. *Fear and Trembling,* 62.

are not intended to make Abraham more intelligible but rather to ensure that "his unintelligibility might be seen more [*desultorisk*] in the round."[8] Kierkegaard thus places his "Speech in Praise of Abraham," which admits to, even asserts, the patriarch's unintelligibility, alongside other readings provided not by the philosophers he is engaged in arguing with but by an unnamed reader, perhaps the pseudonymous author of the work, Johannes de Silentio.[9]

Following a preface (signed by Johannes de Silentio) and preceding the "Speech in Praise of Abraham" is a short, third-person narrative about a man who learned the story of Abraham and Isaac as a child and thought it beautiful, and who read the same story as he grew older with increasing admiration but less understanding. Four different versions of the story of the near sacrifice of Isaac then follow, as narrative fragments reflecting the "ways this man of whom we speak thought about these events."[10] Each begins early in the morning on the day Abraham and Isaac set out for Moriah. In each version the man imagines a different kind of Abraham carrying out the command (until rescinded) in a different manner and with different consequences for the father and the son. The imagined Abraham of the first version pretends he is acting out of his own desire, and not God's, in order that Isaac will still have faith in God, even if he sees his father as a monster. In the second, Abraham is unable to forget what God has demanded of him and afterwards, as he ages and Isaac thrives, "[sees] joy no more." In the third, reflecting on the near sacrifice of Isaac and also his earlier expulsion of Hagar and Ishmael, Abraham begs God's forgiveness for his willingness to sacrifice his son and yet fails to comprehend how it was a sin to be willing to sacrifice the best he owned; night after night, caught between two contradictory ideas, he can find no peace. In

8. *Fear and Trembling,* 136, and translator's notes 118, 158. "In the round" is Hannay's way of expressing Kierkegaard's use of "desultorily" which he thinks is used "in the sense of 'skippingly' or 'disconnectedly,' perhaps 'from different points of view.'"

9. This section is written in the third person, unlike the preface and the rest of the book, which are all in first person. Among the few scholars who comment on the section, some assume the unnamed man and the pseudonymous author are the same. See, for example, Edward F. Mooney, "Art, Deed, and System: The Prefaces to *Fear and Trembling,*" *The International Kierkegaard Commentary 6: Fear and Trembling and Repetition,* ed. Robert L. Perkins (Macon: Mercer University Press, 1993), 67-100; and Amy Laura Hall, "Self-deception, Confusion, and Salvation in *Fear and Trembling* with *Works of Love,*" *Journal of Religious Ethics* 28 (2000): 37-61. On the other hand, some scholars regard the two figures as distinct. See, for example, Kevin Newmark, "Between Hegel and Kierkegaard," 219-31.

10. *Fear and Trembling,* 48.

the fourth account, we are presented with an Isaac who glimpses his father's anguish as he prepares the sacrifice and who, because he sees his father's hand shake, loses his faith.

In a recent article, Amy Laura Hall argues that the four versions function to give readers of *Fear and Trembling* the same experience of disorientation and confusion experienced by the narrator. "We are to 'understand the story less and less' as we read four possible variations of the scene."[11] Thus, the form here is as provocative as the content. Perhaps as readers of *Fear and Trembling* we become more like the man for whom the story of Abraham and Isaac finally "put everything else out of his mind. . . . What he yearned for was to accompany them on the three-day journey."[12] We are told that the man is not occupied by "the finely wrought fabric of imagination, but the shudder of thought"; that is, it is not the qualities of story or narrative possibilities that engross him but rather the faith of Abraham.[13] Nonetheless, while his imaginative reconstructions of the narrative are not the *reason* for his consuming interest in Genesis 22, they are the *means* by which he lives it out, as each imaginative narrative expresses a different interpretive possibility.[14] The man imagines the thoughts and emotions of the characters involved (thoughts and emotions about which the biblical narrative itself is silent), the manner in which Abraham carries

11. Hall, "Self-deception, Confusion, and Salvation," 43. Drawing on Kierkegaard's papers, Jung Lee argues that these four versions show an Abraham without faith. While the Abraham in each narrative fragment does what is demanded, he does not have an "optimistic attitude" ("Abraham in a Different Voice," 400, n. 86).

12. *Fear and Trembling*, 44.

13. It is also worth noting that the man is said to have no Hebrew and not to be a "learned exegete" who might more easily understand the story of Abraham. If this comment is read in light of de Silentio's later criticism of "pious and tender-minded" exegetes who make "drivel" out of Luke 14:26 through grammatical gymnastics (99-100), then such an observation seems more scathing than humble. For a very different and provocative reading of this comment about the unnamed man knowing no Hebrew, see Kevin Newmark's "Between Hegel and Kierkegaard," in which he argues that *Fear and Trembling* is about the "hermeneutic possibility of meaning." That the philosophical ramifications of translation, grammar, and language were relevant to Kierkegaard is evident both in his biography (he requested of the king that he be permitted to submit his thesis in Danish and not Latin, a request that had nothing to do with his mastery of Latin) and in the wealth of material on the subject mined by postmodern philosophers.

14. Each version is followed by a brief and parallel description of the weaning of an infant by its mother. Possibly there is an analogy here between reading Genesis 22 and weaning, in that the encounter with this harsh text forces us beyond familiar comfort and security but does so in order that we can mature and become responsible ourselves.

out the command, what Isaac notices during the events, as well as the subsequent consequences for each person. It is through these imaginative and narrative means that the man keeps himself involved with the story, and with the faith (as incomprehensible as it is) of Abraham.

This section, with its four vignettes, is called by Kierkegaard the "Exordium," or as Alastair Hannay translates it, "Attunement."[15] Amy Laura Hall is, I think, right that these early sections of *Fear and Trembling*, though often overlooked by those who teach the text, are crucial, both in their content and in their structure:

> These complex preliminary sections are intended to disconcert the reader and distinguish the reader's story from the scriptural story of Abraham and Isaac. . . . We must trudge through de Silentio's extensive qualifications of our relationship to the father of faith.[16]

Of these first sections of the book the "Exordium" is perhaps the most overlooked.[17] The term "Exordium" can merely indicate an introduction, but it carries also a connotation of beginning more "at order" or possibly "out of order" — which might be a more appropriate and less ironic title considering the disconcerting character of this particular "introduction." "Attunement," as Hannay translates it, can mean "bringing into harmony" or "making [one] aware of, or responsive to" something. At the very least, it may suggest that these stories are a necessary "tuning up" for author (and reader) or, as Edward Mooney describes them, a series of "false starts" before we can begin to grasp the challenge of the story as Kierkegaard will lay it out.[18] These narrative fragments, like the preparatory notes before an

---

15. Most recent English language scholarship uses Howard V. Hong and Edna H. Hong's translation, *Fear and Trembling* and *Repetition* (Princeton: Princeton University Press, 1983). For reasons of personal preference, the primary translation I follow is by Alastair Hannay. Sometimes, especially when referring to another secondary source, I will represent the different word choices in these translations.

16. Hall, "Self-deception, Confusion, and Salvation," 41. Hall's purposes are very different from mine and a full account is outside the scope of this study. She is arguing for a particular and challenging reading of Kierkegaard's religious ethics. Nonetheless, the attention she gives the early sections of *Fear and Trembling*, as well as her awareness of the effectiveness of its form, are very helpful.

17. Some significant exceptions to this are found in Hall's recent essay, Mooney's "Art, Deed, and System," and Newmark's "Between Kierkegaard and Hegel."

18. Mooney, "Art, Deed, and System," 77. In a new Cambridge translation of *Fear and Trembling*, the "Exordium" section is titled "Tuning Up." See C. Stephen Evans and Sylvia

orchestra performance, allow for essential adjustments in order to reach the proper pitch — to present and perceive the main reading. They prepare us to see Abraham more "in the round."[19]

A somewhat bolder reading of this section might be to suggest that Kierkegaard is putting his primary reading in the context of many others in order to achieve harmony or accord. The accord, the right relationship with the biblical text, is achieved in the act of journeying, again and again, to the mountain in Moriah, recognizing through these journeys Abraham's unique greatness. "Yet no one was as great as Abraham; who is able to understand him?"[20] In a provocative essay, Kevin Newmark suggests that the "reader," the man described in the third person in the "Attunement," is distinct from the pseudonymous author, Johannes de Silentio, who writes in the first person and who is replying to Hegel's reading of Abraham in the rest of the book. While not the primary claim of his argument, this distinction allows Newmark to draw a connection between the "allegorical reader" and Abraham. The "reader" represents "the Individual who cannot express intelligibly in the language of the General his relationship to the Absolute." This is the legacy of Abraham's faith, Abraham's unmediatable faith.[21] This "reader" has nothing to say in the dialectical exchange between Hegel and de Silentio, he is excluded by the singularity of his faith. Yet only in such a reader (such a reading) do we find the possibility of "recalling" Abraham. For while the father of faith cannot be fully seen, fully present, we have in our struggles to recall, to read, to tell this story a kind of analogous experience.

Regardless of whether the man described in the "Attunement" and the pseudonymous author, Johannes de Silentio, are distinct, the content and form of the opening section of *Fear and Trembling* present the reading of Genesis 22 as a lifelong activity. And while Abraham's unintelligibility does not make it impossible to become better readers of his story (weak and mistaken readings can certainly be corrected or improved upon; some are for Kierkegaard the occasion for his own claims), it does make it impossible finally and fully to understand his story, to exhaust its possibilities

Walsh, eds., *Fear and Trembling,* Cambridge Texts in the History of Philosophy (Cambridge: Cambridge University Press, 2006).

19. It may also be important that there are four versions — possibly an implicit rejection of the three phases in a dialectical argument. Timothy Jackson called my attention to this possibility, which I believe deserves more attention.

20. *Fear and Trembling,* 48.

21. Newmark, "Between Kierkegaard and Hegel," 225.

with the tools of moral philosophy. The unnamed man in the "Attunement" who encounters the story as a child continues to read and reread as an adult; "every time he came home from a journey to the mountain in Moriah he collapsed in weariness."[22] In his experience we are shown something about the nature of engaged reading and the nature of the text of Genesis 22. Attentiveness is not merely important: it is a necessary and grueling demand and one in which the inevitable failure to succeed in interpreting the story does not negate the necessity of laboring to do so. The reader's relationship to Abraham is located somewhere in the relationship between the failure to comprehend and constant engagement. And while grappling with Genesis 22 may be exhausting for this fictional reader, or for any attentive reader, such readings can never exhaust (or explain away) the text.

These ideas about reading the *akedah* conveyed in the "Attunement" are further developed through the rest of *Fear and Trembling*. In order not to lose his hero whom he loves, de Silentio observes in the "Speech in Praise of Abraham," the poet "struggles night and day against the wiles of oblivion," and in this way the hero is not forgotten even if he is often misunderstood, and "his lover still comes, and the more time goes by the more faithfully he sticks by him."[23] Again, the struggle to read (as well as [re]tell) a story faithfully is the process by which the story and its hero come into and remain in relationship with the reader. The "hero" here is a more typical (tragic) hero, perhaps the knight of resignation. But Abraham, who "expected the impossible [and] became greater than them all,"[24] is different. Even more then, it seems, must readers of *his* story both work and yet be unconvinced of their own mastery.

> Now the story of Abraham has the remarkable quality that it will always be glorious no matter how impoverished our understanding of it, but only — for it is true here too — if we are willing to "labour and be heavy laden."[25]

In addition to this necessary labor of reading is a related obligation to tell of one's readings (this, of course, on the condition that you are among those who speak of the story with "fear and trembling"). "And out of re-

22. *Fear and Trembling*, 48.
23. *Fear and Trembling*, 48-50.
24. *Fear and Trembling*, 48-50.
25. *Fear and Trembling*, 58.

spect for greatness one should indeed speak."[26] To grapple with the story of Genesis 22, to journey over and over to the mountain with Abraham and his son, without understanding him, and to tell of this journey (his and, it would seem, our own) without assuming we are making him intelligible, seems to be the intended relationship of reader to text in *Fear and Trembling*.

As seen in the preceding reflections on the "Attunement," the form as well as the content of Kierkegaard's writing is important in his own address to Genesis 22. Thus the designation of genre given as the volume's subtitle (*Fear and Trembling: Dialectical Lyric*) is noteworthy. The expected phrase in the context of dialogue with philosophers (especially Hegel) would surely be "dialectical *argument*." Why then does he substitute "lyric"? Several possible reasons suggest themselves. First, Kierkegaard is presenting a position that may not be generally accepted or rationally demonstrable but can nonetheless illuminate Genesis 22 for his readers. He is exploring a new approach to the story of Abraham's trial, to the relationship of faith to reason, and to human existence. But this approach is not an argument as much as a meditation; it is personal and particular. It is something other than a work of speculative philosophy; it has literary or poetic qualities. Second, while there is no clear and widely accepted definition of lyric,[27] it is typically associated with music; its sound and form (and often, performance) are somehow constitutive of its meaning or purpose. (This association, incidentally, supports the musical translation of "Exordium" as "Attunement" in Hannay's translation.) Third, as a species of poetry, lyric is personal (not universal) and intimate (not epic). Hegel himself described lyric poetry — and Kierkegaard doubtless knew this — as an "intensely subjective and personal expression."[28] It is emotionally evocative, conveying (often strong) passions, what Wordsworth described in his *Lyrical Ballads* as the "spontaneous overflow of powerful feelings." Fourth, in the context of European Romanticism the designation "lyric" suggests not only a personal and particular voice, but a self-conscious and inward focus.

Fear and Trembling is thus a unique mixture of the philosophical and

26. *Fear and Trembling*, 103. Here he is arguing that one who knows the greatness of Abraham should speak, in case that greatness (with its terrors) is forgotten.

27. For a discussion of the history of attempts to define this category of poetry, and the challenges in doing so, see "Lyric" in *The New Princeton Encyclopedia of Poetry and Poetics*, ed. Alex Preminger and T. V. F. Brogan (Princeton: Princeton University Press, 1993), 713-27.

28. Quoted in "Lyric," 714.

the literary. Over thirty years ago, Louis Mackey argued that Kierkegaard needed to be studied with, and perhaps primarily with, the "tools of literary criticism."[29] He followed this work fifteen years later with studies showing the limitations of those same tools. As Roger Poole writes in a review of twentieth-century literature on Kierkegaard, "It is very much to Mackey's credit that he lays out so plainly both the necessity for a literary approach and the inevitability of its falling short."[30] It is not surprising that *Fear and Trembling*, with its unique blend of imaginative story-telling, posing of narrative possibilities, and dialogue with other literature, has itself become such an important primary text.[31] Yet it is also clearly self-defined as a philosophical treatise. Towards the end of the work, in Problema III, when Johannes de Silentio is retelling Aristotle's story of the bridegroom who doesn't go through with his marriage, he explicitly tells us that he is no poet: "But here I break off. I am not a poet. I only practice dialectics."[32] It is clear that, regardless of the need to tell the story of Abraham, the demand to "speak" because of the patriarch's greatness, Kierkegaard's de Silentio is not offering poetry as antidote, the better alternative, to speculative philosophy. The poet can only recall what has been done, can only try to tell the story. His telling of the story may be the companion of Abraham's act of faith, but, as Abraham is un-mediatable (silent), such (re)tellings of the story cannot inform us. Neither the speculative and philosophical nor the imaginative and personal approaches to biblical text capture or mediate the story, but these attempts, these acts of reading (when undertaken with rigor and sensitivity) give us a relationship to the text that forms us — forms us in ways related to the way the trial formed Abraham.

The reading of Abraham presented in *Fear and Trembling* is intended to be radically transformative of our assumptions about ourselves as well as

29. Louis Mackey, *Kierkegaard: A Kind of Poet* (Philadelphia: University of Pennsylvania Press, 1971), ix.

30. "Twentieth-century Receptions" in the *Cambridge Companion to Kierkegaard* (Cambridge: Cambridge University Press, 1998), 67.

31. The narrative and imaginative reflections on Genesis 22 continue after the "Attunement" (and thus are clearly to be attributed to de Silentio), particularly in the "Speech in Praise of Abraham." Another literary characteristic of the text is its constant reference to other stories from the classics throughout (especially in the *Problema* sections). Biblical references also abound; interestingly, they do not function in any significant way differently from other allusions. In one place it is even unclear whether the reference in *Fear and Trembling* is to Ovid or to Jeremiah (150, n. 16).

32. *Fear and Trembling*, 116.

of Abraham. As Hall has suggested, in *Fear and Trembling* we "are ourselves called into question." After all, de Silentio himself forewarns us that "the form and content" of the work "are intended to disconcert."[33] It is also clearly intended to demonstrate the inefficacy of speculative philosophy in addressing a story like that of Abraham — especially in its misleading domestication of religion and morality. But this "dialectical lyric" does not make a case for a particular reading; rather it offers a potent argument about (and demonstration of) the power of reading well (and the dangers of reading poorly). When writing about "Kierkegaard and Evil" Paul Ricoeur emphasizes that in *Fear and Trembling* Kierkegaard works out his concept of faith as a way of being in relationship with God "not by means of an abstract discussion about theological concepts, but by way of an *exegesis*."[34]

So with a lyrical exegesis of Genesis 22, Johannes de Silentio offers a critique of the comprehensive claims of speculative philosophy and the pseudo-Christianity of "our age."[35] This critique maintains that the claims of philosophy, the arguments of dialecticians, do not help us understand Abraham. Nor can the poets or exegetes help us understand him fully. The advantage that the poet (and perhaps some exegetes) may have over at least the philosophers de Silentio is concerned with, does not come from what is *produced*, but lies in the activity itself, the willingness to value direct engagement with the story and with its characters. It is one's sustained though challenging relationship with the story that is important. In one instance, where he is criticizing some rival interpretations of the *akedah* that speak of the "whole thing" as "just a trial," de Silentio's concern is with how quickly such a reading allows one to be finished with the story:

> A trial — that can say a lot or little, yet the whole thing is as quickly done with as said. One mounts a winged horse, that very instant one is on the mountain in Moriah, the same instant one sees the ram. One forgets that Abraham rode on an ass, which can keep up no more than a leisurely pace, that he had a three-day journey, that he needed time to chop the firewood, bind Isaac, and sharpen the knife.[36]

33. Hall, "Self-deception, Confusion, and Salvation," 41-42.

34. Paul Ricoeur, "Kierkegaard and Evil," in *Søren Kierkegaard*, ed. Harold Bloom, 53. Emphasis is Ricoeur's.

35. There is a strange complication here as de Silentio "has no faith," no personal relation with God — and yet the book presents his ongoing reading-relationship with the text as authoritative.

36. *Fear and Trembling*, 80.

Readings of Genesis 22 that are quickly formed and that reduce a story to an idea or a proposition are inadequate. They do not do justice to the elements of the narrative itself, and thus they do not really attend to Abraham (his experience as depicted by this story). Our address to the narrative cannot be merely speculative, preoccupied with questions about why God tried Abraham or what relationship pertained between God's command and Abraham's ethical life. On the other hand, attentive or engaged reading (and retelling) is also insufficient. The kind of reading that Kierkegaard's *Fear and Trembling* implicitly argues for is neither limited to any one approach nor simply expanded to recognize a plethora of possible approaches. Rather, reading Genesis 22 is portrayed as a demanding and terrible obligation.[37] De Silentio argues that those who read this story about Abraham must be willing "to labor and be heavy laden." The labor of reading the *akedah* is an ongoing (and repeated) act, best undertaken when we are "laden" with the awfulness of taking the story seriously, as we try to walk up the mountain with Abraham and Isaac. But also laden with an awareness that all our efforts to understand the story and its hero will fall short, will inevitably fail, and may lead us deeper into self-doubt. It is through these labors of reading that we stay in relationship with Abraham. It is through this ongoing (absurd) effort that reading Genesis 22 offers a formative relationship to the father of faith.

Philip the Chancellor

Many medieval readings of the *akedah* could be presented here if the main purpose of this study were to offer a comprehensive overview of such interpretation in the Middle Ages. My aims here are rather, through focused consideration of one medieval treatment of Genesis 22, to supplement the presentation of medieval readings in the work of the contemporary ethicists examined in previous chapters and, more importantly, to illuminate a medieval methodological legacy. By examining this legacy I hope to demonstrate both its possibilities and the distortions resulting from our own uncritical adoption of certain ways of appropriating the text in contemporary Christian ethics.

37. Kierkegaard says elsewhere that "the most important ethical and religious truths cannot be communicated directly, as though one were writing on a blank sheet of paper. They demand instead creative endeavor by author and a corresponding effort by the reader that involves 'bringing to light by the application of a caustic fluid a text which is hidden under another text'" (*The Point of View for My Work as An Author,* 40, in the *Cambridge Companion,* 257).

It must be admitted that no Christian medieval reading of Genesis 22 has comparable influence in contemporary moral theology to Kierkegaard's nineteenth-century "dialectical lyric," *Fear and Trembling,* which, in the words of Ronald Green, "shapes modern access to the Genesis text."[38] Nor does medieval exegesis of Genesis 22 (or of the biblical text more generally) seem to be an acknowledged or explicit source in much contemporary ethical reflection. Yet, as we have seen, both Ronald Green and Timothy Jackson view such readings as important to their own discussions of the *akedah.* For Green, Thomas Aquinas's treatment of the sacrifice of Isaac is the watershed moment in the history of interpretation that "opens the door" to all modern concerns about the relationship of biblical authority to human moral reasoning. For Jackson, the "traditional view" of the *akedah* (which he seems to associate with medieval readings like Aquinas's) is the principal foil to his own reading. It seems likely, however, that — acknowledged or not — medieval readings continue to influence the ways contemporary (Christian) ethicists treat the Hebrew Bible, perhaps especially in the case of Genesis 22, if in distorted (from the perspective of my proposals and perhaps also from the perspective of the medieval theologians) ways.

The centerpiece of this section of my argument is a close reading of a discussion of Abraham's sacrifice by the thirteenth-century medieval theologian Philip the Chancellor. For my purposes, study of Philip's treatment of Genesis 22 will supplement both Jackson's characterization of the "traditional" view of the story and Green's understanding of Thomas Aquinas's treatment of the story and will help demonstrate certain contemporary interpretive moves and the assumptions about the character of the biblical text that warrant such moves.

We begin, then, by revisiting Timothy Jackson's argument in *Love Disconsoled.* Before beginning to develop his own reading of Genesis 22, Jackson briefly describes what he calls the "traditional view" of the story (which he assumes to be singular, or univocal). This view, as he presents it, can be summed up by saying that Genesis 22 teaches "that one must be willing to surrender anything, including persons dear to you, before God."[39] The relationship between humans beings and God is described as

---

38. Ronald Green, *Religion and Moral Reason* (New York: Oxford University Press, 1988), 122.

39. Jackson, *Love Disconsoled: Meditations on Christian Charity,* Cambridge Studies in Religious and Critical Thought (Cambridge: Cambridge University Press, 1999), 180.

"trumping" the relationships and moral obligations people have to one another. In Jackson's description, this amounts to a kind of divine command theory in which God's commands can not ever be properly called unjust for the simple reason that "God is the utterly sovereign Creator to whom everything is owed." (As we will see in Green's discussion of Aquinas, there is a possible distinction between seeing all God's commands as just because he is "utterly sovereign" and because God is someone to whom human beings owe a just debt, someone to whom "everything is owed." But this is not a distinction that enters into Jackson's depiction of the traditional view.) Jackson does not explicitly equate his characterization of the "traditional view" with any particular or sustained medieval argument, but he uses Aquinas as his main spokesman for it by quoting the following passage from the *Summa*:

> God is Lord of death and life, for by His decree both the sinful and the righteous die. Hence he [like Abraham] who at God's command kills an innocent man does not sin, as neither does God Whose behest he executes: indeed his obedience to God's commands is a proof that he fears Him. (ST II-II, Q64:art 6, ad i)

Here Jackson quotes Aquinas as if the great medieval theologian were using the biblical text to prove God's complete sovereignty. As the following close reading of Philip the Chancellor will illustrate, it seems unlikely that such a purpose would have occurred to a medieval theologian: the authority and sovereignty, as well as the justice, of God are completely assumed. What needs to be worked out, as we will see in Green's more complete presentation of Aquinas and in a close reading of Philip, is *a better understanding* of the moral (and reasoned) implications of God's justice and Abraham's righteousness, especially for our own understanding of moral theology. Medieval interpreters taking up this task delve into far more subtle issues — refining ideas about justice, law, and authority — than can be summarized by a simplistic notion that God's power trumps human ideas of justice.

Of course, Jackson's purpose in describing the "traditional view" of Genesis 22 is certainly not to comprehensively and accurately represent such treatments; rather, he intends to describe a common and prevalent reading of the story in its history of interpretation and then to identify three problems he believes this view presents. The first problem Jackson identifies is that such a view would indicate that the world, and human beings in particular, have no intrinsic value such that God "is inclined, much less bound, to respect [them] for their own sakes." Second, this view "would seem to corrupt individual consciousness" as it presents God's authority as deriving from "a cavalier and inscrutable power" and encourages the "veneration of a homicidal Abraham." Third, and, for Jackson's proposals most importantly, this view shows God as capable of commanding anything "with sublime indifference," which removes any meaning from the concept of God's love.[40] While I am sympathetic to these criticisms and both acknowledge and join Jackson in his concern regarding the prevalence of such readings in popular tradition, we will see that these concerns cannot be properly applied to a treatment like Philip's, or indeed (through the second-hand presentation by Green), to that of Aquinas. It would seem that we need to nuance our ideas about the "traditional or pious view," or at least our association of such a view with medieval and other past treatments of the text — particularly if we are to better understand the legacy of these past readings in our own treatments of the akedah.

If Jackson's description of a "traditional view" of the text is broad and generalized, Green's presentation of medieval readings is almost exclusively focused on the treatment of Genesis 22 in the work of Thomas Aquinas, which he identifies as a turning point in the history of the story's interpretation. He argues that Aquinas, in his reading of the sacrifice of Isaac (and in his theological thought overall), makes possible a fundamental tension between revelation and human reason by identifying these as distinguishable sources of moral information. On one hand, the moral obligations recorded in the biblical text, revealed divine law, are always and unchangeably valid because God is just and eternal. On the other, the humanly established laws that rest on our rational perception of created order and the laws of the natural world (what we perceive as "natural law") are also valid and authoritative. These sources of moral obligations — biblical revelation, and human rational apprehension of natural law — originate, of course, in the same ultimate source, which is God. The same God who reveals himself in the Bible created the order of the universe and gave human beings the capacity to apprehend it. And while Green acknowledges that Aquinas would not think of it this way, being deeply steeped in the biblical perspective of his Christian medieval world, he asserts that Aquinas's claims about the potential of human moral reason puts these

40. Jackson, *Love Disconsoled*, 181.

two sources into conversation with one another in such a way as to open the door to possible tensions between them. Green sees in Aquinas's treatment of the Genesis 22 story the first hints of a (very qualified) "moral discomfort," in his sensitivity to the fact that the command of God to Abraham may not seem to be consistent with a normal human idea of what is morally permissible.[41] Also remarkable, according to Green, is the fact that Aquinas does not use the "implicit moral justifications" found in earlier traditions about the text: he does not make claims about Abraham's belief in the resurrection of Isaac as found in, say, the Letter to the Hebrews, nor does he, in Green's words, "stick to the clear sense of Scripture" and argue that God did not intend for the sacrifice to be carried out.[42] Instead, what Green sees in Aquinas is the "first explicit effort to harmonize revelation and moral reasoning."[43] It is this effort that Green characterizes as a "strain."[44]

The "problematic appearance" of God's command stems from two sources. The first is its relationship to the Decalogue, with its *revealed* commandment against killing an innocent person. The obvious problem that human reason can identify here is an apparent contradiction between God's revealed law in the Decalogue and his particular command to Abraham in Genesis 22. Aquinas also considers in this regard God's ordering his people to take the vessels of the Egyptians in Exodus 12:35 and God's command to the prophet Hosea to marry a promiscuous wife in Hosea 1:2. These three biblical stories and the related challenges they appear to present received attention from several theologians in Aquinas's day, perhaps because of shared familiarity with earlier influential readings such as that of Bernard of Clairvaux in his treatise, *De praecepto et dispensatione*. We will see that Philip also connects these three narratives in his reading of the sacrifice of Isaac and makes specific allusion to Bernard's earlier treatment of them. But while Green relays Aquinas's discussion of all three stories, he does not acknowledge that Aquinas was following established interpretive precedent in associating them; it is clear that Aquinas attends to the cases in question not because he is the first to have some sense of "moral dis-

---

41. Green, *Religion and Moral Reason*, 109 (as we will see, for Philip this is less an occasion for discomfort than an opportunity to work out and refine the implications of this story for moral theology).

42. Green, *Religion and Moral Reason*, 113.

43. Green, *Religion and Moral Reason*, 113.

44. Green, *Religion and Moral Reason*, 111.

comfort" with them but rather because he is following a tradition that identifies these stories as presenting apparent contradictions.

The second source of apparent difficulty lies in Aquinas's argument that a law derives its authority from its inclination towards preserving and promoting the common good. God's revealed laws are always valid, as God is just; God's laws are always "rational ordinances for the common good and thus potentially accessible to human reason."[45] On the grounds of Genesis 22, how can the apparent contradiction make sense? Even while in one place Green characterizes Aquinas's task as "justifying the ways of God"[46] to human beings, in another he more accurately notes that the question that worried Aquinas is demonstrating that the "natural law and the standards of human reason have the stability and clarity" he claims for them.[47] Regardless of Green's inconsistency on this issue, for a medieval theologian like Aquinas, it is never the consistency, validity, and authority of God's commands that need to be defended, but rather our human ability *to apprehend* that these commands are consistent, valid, authoritative. It also appears that if anyone's acts are being justified, they are Abraham's (not God's): this will be apparent in Philip's discussion as well.

Green argues that Aquinas resolves these apparent contradictions by distinguishing between the unchangeable basic or highest-order principles of natural law (also revealed in divine law) and specific applications of these principles. These principles are always valid everywhere for all rational beings. On the other hand, in their application, "complex special cases may lead to conclusions seemingly different from the highest order principles."[48] So with regard to the law against killing, it can be argued that the just execution of a criminal does not break this law; the criminal's life is forfeited for the common good. In Aquinas's biblically informed perspective, the same kind of conclusion applies to all human life, which, since the sin and fall of Adam, is justly forfeit to God. Thus, for God to demand one of those lives is just, not merely because God is all-powerful but because of a prior *human* act. On this reading, God's act in commanding the execution of one of these forfeit lives is just in the same way it would be just for a proper human authority to order the execution of a particular criminal.

45. Green, *Religion and Moral Reason*, 110-12.
46. Green, *Religion and Moral Reason*, 113.
47. Green, *Religion and Moral Reason*, 111.
48. Green, *Religion and Moral Reason*, 110.

It is not as obvious to me as it seems to Green, that Aquinas is "straining" here. The claim that human life is forfeit to God because of "the sin of our first parent" is consistent and common in medieval Christian theology. That the "innocence" of a person is in relationship to the laws and judgment of the authority who is assessing him or her is also a logical and common move. And finally, claiming that Abraham, in carrying out the command of a *rightful* authority, is not guilty of wrong-doing, "is no murderer any more than God is,"[49] is still a widely accepted legal and logical principle. Green is careful to point out that this argument, whatever our modern instincts may say about it, does not result in a divine command ethics in which God can essentially command anything because it is God's command that designates things as right or wrong. But he again refers to Aquinas's "handling of these episodes" as "strained," claiming that this strain is not surprising in that what Aquinas is doing is "unprecedented" in a "context where [the ways of God], however primitively recorded in the earliest texts, have always instinctively been regarded as just."[50] For Aquinas, as Green goes on to make clear, there are unchangeable basic standards of right and wrong. In this particular situation, the command God gives in Genesis 22 (and the commands in Exodus and Hosea) would be morally justifiable to a *similarly situated* human being.

While arguing that Aquinas's treatment of Genesis 22 "opens the door to ideas that would eventually tear apart the unexamined synthesis between moral reason and revelation,"[51] Green acknowledges that "where biblical revelation, at least, was concerned, Aquinas was no revolutionary."[52] There is no questioning here of the authority or relevance of the biblical text; Aquinas, with other Christian medieval thinkers, inhabits a world defined by, immersed in, biblical faith. But now, in addition to belief in biblical authority, we find belief in human moral reason, and thus, attention to how what is revealed in the biblical text can be apprehended by that capacity. There is no doubt in Aquinas's mind that human reason, when applied properly, carefully, and attentively to what God does and commands in the Bible, will detect perfect consistency.[53] Perhaps it is for this reason that

---

49. Aquinas, Q 100, art. 8, reply obj 3. Quoted by Green, *Religion and Moral Reason*, 112.

50. Green, *Religion and Moral Reason*, 113.

51. Green, *Religion and Moral Reason*, 114.

52. Green, *Religion and Moral Reason*, 111.

53. Green, *Religion and Moral Reason*, 111.

"straining" does not seem the best characterization of Aquinas's treatment of Genesis. With what Green calls the "naive confidence . . . evident in Aquinas . . . that human moral reason and revealed morality are one," tension or strain is unimaginable. Nor is it accurate to characterize Aquinas's treatment of these issues as unprecedented. In such readings of the biblical text in medieval moral philosophy, the task is to continue to refine human understanding. A close reading of another medieval treatment of Genesis 22 provides an illuminating example of how this task of refining moral theology through reading the Hebrew Bible was carried out, so let us turn now to Aquinas's near-contemporary Philip the Chancellor.

Several of the important characteristics of medieval ethical readings of biblical text can be found in the treatment of Genesis 22 by Philip, an early-thirteenth-century (d. circa 1236) Parisian secular theologian.[54] Philip's milieu is interesting for several reasons. It is in the university in Paris, very shortly after Philip's time (around 1235-1240), that an explicit distinction is made between the study of *pagina sacra* ("non-scientific" biblical exegesis) and *theologia* (defined, on the other hand, as a [or *the*] science). Until this separation, theology "existed only as biblical exegesis."[55] Like other theologians of his time (as well as many who come before and after), Philip focuses on Genesis 22 precisely because of the possible *appearance* of contradictions — within biblical revelation itself and between revealed or divine law and human reasoning about justice and, interestingly, between what God wants and what God commands. The appearance of such possible contradictions becomes for Philip an occasion for the careful refinement of the terms and concepts by which human beings reason about right and wrong and about God's relationship to us as well as to natural law, written law, and reason itself. He also, typically enough, gives careful attention to preceding authoritative discussions of this text. While none of these characteristics are unique to a medieval treatment of the text, the basic assumptions about the justice of God most accessibly and perfectly presented through the authority, integrity, and universality of the biblical text are the necessary foundations of an argu-

---

54. "Secular" here indicating that he was not a member of a religious order though he was, of course, a cleric.

55. For a more complete discussion of this split and its ramifications for medieval biblical exegesis, see the source of my information here, Gilbert Dahan, "Genres, Forms and Various Methods in Christian Exegesis of the Middle Ages," in *Hebrew Bible / Old Testament: The History of Its Interpretations*, vol. 1, *From the Beginnings to the Middle Ages (Until 1300)*, ed. Magne Sæbø (Göttingen: Vandenhoeck and Ruprecht, 2000), 212-13.

ment such as Philip's and are discernible both in his method of discussing the text and in his conviction in doing so.[56]

The specific form of Philip's discussion of Genesis 22 is that of a medieval *quaestio*.[57] He begins by describing the apparent problem: The Lord commanded that Isaac be sacrificed. A command like this is contrary to the precept not to kill and thus is contrary to natural law. Since the Lord commands this action that conflicts with natural law, he is able to command others. The possibility that concerns Philip the most, it seems, is that it might appear that God could command a person to commit adultery. This apparent conclusion results in following a certain logic based on reading Genesis 22 in conjunction with an over-simplified (as Philip will demonstrate) understanding of natural law and its prescriptions that leads to misguided analogies between such precepts. The statement of the apparent contradiction and the consideration of the resulting possibilities with regard to adultery as identified by Philip are then followed by a series of objections (containing occasional digressions) which are in turn answered in a series of "contras." Philip uses both of the divisions or forms within the *quaestio* to work out a variety of refinements, ultimately demonstrating, in his responses to the objections (the "contras"), the appropriateness (accessible to human reason) of both God's command and Abraham's obedience. One of the most interesting characteristics of a treatment like Philip's (especially when one compares it to more recent treatments like Kierkegaard's, or especially Jackson's) is that the reading and interpretation of the biblical text remain strikingly straightforward. It is the straightforward reading of the text that forces or allows a medieval moral theologian like Philip to refine, and then refine some more, his moral philosophy, his definition of natural law, and his

---

56. Philip the Chancellor, *Summa de bono, de justitia,* Q. 8 (on obedience), art. 11.b. I am following the (unpublished) translation of Jean Porter, based on the excerpted Latin text published in Odon Lottin's *Le Droit Naturel chez Saint Thomas d'Aquin et ses Predecesseurs,* 2nd edition (Brussels: Beyaert, 1931), 111-14. The complete text of the *Summa de bono* is available, with introduction and notes in French, as *Philippi Cancellarii Parisiensis Summa de bono,* 2 vols., ed. Nicolai Wicki (Bern: Francke, 1985); the text under consideration can be found in volume 2, 1024-29, of Wicki's edition.

57. While Philip was working in the 13th century during the period when the exposition and the disputed question were beginning to be distinguished, even after this distinction is complete the intermingling of forms is present: "exegesis often develop[ed] along the lines of doctrinal research, argumentation, arguing from suitabilities, and, lengthily at times, refuting errors." See M. D. Chenu, *Toward an Understanding of Saint Thomas* (Chicago: Henry Regnery, 1964), 253.

reading of the traditions he has inherited. The text (with his accompanying assumptions about its accessibility to human reason) forces refinement of his moral theology rather than the other way around; his commitment to particular ethical ideas does not force "refinement" of his reading of the text.

Philip defines natural law later in this same *quaestio* as that which is both prescribed by and written into natural reason. One of the fundamental prescriptions of nature, or, equivalently, natural reason, is to preserve the species, and this prescription appears to be relevant to his discussion of both the command to Abraham and the hypothetical command to commit adultery. Following his statement, Philip offers the general position against the apparent problem that he will go on to develop: that some actions cannot be rendered good no matter what, but that killing can be rendered good in some circumstances. By "good" one assumes here that he means killing can sometimes be directed towards the preservation of the species, or more generally described, the common good. He then begins to clarify by describing killing as an action that does not have a "deformity" within itself and thus can receive "compensation" if it is directed towards a good. His examples of such a good are the killing of criminals for the good of society and the killing of heretics for the growth of the church.

What about the command of God in Genesis 22? The key refinement that Philip offers to explicate the reasonableness or appropriateness of laws or commands is the proposition that "some prescriptions are [given] with respect to a purpose, and some, with respect to a subject matter." The purpose, the ultimate reason, for any proper prescription is God, and, following from that, ?God's purposes, which are represented by the basic principles of natural law. Thus "God can in no way command anything contrary to those prescriptions which pertain to purpose" since to do so would be a self-contradiction. Going back to Philip's concern with adultery, this means that God cannot command someone to have sexual relations for the sake of lust. That would be contrary to the purpose, which must first of all be Godself, and secondarily the preservation of the species. On the other hand, God can command something contrary to prescriptions with regard to the subject matter of the command. The biblical examples that Philip draws on to demonstrate this point are Jacob's four wives and Abraham's sexual relationship with Hagar.[58] Such ex-

---

58. For a contemporary reader, important feminist concerns are and should be raised

amples are commands that Philip characterizes as against natural law as human reason apprehends it; nonetheless, it is appropriate that God can command them in the same way God can perform miraculous works. The purpose of the commands — ultimately Godself — remains God so there is no contradiction even if such precepts, or works, are (in one sense) not natural. In this way, Philip distinguishes the possibility of God commanding someone to commit adultery (which he characterizes as having a licentious purpose within it) from God's actual command to Abraham about Isaac. The action of killing carries no purpose within itself, and God did not command Abraham to have a purpose other than God; thus nothing in the command was inappropriate. Isaac's innocence was a circumstance with regard to the "subject matter" of the command, and this, like Hagar's not being Abraham's wife, does not make the command to sacrifice him contrary to the precept not to kill the innocent. Or viewed from another perspective, it appears that the command could not have been that Abraham *desire* to kill Isaac for the sake of killing him or that he kill him *because* he was innocent.

If a distinction between the "purpose" of a precept and the "subject" of it demonstrates to human reason that God's command to Abraham was appropriate, what then follows concerning Abraham's actions in obeying it? Philip refines the way in which obedience to a superior authority is proper, even if the appearance of that authority's commands is confusing to the one following it. To illustrate this, he argues that if a person is guilty according to the law and the proofs it demands, a judge (who is a minister to the authority of that law) must act according to the law even if, "according to his own knowledge," he believes the person to be innocent. In such a case it is not the judge who executes the person but the law, which has rightful authority to do so (and to which the judge owes obedience). This assumes, of course, a just law that is directed towards the common good. In carrying out the authority of the law, a judge is acting reasonably and properly. The law and its proofs are reasonable and authoritative. More so then is God, in commanding Abraham. For Philip, a legal and logical analogy allows him to establish that Abraham is both good and reasonable in his obedience to God and thus, through refining human understanding of the reasonableness of obedience to rightful authority, the actions of Abraham are made sensible (as well as good).

---

by such an argument. The importance of contemporary ethical insight in the reading of Genesis 22 is discussed in the next chapter.

Another possible interpretation of the text (raised in the series of objections that Philip considers) is that the action of killing is simply made good by God's having commanded it. The argument for this possible interpretation lies in an analogy to God's command to Adam in the garden of Eden which made an act "not evil itself, but indifferent and lawful" — that is, the act of eating a particular fruit — into an act that was evil. If an order can make a neutral, even wholesome, act like eating a piece of fruit into an evil one, then, this objection continues, an order can make an evil act good — *especially* when such an order is given by God. The use of "especially" here is noteworthy, as it indicates that in this interpretation to which Philip will respond we are not getting simple divine command theory but a more generally applicable "command" theory of law.[59] The concern in this objection is whether an order from any rightful authority (noting that God is the *most* rightful authority) can change the fundamental character of an act, or it seems, can change a fundamental principle of natural law. Philip counters this interpretation by reiterating and continuing to refine distinctions between the subject and the purpose of a command or act and the fundamental prescriptions of natural law and their application in particular situations. An act like killing is understood to be evil in some respects, but "not simply." Certain circumstances can give such an act, which does not have a "deformity" within it, that is, does not necessarily contain a purpose other than God, compensation. Thus the killing of Isaac is not made good "simply": the nature of killing an innocent is not changed generally by God's command. But it is made good "for him to whom it was commanded." From this position or refinement, Philip is able to make an indirect allusion to the outcome of the story of Genesis 22 (that God stops the sacrifice), saying that "the Lord wished Abraham not to sacrifice Isaac" while simultaneously claiming that Abraham's obeying of the command was a good act (for Abraham and Abraham only). Again, it is apparent that a relatively straightforward reading of the story, coupled with some traditional theological convictions about God's goodness, justice, unchangeability, and authority, becomes for Philip the occasion to explicate and refine the understanding of natural law, the nature of precepts, and the role particular circumstances play in their application.

There are other points of interest in the study of Philip's treatment of Genesis 22 for my own project in this volume. First, his interest in and re-

59. This parallels the argument discussed above regarding the judge and the law.

spect for other parts of the biblical text (particularly other parts of the Hebrew Bible) deserve consideration. Obviously, he is concerned with the two other traditionally associated texts (Exodus 22 and Hosea 1); the Adam and Eve story also merits brief discussion in his response to an objection. Additionally, he pays constant, if not always explicit, attention to the Decalogue — for while the precept against killing is primarily discussed in terms of its embodiment of the fundamental principle of natural law regarding the preservation of the species, Philip's distinction between the command "do not commit adultery" and the imperative "do not kill" constantly brings to mind these "written" laws of God given on Mount Sinai and preserved in the biblical text. For a medieval theologian such as Philip, the fundamental prescriptions of natural law are unchangeably recorded in these writings. Law texts and other narratives in the biblical canon must therefore be read alongside Genesis 22, and all must make sense, fit together, in a way that is not contrary to reason.

Second, Philip's treatment of the *akedah*, like that of Aquinas, does not turn to the New Testament or the idea of resurrection to "solve" or resolve the moral reasonableness of Genesis 22. The only New Testament reference in Philip's treatment comes in the context of an argument about a possible analogy between God commanding Abraham to commit an act like killing Isaac and, hypothetically, commanding him not to believe that God was to be incarnate. Here Philip is exploring possible parallels between commands concerning articles of faith and commands concerning acts that have a deformity within them. Certainly, nowhere in Philip's consideration of Genesis 22 is there any equivalent to Jackson's argument that Abraham's act was good because he believed in Isaac's resurrection or that God's ironic and schooling actions and disconsoling love only finally make sense in light of the cross and resurrection. Historically and theologically it is clear that no Christian medieval philosopher like Philip regards the New Testament as superfluous to the understanding of the Old; nor would he be troubled by concerns about supersessionism as we have come to define it. On the other hand, for a theologian, philosopher, and reader of the text like Philip, it seems critical that the Hebrew Bible (or specifically here Genesis 22) and the actions and commands of God recorded there be understood as accessible to human reason. The story of Abraham's near-sacrifice of his son, like all biblical texts, (must) make moral and reasonable sense according to natural law. The fundamental precepts that make this possible (as well as make this story an occasion for discussing its apparent contradictions) are unchanging, whether accessed through knowledge of God's written law (other biblical texts) or nature and human reason. The events described in the New Testament, whatever else they do, did not change these fundamental prescriptions, and the refining of our understanding through engagement with the texts of the Hebrew Bible like Genesis 22 must be done on the *text's own terms*. Or at the very least, we can say that Philip shapes his consideration of Genesis 22 in this way.

A third characteristic in Philip's treatment of Genesis 22 that warrants attention is the role and status he assigns other earlier readings of the text in the history of its interpretation. As noted previously, his connecting of the *akedah* with the events narrated in Exodus 22 and in Hosea 1 seems to follow associations of those stories in previous discussions. That Bernard of Clairvaux's *De praecepto et dispensatione* is one of the sources from whom Philip inherits this grouping is made explicit in that one of the objections that Philip discusses arises from a reading of Bernard's treatment of these texts. The objection arises that Bernard "seems to say," among other things, that God ordered something contrary to "do not commit adultery." According to Philip's account, Bernard distinguishes between prescriptions that are "stable, inviolable, or incommutable." He then characterizes the commands "do not kill," "do not commit adultery," and "do not steal," as "inviolable," meaning these precepts come from divine, and not human, authority. They can only be changed (or indeed nullified) by God. Such acts as those described in Exodus 22 and Hosea 1 are only excused because of God's command and authority, by which it seems God can (as in Hosea) order someone to commit adultery (the possibility that so concerns Philip). Philip does not handle this tradition from Bernard by claiming it is mistaken. His very discussion of it confirms the authoritative status he assumes it must have. Rather, he ascribes to this reading of Bernard the same distinction between the purpose and the subject of commands that he discusses earlier when directly reading this biblical text. Yes, he agrees, "on the authority of St. Bernard, only God can command contrary to inviolable necessity." But he then goes on to reply that God could and can only command so because he commands with regard to subject matter and not purpose. The purpose remains God. For example, God commands that Hosea join himself to a prostitute (Gomer is the subject here but the purpose is still God), but it does not follow that God can command someone to "fornicate," where the purpose of the act is lust, not God. This distinction is not new; it repeats the distinction already made by Philip in this same *quaestio.* But it is here applied to the traditional interpretation of Genesis 22 inherited from Bernard with the same care he earlier used in applying it to the biblical text. Bernard's reading is not characterized as mistaken but is rather assumed to be authoritative; to understand it properly, as Philip demonstrates, we must recognize the distinctions regarding the subject and the purposes of precepts. In other words, from Philip's point of view, our traditions are authoritative, but our understanding of them may need refining. So much more so, then, with the biblical text itself!

Returning to Jackson's objections to the "traditional view" as he sets it up, it is evident that these do not apply properly to a reading such as Philip's.[60] First, the concern that human beings and human lives have no intrinsic value that God is inclined or bound to respect seems inappropriate. Philip would no doubt avoid any language that "binds" God in any way, but his identification of the "preservation of the species" as one of the most fundamental precepts of natural law (and thus God's law) seems to make such a concern foreign. Additionally, Philip goes as far as to say God does not wish Isaac's death. To imagine God disregarding human life would be to imagine a divine self-contradiction. Instead, Philip's argument regarding the compensation that makes some acts of killing appropriate tends to support the claim that human life has a value, for it is this value that must be compensated.

With respect to Jackson's second objection, that the "traditional" reading presents a God whose authority is inscrutable and an Abraham who is homicidal, it is clear that both characterizations are strongly contradicted in Philip's treatment. That God's authority and commands are appropriate, just, and accessible to human reason are the foundational assumptions of Philip's treatment. And Abraham's obedience to rightful, just, and reasonable authority (God's) is characterized by Philip as good and appropriate. Never is he homicidal (wishing innocent Isaac's death on its own account), nor does God command him to be so. This would be in direct contradiction to Philip's careful distinction between the subject and the purpose of an act or precept.

Third, Philip's treatment does not present us with Jackson's objectionable portrait of a God who is "sublimely indifferent." Compensations, purposes directed towards the good (construed both as the good of the

---

60. I am not here claiming that Jackson would identify Philip as fitting into his characterization of this view but rather using his objections as useful discussion points with respect to Philip's approach.

species and as Godself), the wish for Isaac not to be killed: all these directly contradict any notion of God's indifference. Philip, at least, can be cleared of the charges Jackson brings to "the traditional view" of Genesis 22. Indeed, Philip's treatment does not fit Jackson's characterization at all. Nor, from our reading of Green, would Aquinas's, though it is a citation from Aquinas that Jackson uses to express such a view. Again, I do think the view Jackson describes is both prevalent and problematic, but associating it with the period of Philip the Chancellor and Thomas Aquinas seems capricious when the moral reasonableness of the biblical text was so thoroughly assumed.

Whether or not Ronald Green would read Philip's treatment of Genesis 22 as "straining" as he does Aquinas's, we cannot know. But from this study, it does not appear that such a characterization would fit. This is not to say that Philip's assumptions and concerns do not strike contemporary ears as peculiar. For Philip the killing of heretics is justified by the growth of "the church"; this is for him an apparently obvious example of when killing receives compensation. To the twenty-first-century reader, such an argument seems both strange and fanatical (and yet frighteningly familiar). So, of course, does Philip's view of Jacob's wives and Abraham's sexual relationship with Hagar. In fact, the central attention given to adultery in the consideration of a story about child-sacrifice seems eccentric, to say the least, to contemporary ethicists whose concerns about the story typically focus on the potent(ial) violence it presents. But in Philip's treatment, one that rests on the refinement of an understanding of precepts with regard to purpose and subject, the connection is, well, rational. Adultery receives attention as a foil to killing for several reasons. It is the subject of another precept that is also both characterized as revealed (part of the Decalogue) and believed to be accessible through reason and natural law. And it is a precept that also demands examination through apparently problematic biblical texts. But unlike the command not to kill, Philip believes "do not commit adultery" contains a reference to purpose (the purpose of lust in sexual relations) and thus committing adultery, by definition, contains a deformity within it. The attentive comparison then of the precept against adultery with the precept against killing makes sense in Philip's treatment; it is through this comparison that he can elucidate the distinction he needs in order to demonstrate, through reasoned argument, that God did not command anything inappropriate in Genesis 22. All this is to acknowledge the evident strangeness of some of Philip's treatment to the contemporary reader[61] but at the same time to assert that within the argument itself, taken on its own terms, there is no "straining." Instead it is an elegant piece of reasoning and refinement of human understanding of the nature of prescriptions, commands, and law that takes as its starting point and touchstone a relatively straightforward reading of Genesis 22.

In addition to supplementing the discussions of medieval/traditional treatments of Genesis 22 in the work of Timothy Jackson and Ronald Green, the examination of Philip's *quaestio* concerning the sacrifice of Isaac, and whether God can command something against natural law, points us in the direction of one of the central issues of this volume — the status of the biblical text in Christian ethics. Philip's treatment illuminates this issue because, for a theologian like him, the unique and complete authority, inerrancy, and universal accessibility to reason of the biblical text are the assumptions that make both the occasion and the method of his treatment possible. Thus, a difficult text (difficult in that it appears to contain a theological and ethical contradiction) like Genesis 22 becomes the reason for explicating and refining moral philosophy rather than an occasion of moral discomfort. The discussion of Philip Quinn, whose treatment is probably most similar to Philip's, provides a useful counterpoint. Quinn, while calling for more attentive and sensitive reading of the biblical story, turns to the theological propositions of his tradition to refute the "actuality" of it. Rather than becoming an occasion to nuance and refine moral theology, the reading of the *akedah* runs up against it, and is finally trumped by it. Contemporary ethicists like Quinn do not have the kind of pre-critical view of the biblical text that Philip had; they do not expect that through reasoning and refining our own understanding of ethics the story will be resolved or de-problematized. Perhaps this is one reason Kierkegaard's reading has become such an important interpretation of the story in contemporary ethics: it grants authority to the text but rejects its accessibility to human reason, taking it completely out of the realm of ethical requirements. Ironically then, the modern text that takes the *akedah* narrative (and its biblical context) most seriously is also the means by which Genesis 22 is discounted as a relevant or authoritative source of *moral* reasoning.[62]

---

61. On the other hand, there are aspects of Philip's reading that sound familiar and appeal to a contemporary reader — particularly his insistence that the particularities of a situation are crucial to understanding the application of a general principle of ethics.

62. This distinction is the reason for Green's "Enough Is Enough! *Fear and Trembling* Is Not about Ethics," *Journal of Religious Ethics* 21 (1993): 191-209.

Another characteristic of contemporary treatments of the biblical text illuminated by comparison to that of Philip the Chancellor is the approach to inherited interpretations. Like Philip in his discussion of Bernard of Clairvaux, contemporary interpreters often take into account earlier views. As can been seen in work like Green's or Jackson's, historical interpretations of Genesis 22 are still quite important to them: for Green, they provide comparative evidence about human reasoning and religion; for Jackson, figures like Kierkegaard and Blake are central conversation partners. Yet neither of these scholars sees himself as participating in the same task as the historical sources he critiques and selectively retrieves. What seems striking to us about Philip's reflections on Bernard (though this is typical of his time) is that, even within an objection, he not only assumes Bernard's authority (and the appropriateness of his interpretation) but also assumes a common task. Thus, when Philip attributes to Bernard's interpretation his (Philip's) own distinctions of "purpose" and "subject," Philip is not apparently being disingenuous but rather envisions his own work, his own refinements, as contributing to a common project, shaped by shared reading of a common text — the story of Genesis 22.[63] In contemporary Christian ethics, most of these connections and assumptions are fractured, lost, and sometimes, impossible. Presuppositions about the accuracy and authority of previous interpretations and inherited traditions are various and often contradictory. Different ethicists in different traditions and with different training are influenced by, and may even take as authoritative, a variety of earlier figures and interpretations, but just as often these interpretive sources are examined for the purposes of critique (perhaps with some selective retrieval) and presented as foils to the interpretation presented in the contemporary work. Instead of refining our understanding of what has come before us, the contemporary task has often become one of distinguishing ourselves from it.

If there is one interpretation of Genesis 22 that comes close to having "authority" for contemporary (Christian) ethicists, as Bernard of Clairvaux did for Philip the Chancellor, it would seem that source is Kierkegaard's *Fear and Trembling*. If so — if, when it comes to the sacrifice of Isaac, Kierkegaard is our Bernard — it is important to consider some of

---

63. It can't be ignored, however, that "objections" or contrary arguments are built into the very form of a medieval treatment like this — no ideal or naïve assumption here of universal agreement, but rather a shared commitment to text and confidence in reasoning that can achieve agreement with these (re)sources.

the ways this possible parallel can illuminate our own readings. Since the above study examined Bernard only through Philip and Philip's assumption that his work and Bernard's are in essential continuity, comparing Kierkegaard to Philip may serve to illuminate these possibilities. Both these sources assume the absolute authority of the biblical text, and thus of Genesis 22, but for Kierkegaard this does not mean it must be accessible to human reason while for Philip, its reasonableness is not only a basic assumption, but a necessary one.[64] Another difference worth noting is the ways in which these two treatments envision the labor of moral reflection in light of Genesis 22. For Kierkegaard's Johannes de Silentio, grappling with this story is an exhausting struggle. Philip is not plagued by any experience of the "awfulness" of this story or God's command, or any doubts about the endeavor to reason it through. For Philip, the labor of the task lies not in making sense of an "absurd" story but in the careful working out of refinements in our understanding of ethics and law. In a strange way, serious moral reasoning is important for both. It is his moral reason, coupled with attentive reading, that shows Kierkegaard's de Silentio the awfulness of the command and keeps him reading, and rereading, Genesis 22. For Philip, the reading of the story is the occasion for the exercise of moral reasoning, and reveals our need to continue refining ideas about natural law, the nature of commands, and justice. In addition to sharing an emphasis on moral reasoning (though in very different ways in relation to interpreting the text), both demonstrate, again very differently, that the task of reading this story in Christian ethics is ongoing. *Fear and Trembling* presents a portrait of a personal ongoing attempt to stay engaged with the story, whereas in Philip there is an ongoing (more communal) refinement of tradition and human understanding of the law motivated by its reading.

The differences between Kierkegaard and Philip not only reflect different views regarding the reasonableness of Genesis 22, they also reflect very different sensibilities. For many contemporary ethicists, Kierkegaard's elucidation of the awfulness of the command to Abraham is critical; his explicit attention to the reader (caught between reason and God's command) appeals to modern and postmodern awareness of and interest in

---

64. It is not unusual to hear acknowledgment and even frustration that there was no explicit theory of the relationship between reason and revelation in medieval theology. But this is not surprising if the relationship was a foundational assumption of the interpretation. On the other hand, it seems more problematic that contemporary Christian ethicists use the biblical text in their work without grappling with this question in meaningful ways, as they cannot claim to have any shared underlying view of this complex issue.

the self/subject. On the other hand, Philip's focus lies not on the reader of the text but on the text and its relationship to a system of law and ethics, and this through attention to *its* subject, the actions of God (and Abraham). And while Philip's concerns (at least on a superficial level) about adultery or his acknowledgment of the legitimacy of killing heretics immediately arouses contemporary suspicion, his assumption that reading this story will contribute to our understanding of human morality seems an important one, particularly if contemporary Christian ethicists hope to maintain a crucial role for the biblical text in their work.

It may also be helpful to compare the form of these very different treatments of Genesis 22. Kierkegaard's "dialectical lyric" is a provocative combination of the philosophical and the poetic. It is a creative work, beginning with the very creation of Johannes de Silentio, and yet this pseudonymous author describes himself as a "dialectician," a moral philosopher. *Fear and Trembling* is, in fact, (intentionally) *sui generis,* its very uniqueness corresponding with the view it presents of Abraham as un-mediatable and the reading of his story as inimitably personal. The form of Philip's treatment of Genesis 22 is, by contrast, entirely unoriginal — a medieval *quaestio* with its expected elements, order, and function. Philip's reflections on Genesis 22 fulfill formal expectations that are not created by Philip but are, rather, part of an inherited and communal tradition of medieval scholars and theologians. The goal was not to create something new, to emphasize any personal experience of reading, or certainly to pronounce on any perceived "absurdity" in the biblical text. In fact, Philip's concerns were directly opposed to such aims: his discussion assumes both the reasonableness of the biblical text and the ability of human reason to refine thought and ultimately settle disputes. The *quaestio* is, for a medieval theologian like Philip, one of the accepted ways these assumptions are expressed. As we have seen, such a text was understood to be part of a greater whole, not merely the whole of one's own work, or even of the collective effort of medieval theologians in establishing and systematizing a whole theology; it was actually understood as part of the entire process of re-claiming what could be re-claimed of knowledge lost, lost in the Garden and scattered throughout history. There is also, in the form of the *quaestio,* in both its repetitiveness and in the expectedness of its elements, a meditative character. In Philip's discussion of Genesis 22, for example, there are a rhythm to the objections and replies and a discipline in the adherence to the constraints of the *quaestio.* While the occasion for this treatment is an apparent contradiction, and the aim is the refinement of human reasoning in such a way as to resolve that contradiction, the nature of this discussion functions constantly to bring the reader back to reflecting, methodically and carefully, on the biblical text.

As easy as it is to contrast the form of Philip's treatment of Genesis 22 with that of Kierkegaard in *Fear and Trembling,* comparing it to the other contemporary treatments discussed in previous chapters is more complicated. At first glance, it would seem that Green, Quinn, and Jackson have more in common with Kierkegaard than with Philip the Chancellor, a connection highlighted by their modern sensibilities and their own aspirations to originality. And yet these, like other contemporary treatments of the biblical text in ethics, share a surprising number of characteristics with the medieval *quaestio* as well. Like Philip, contemporary ethicists are drawn to consider Genesis 22 because of the appearance of contradiction: for Green, it is the "hard case" for Jewish and Christian ethical interpretation, while for Jackson, the occasion for his reading is the perceived need to "square" Genesis 22 with his understanding of the New Testament love commands. Like Philip, these contemporary treatments draw on their own traditional "authorities," all being deeply indebted to Kierkegaard, among others. And like Philip, these contemporary religious ethicists share aspirations to analytical clarity and completeness. Their reflections can with some imagination be viewed as examples of a contemporary *quaestio,* even if they are less obviously or formally constrained than Philip's. Like their medieval counterparts, most contemporary ethicists assume that reasoning, arguing, and refining ethical propositions and theories will work to convince others of their appropriateness. More subtle are assumptions about the role of the biblical text, especially the Hebrew Bible, shared and not shared. For Philip the Bible was authoritative, inerrant, and neither historically nor culturally bound (though incidents and prescriptions could be understood sometimes only in their particular circumstances); its ethical authority and appropriateness were accessible to human reasoning. The role and status of the Hebrew Bible in contemporary Christian ethics are much less clear. Contemporary treatments of a biblical narrative such as the near-sacrifice of Isaac may sometimes be more elegantly written, more creative, and even more morally sensitive than a medieval *quaestio* like Philip's, but their attitude towards the text, and the role this attitude may play in shaping the proposals or theories offered, is less manifest. On the one hand, contemporary ethicists like those examined previously share with Philip and other medieval scholars an intellectual approach to the biblical text. Reasoning and analyzing the biblical text (and not some special grace, inspiration, or secret knowledge) are the means by which it is interpreted. This common approach to interpretation can be seen in tendencies to refine terms and make systematic proposals. On the other hand, contemporary ethicists do these things without the same convictions as their medieval counterparts about the integrity, authority, and universality of the biblical text in ethical reflections. Green treats interpretations as anthropological data, and, even as such, he does not explore the role or status of the biblical text (or the interpretations of it) in the traditions about which he is writing. Quinn's proposed reading of the dark depths of Genesis 22 is functionally dismissed when weighed against a theological logic that proves to him that the story cannot present an "actuality." And Jackson's ideas of Christian agapic love compel him to characterize God's command as "ironic" — a means of tricking Abraham out of an ethical stance not governed by love — and to view this story from the Hebrew Bible as one that only makes sense in light of the New Testament. All three ethicists look at Genesis 22 precisely because it is a biblical text, a challenging biblical text. But because none has a clear sense of the role or status of that text in their ethical reflections, these reflections can take a variety of turns that tend, at the very least, to use the biblical text to support their own ethical claims, or worse, to interpret the Hebrew Bible only though the lens of their own religious or theological convictions, or their assumptions about what is reasonable. The text itself never appears in these contemporary accounts as an occasion for challenging, refining, or nuancing such ideas.

Comparing contemporary and medieval approaches to the biblical text in ethical work reveals that our emulating (however unintentionally) aspects of the medieval *quaestio* demands scrutiny, as the relationship between moral reasoning and revelation in the two approaches is significantly different. Contemporary ethicists confronting the *akedah* aspire to completeness and analytical clarity, but without any conviction that the biblical text contributes to these goals in any direct way. This fact permits — indeed even requires — that contemporary philosophical, theological, and cultural analysis override any claims of the text itself on our attention, on us, and certainly on our ethical reflections. We may, in a kind of superficial continuity with the practices that precede us, use the Hebrew Bible in our moral theology as if we have shared assumptions about its authority, inerrancy, and unity, and yet all these assumptions have broken down — most primarily and obviously in the field of biblical scholarship.[65] Even

---

65. Clearly other postmodern concerns about the possibilities and limitations of human reason are also relevant forces in this breakdown, though these do not seem to have the

the most devout of contemporary Christian ethicists can scarcely be said to share the medieval theologian's assumption of, and thus inherent commitment to preserving, the status of the biblical text as inspired, inerrant, immediate, and authoritative. In contemporary discussions, the Hebrew Bible most often ends up functioning like any other text (and it is sometimes granted even less status than other texts because it arouses a wide array of suspicions). In an odd way, Green's failure to discuss the role or status of the Bible in the traditions he studies actually ends up expressing a functional reality in contemporary Christian ethics. A medieval theologian like Philip was immersed in textually transmitted tradition, anchored in Scripture, the text of texts. Labor in moral reasoning was carried out primarily, though perhaps not exclusively, through attention to texts. Or, to put this another way, the exposition of authoritative texts was, for the medieval scholar, the way of deriving almost all knowledge, including understanding of ethics. In that world, no text was as authoritative or as influential as the Bible. It was the authority of authorities.[66]

Contemporary Christian ethicists, then, seem caught between the perspectives of Kierkegaard and Philip — drawn to the fractured experience of reading Genesis 22 presented in all its awfulness in *Fear and Trembling* and yet somehow holding onto both the goals of moral reasoning and an assumption that this and other texts of the Hebrew Bible are significant for our moral reasoning. And yet, without an ability to articulate ways that the text has unique or special status for religious ethics, it becomes very unclear what that significance is.

Genesis Rabbah 55

So what do we do? How do we grapple with the special status of the Hebrew Bible in contemporary Christian ethics if we can't do so by holding pre-critical assumptions about its authority and perfection? A return to a pre-critical view of the text is not only impossible but, for most ethicists,

---

same impact on the particular treatments examined in Chapters Two and Three as does the lack of authority ascribed to the biblical text.

66. For one of the best discussions of the authority and role of the Bible in medieval scholarship and a refutation of the notion that the role of the Bible diminished in scholastic thought, see R. W. Southern, *Scholastic Humanism and the Unification of Europe*, vol. 1: *Foundations* (Oxford: Blackwell, 1995), especially chapter 3, "The Sovereign Textbook of the Schools: The Bible," 102-33.

clearly undesirable. One last study may help further illuminate these questions about the role and status of the Hebrew Bible in ethical reflection and even offer possible avenues to explore in addressing these concerns. As Yvonne Sherwood recently argued through her analysis of the sacrifice of Isaac in ancient Judaism, Christianity, and Islam, "the ancient interpreters come surprisingly close to 'us' and also give us some iconic ways of thinking paradoxes still very relevant to 'us.'"[67] Thus, the last historical study of this chapter turns to interpretations of Genesis 22 by the ancient rabbis in *Midrash Rabbah*.

This source has, of course, already been discussed in the context of our review of the work of Ronald Green, where a critique of Green's analysis and conclusions about "traditional Jewish" interpretation was also offered. Like the previous close readings of Kierkegaard and Philip the Chancellor, this study of *Genesis Rabbah* has a dual purpose: it will supplement the (problematic) discussions of this interpretive source in the work of other ethicists and, more importantly, it will offer some possible ways of reflecting on the issues of authority and interpretation of biblical texts in religious ethics. Like the two previous studies of historical interpretation in this chapter, it will be focused and selective. My aim is not, like Green, to represent or comprehend a whole tradition of interpretation. Rather, in serving my dual aims, the following study centers around a close reading of one *parashiyyoth* or chapter of one ancient midrashic compilation — *Bereshith (Genesis) Rabbah*. *Genesis Rabbah* is a collection of rabbinic exegesis usually assumed to have been given its final form towards the end of the fourth century or the beginning of the fifth century CE by redactors or editors, though much of the material it contains may have been composed much earlier. The rabbinic authors and compilers of this material were Jewish scholars and teachers whose approach to Scripture and Judaism (often distinguished within the diverse history of Judaism as "Rabbinic Judaism" and probably what Ronald Green meant by "traditional Judaism") took shape during the centuries immediately preceding and following the first millennium and continues in some expressions of Judaism today. As this commentary shows, the rabbis' interpretive focus was scriptural, historical, and ethical. Their meticulous attention to the text includes minute scrutiny of individual words, phrases, and even letters as well as wide-ranging refer-

67. Yvonne Sherwood, "Binding-Unbinding: Divided Responses of Judaism, Christianity, and Islam to the 'Sacrifice' of Abraham's Beloved Son," *Journal of the American Academy of Religion* 72 (2004): 855.

ences to other canonical texts. They see in this text ways of viewing and understanding their own particular historical situation (which had been radically altered by the rise of Christianity within the Roman Empire).

Unlike the other works of *Midrash Rabbah,* the volumes on Genesis present a verse-by-verse, chapter-by-chapter commentary (rather than a collection of homilies based on the biblical book). The three chapters in *Genesis Rabbah* devoted to Genesis 22 are chapters 55-57. The analysis here will focus on the first of these, *parasha* 55 (while drawing on material from 56, 57 and even 58 when necessary), which comments on only the first three verses of the chapter. The reason for this extreme selectivity owes, as I hope will become apparent, to the richness of the interpretive commentary itself. It is ethically, methodologically, and formally provocative, even in its address to just the first three verses of the *akedah.* Rather than try to summarize general ethical ideas or issues suggested by the whole treatment, or attempt to describe some general methodological or formal characteristics of the *Genesis Midrash* (or "Rabbinic" or "traditional Judaism," for that matter), it is more in keeping with my goals in this volume, and more cautious in the face of this ancient source, to attend carefully to one selective portion and see how it can contribute to contemporary ways of thinking ethically and interpretively about the biblical text.

Genesis Rabbah 55 is unlike the other two texts examined in this chapter in many important ways. Its distinctive provenance is the most obvious: it is from an ancient Jewish milieu and not a modern or medieval Christian one. But while the religious tradition of which a text is a part, as well as its historical context, are of course important in understanding the interpretations themselves, these obvious differences are not the characteristics that will concern us most (though they clearly condition the other characteristics that we will consider). As mentioned already, *Genesis Rabbah* differs from our other historical sources, as well as other *Midrash Rabbah,* in its form — a line-by-line commentary, interpreting as it proceeds through the text chronologically. Authorship and composition issues are more complex for *Genesis Rabbah* than for Philip's *quaestio* or Kierkegaard's "dialectical lyric." First, there are multiple rabbinic voices contained in this compilation, often identified, but certainly not always. They can frequently be heard commenting on the same verse, offering a variety of ways of interpreting it, sometimes even arguing. None is recognized as a more authoritative or "correct" interpreter than another; inclusion in the *Midrash Rabbah* indicates, rather, that all are deemed authoritative. In addition to these textually "audible" voices one must consider also the (rabbinic) compilers and editors — more correctly described as redactors — whose selection and arrangement of this material were likewise a form of interpretation. It is not remotely within the scope of this volume or my own expertise to sort out these layers of authorship and redaction from a historical perspective. But awareness of the complexity of this composition is important both in reading the text well and in considering its possible contributions to our thinking about ethical interpretation of the biblical text. Further comparisons between these very different but illuminating sources will be possible after examining a selection from *Genesis Rabbah*.

Parasha 55:1 of *Genesis Rabbah*[68] begins with a discussion of Genesis 22:1: "And it came to pass after these things that God did prove Abraham." Almost immediately the interpretation of the text turns to the issue of intention; with reference to another biblical text (Psalm 60:6), the purpose of God's proving or trying of Abraham is given as "truth," which is further explained as verifying to the world "the equity of God's justice." God's actions and choice are not arbitrary. In fact, to anyone who posits what we now label as a divine command theory about God's justice (by saying "Whom He wishes to enrich, He enriches; to impoverish, He impoverishes") the rabbis tell us we "can answer, 'Can you do what Abraham did?'" (that is, not refuse what God asked). What is noteworthy here is that at the very beginning of this discussion of the *akedah*, God's justice is appealed to, is equated with truth, and given as the (identifiable) purpose of God's actions in this story. The *akedah* is immediately framed as a story that does not call into question God's justice (or its readers' ability to perceive God's justice) but in fact posits this justice as the very objective of God's actions in Genesis 22. And God's choice of Abraham is shown to be part of this justice — not random but eminently reasonable: Abraham was chosen because he could succeed. This theme is continued into 55:2 where three rabbis offer their interpretations of God's choice, while considering Psalm 11:5 ("The Lord trieth the righteous") through three analogies: a potter who tests sound vessels (since weak ones would obviously break); a flax worker who improves high quality flax by beating it more (whereas inferior flax would split); and, finally, a man who places his yoke only on his strong

68. My primary text and translation for *Genesis Rabbah* is H. Freedman and Maurice Simon (New York: Soncino Press, 1983) though I also refer to and have benefited from the notes in Jacob Neusner's more recent translation, *Genesis Rabbah, The Judaic Commentary to the Book of Genesis, A New Translation*, vol. 2, Brown University Judaic Studies 104 (Atlanta: Scholar's Press, 1985).

cow. All three of these analogies show that choosing to test, beat, or yoke that which is strongest and best is reasonable.

The rabbinic interpretive interest in the justice and reasonableness of God in this story continues with "another interpretation" which is given in a kind of homiletic form in 55:3. Its subjects are a student and a teacher; the student believes the teacher is doing something that he told his students not to do (the main example given is lending money for interest). The teacher goes on to explain to the student that the ban on lending with interest applied to lending to Israelites only and not to people from other nations (presumably the teacher had lent his money for interest to a foreigner). The student (being a student and not the teacher) was not in a position to understand the variety and complexity of teaching on this issue and so was given a command that was simpler and inclusive. He was not therefore in a position to judge or understand the actions of his teacher (who could grasp the more complex law). The difference between teacher and student (of understanding, and of status with respect to complexities of justice based on that understanding) is then applied analogously to God and his people, culminating in the harmonization of Deuteronomy 6:16, "Do not try the Lord your God," with "God did prove Abraham." God has a different status from people with respect to the issue of what God can and cannot do — not because God is outside or beyond ethical obligations but rather because God has a more complete, authoritative understanding of ethics, of what "I wrote in My Torah." Thus God can try a human being, but we cannot try God — not because the laws do not apply to God but because he has a different relationship to them and their object (Godself).

The next notable interpretive move in this text is to explain not just why God's trying Abraham was both just (in that it was not outside the law, outside the ethical) and reasonable (in choosing Abraham because of his strength, his righteousness), but to ascribe a cause to the whole situation. God tries Abraham, we learn, either because Abraham has begun wrongly to doubt himself or because the members of God's court have begun to doubt him. At one point, in a narrative expansion, *Genesis Rabbah* shows an Abraham who remembers that he celebrated but did not sacrifice anything to God and thus has "misgivings" (a wordplay involving "after," as in "after these things") about his own righteousness. God answers these doubts by saying "I know that even if thou wast commanded to offer thy only son to Me, thou would not refuse." This brief episode is followed by a similar one where the angels of God's court point out Abraham's failure to make an animal sacrifice when rejoicing and God answers them, "Even if we tell him to offer his own son, he will not refuse" (55:4). Neither of these narrative expansions appears to demonstrate that Abraham "deserves" to suffer this final trial because of a prior act (the notion that failure to perform a ritual at a feast might merit the loss of one's son in a particularly horrific way would, of course, be awful); instead, they offer more ethically complex interpretive suggestions. First, it is clear that the trial is not meant to show or prove anything to God; God, in fact, is the only being who seems to have complete faith in Abraham. Second, the trial is not meant to do anything for God. It is an event set in motion for the sake of Abraham, to prove the extent of his faithfulness either to himself or to the heavenly court. Third, it casts Abraham in an even more positive light. Not only is he righteous, strong, and faithful; in this lovely, humanizing narrative addition, he becomes self-critical and reflective (remembering his rejoicing and failure to sacrifice) and humble (seeing his own faithfulness as lacking).

This section of *parasha* 55 continues with another narrative expansion, providing two different versions of an exchange between Isaac and Ishmael. The two sons of Abraham are arguing over which one is most beloved. In the first version Ishmael claims that he is beloved because he was circumcised at the age of thirteen and thus could have protested, but did not. At this point in the argument, Isaac, who had claimed that being circumcised at eight days showed him to be more beloved, cries out, "O that God would appear to me and bid me cut off one of my limbs! then I would not refuse." And God answers him: "Even if I bid thee sacrifice thyself, thou wilt not refuse." This obviously sets up the coming event — showing God's confidence, again, in the faith of those chosen to participate in this trial, and Isaac's willingness, even desire, to prove his devotion. The trial is thus cast as an opportunity for Isaac also to prove himself — not to himself, perhaps, or to a heavenly court, but to his brother — and to demonstrate a faithfulness that he feels he hasn't had the chance thus far to show. The second version reads much as the first, but in answering Ishmael's claim Isaac gives additional information about his age at the time of this conversation, God's answer then indicating that the trial directly follows this exchange between the brothers:

> Isaac retorted [to Ishmael]: "All that thou didst lend to the Holy One, blessed be He, was three drops of blood. But lo, I am now thirty-seven years old, yet if God desired of me that I be slaughtered, I would not refuse." Said the Holy One, blessed be He, "This is the moment!" Straightaway, God did prove Abraham. (55:4)

Even more than the first version, this shows Isaac's willingness to be the subject of such a sacrifice and indicates that this willingness was relevant to the occasion (timing) of the final trial of Abraham. Not only is God's purpose in commanding this last terrible trial understood from the outset as just and reasonable (God acting within God's own law in ways accessible to our comprehension); the trial is also understood to be occasioned by and a response to human actions and speech (indicating human needs/wishes).

The addition of Isaac's age contributes to an ethical reading in several ways. First, as Green noted in his reading of this midrash, it demonstrates Isaac's willingness as a full adult and absolves Abraham of the charge of forcibly binding and (almost) slaughtering a helpless and/or unknowing child. And if there is any doubt that words said in competitive argument with an older brother are reliable, we now can imagine that a man of thirty-seven could not be overpowered by a very elderly father; when Isaac eventually ends up bound with knife above his throat, he proves as faithful as his words. Additionally, the method by which the rabbis calculate Isaac's age here — using Sarah's age at his birth (90) and her age when she dies (127) — foreshadows the rabbinic association of the death of Sarah with the events on Mount Moriah. Attributing Sarah's death to these events, which will happen later in *Genesis Rabbah*, adds to the ethical ramifications of these events.[69] That the command regarding Isaac's life was rescinded does not mean that there were no (ethical or unintended) consequences of these events. There were in fact (tragic) costs, however displaced.

Another interpretative dimension opened up by the "controversy" involving Ishmael and Isaac lies in the meaning of "beloved." As readers, we, like the rabbis, know that this word, this designation, has great import in this story: it will eventually be the "beloved" son of Abraham that will be taken to Mount Moriah to be offered as a burnt sacrifice. Both sons are claiming to be most beloved, though of whom, father and/or God, is left unclear.[70] But the

69. I owe my knowledge of this calculation to the Freedman and Simon translation of *Genesis Rabbah*, 485, n. 1, and my eventual interest in the issues raised by associating Sarah's death with Moriah to the work of Sebastian Brock ("Genesis 22: Where Was Sarah?" *Expository Times* 96 [1984]: 14-17) on other ancient (Syriac Christian) sources, and more recently to Yvonne Sherwood's "Binding-Unbinding," esp. 851-54, and "And Sarah Died," *Derrida's Bible (Reading a Page of Scripture with a Little Help from Derrida)* (New York: Palgrave Macmillan, 2004), 261-92.

70. For further discussion of what it means to be the "beloved" son, see Jon Levenson, *Death and Resurrection of the Beloved Son: The Transformation of Child Sacrifice in Judaism and Christianity* (New Haven: Yale University Press, 1993), and Chapter 5, below.

evidence given by each to demonstrate that they are most beloved is their respective willingness to sacrifice themselves physically to God. Ishmael claims
he is most beloved because he could have protested his circumcision but did
not. And this elicits from Isaac the claim that if God wanted his limbs, his
life, he would not refuse. The willingness to sacrifice to God, to give blood,
limb, and life when and if asked, is somehow linked (whether causally or evidently is unclear) to being beloved (whether by their father Abraham or by
God or both). If these narratives are read in light of *Genesis Rabbah* 55:7,
which comments on Genesis 22:2 "Take your son, your only son, whom you
love, Isaac," Abraham evidently loves both sons. As the midrash recounts
each phrase of God's command, it interjects the replies of Abraham. Thus, in
response to the phrase "'Whom thou lovest' [Abraham asks] 'Is there a limit
to the affections?'" and God then specifies: Isaac. Immediately following this
recounting, along with the narrative additions, the commentary asks a rhetorical question focusing on this slow-paced, indirect manner of God's indication of the subject of his command: "And why did He not reveal it to him
without delay? In order to make him (Isaac) even more beloved in his eyes
and reward him for every word spoken." According to the rabbis, God's very
pacing and ordering of speech, the command as it is spoken in Genesis 22:2,
works on Abraham, making Isaac more beloved, and in turn, Abraham is rewarded for every word he speaks/hears. As with the question of belovedness
and sacrifice in the argument between the brothers, the actions/dispositions
and the rewards are seemingly collapsed. The increased belovedness of Isaac
to Abraham is tied so directly to Abraham's reward that they appear to be the
same thing. The trial becomes not some horrendous act that God demands
and that Abraham and Isaac participate in to justify future rewards but
rather the opportunity of increasing belovedness, which seems, considering
the argument between Isaac and Ishmael, to be interpreted as reward in and
of itself.

Parasha 55:6 concludes its commentary on the first verse of Genesis
22 with an extended comparison between Abraham and Moses, a comparison that emphasizes Abraham's unique greatness. But in one final interpretation of the phrase "That God did prove Abraham," Rabbi Akiba
points out that the trial was deliberately performed in such a way that no
one could say Abraham did not know what he was doing. The sacrifice was
not to be immediate but involved a long journey and many preparations.[71]
The opportunity for reflection on Abraham's part is, according to this in-

71. This information comes from the Freedman and Simon translation, 486 n. 1.

terpretation, an integral part of the efficacy of the trial — both so that others may not misunderstand or misjudge Abraham (Rabbi Akiba's focus) and also to add to the meaningfulness of the events for Abraham himself. Unthinking, unreflective obedience does not seem to appear to these commentators as laudable. And reflective obedience itself is regarded as neither a means to an end nor a once and for all assent to a proposition of faith, but (perhaps) the end itself, the strengthening or increase of belovedness, and a lived relationship.

One last issue raised by the rabbis in *parasha* 55 deserves attention. While the idea of reward seems, at the least, de-emphasized, and mostly equated with the occasion itself (and its inherent increase of belovedness), the idea that actions are interrelated and consequential for the history of God's people is an important contribution of this chapter. The verse that occasions these comments is Genesis 22:3: "And Abraham rose early in the morning and saddled his ass." After a brief consideration of why Abraham did this work himself, the rabbis turn to more weighty matters: "Let saddling counteract saddling" such that what Abraham does as he prepares to fulfill God's command counteracts what Balaam did (after saddling his own ass) when he prepared to go out and curse Israel. And let the knife taken up by Abraham counteract the sword taken up by the Pharaoh to kill God's people. Comparisons are drawn, also, between Abraham and Saul, who both, in their respective narratives, take two men with them, and finally, between Abraham cleaving the wood (an act inferred by the fact that the word for wood is plural and thus must be two pieces cut up)[72] and God dividing the waters of the sea. Actions in the world are never entirely new and original, nor do they exist in isolation. Abraham's actions interconnect with the actions, good or bad, of others. These comparisons are not posited as reasons for the trial but are rather intended to explicate the results of actions in history. What happened on the top of a mountain, involving only Abraham, Isaac, and God (and the angels and the ram) has implications for a whole people; these actions matter historically, socially, religiously, ethically.

At the very end of this discussion comes an exclamation "Enough of this!" (ascribed to Rabbi Levi) — a vehement reaction against the preceding comparison between God and Abraham. "In truth Abraham acted according to his powers and the Holy One, blessed be He, according to His powers" (55:8). God's actions respecting both what is possible and what is

---

72. Freedman and Simon, 484, n. 3.

just are to be differentiated from Abraham's; a comparison between human actions and God's acts is not respectful of the possibilities or justice
of either.

These many voices of interpretation provide one of the most exciting
characteristics of *Genesis Rabbah* and distinguish it from other interpretive
texts as well as from Ronald Green's representation of "traditional Judaism." Certainly there is a shared interest in these sections of midrash in
theological and ethical concerns (God as just, reasonable, and ontologi-
cally different from human beings). And perhaps this is all Green meant to
indicate by saying that traditional Judaism spoke with "one voice" about
the *akedah*. But even in this incredibly selective look at ancient midrash,
one that focuses on only one *parasha* of one particular text in *Genesis
Rabbah*, it seems that many readers/speakers are deemed necessary to express the meaning of this biblical text. Multi-vocal expression (including
even internal debate, such as sudden "Enough!"in 55:8) seems built into
the form of the reading. Thus, in 55:2, three different analogies are made to
explain how God's choice of Abraham is a reasonable one. Clearly, all make
a similar point — that it is reasonable (and just) to test or try the soundest
or strongest — but each analogy, attributed to its own rabbi, adds its own
interpretive layer when applied to the trial of Abraham. Rabbi Jonathan's
potter tests the best that he has made (since the weak vessel will obviously
break). The analogy of potter/vessels suggests a creator/creation idea in
which Abraham is not only one of the best and strongest among men; he is
that way because he was made that way. His trial is not ultimately tied to
his own prior acts (of righteousness) but rather to his having been shaped
in a certain manner. Rabbi Jose ben Rabbi Hanina's flax-worker beats the
high quality flax (weak flax only breaks under this treatment) expressly for
the purpose of improving it. The trial, by this analogy, is itself good for
Abraham. It improves him somehow — perhaps in that it reveals him to
himself, or makes Isaac more beloved. Finally, Rabbi Eleazar speaks of the
strong cow that is chosen expressly for the yoke by its owner. This analogy
seems to indicate not only that Abraham is being improved, but that
through this trial he is doing the work of God. All three analogies, by all
three rabbis, make possible different interpretive responses to Genesis 22,
and *Genesis Rabbah* in no way indicates that one analogy is more accurate
than another. In fact, the presence of all three indicates that all are
interpretively relevant, that all these possibilities inhere in the biblical text
itself. The various perspectives offered on the passages under consideration are sometimes introduced with the phrase *davar aher* ("another in-

terpretation") (55:3). This formulaic expression and others like it ("another version" is used before the second account of the argument between Ishmael and Isaac [55:4]) are found frequently throughout *Genesis Rabbah*. Such terminology reflects an acknowledgment of multiple interpretations (and when those interpretations take the form of narrative expansions, multiple versions) of a given text. That "another" response is announced as such not only declares its presence but also seems to attribute value to it.

In the chapter of *Genesis Rabbah* selected for this close reading, the multiplicity of perspectives is seen most vividly when commentary is offered on the name of Moriah (the mountain of sacrifice). The section (55:7) begins with reference to two rabbis who "discussed this" and then offers their slightly different explanations for this choice (one describes it as the place from which instructions went forth into the world and the other as the place from which religious awe went forth). Then further discussion is reported between these same authorities — two more exchanges in which each continues and nuances his line of explanation and wordplay. These are followed immediately in the same section by four more explanations by four other rabbis (all different, though some related, and all involving wordplay on the word "Moriah"). The section then concludes with one more explanation attributed to the (plural) "rabbis." All this is worth mentioning in detail for several reasons. It showcases the kind of serious yet playful ways the rabbis read the text — six teachers all making different clever plays on one word, all with serious religious and possibly ethical interpretive claims. It dramatically illustrates the presence of different voices and different (though not contradictory) interpretive claims: Moriah gives instruction, light, even God's speech; Moriah inspires religious awe, reverence, and offers retribution in the world; from Moriah other nations are either instructed or overthrown; Moriah corresponds with the "heavenly temple," it is the seat of the world's domination, the place where incense would be offered. In one word are all these ideas found — instruction and retribution, reverence and worship, guidance and destruction — and set forth by different readers of the text. It takes all these interpreters, all these voices speaking, severally and with each other, to express the content of the word "Moriah."

This kind of wordplay is a central component of the rabbinic response to Genesis 22 (and the biblical text more generally). The entire discussion about Abraham's (or the heavenly court's) "misgivings" about his faithfulness discussed above is occasioned by a play on the Hebrew word *'ahar* (which means "after," as in "After these things" — the first words of the *akedah*). The play is in connecting *'ahar* with the word *hirhur,* which means misgivings. The apparent pun provides all the occasion necessary for a discussion about "misgivings experienced on the occasion" — Abraham's own self-criticism and doubt of his faithfulness.[73] And when Rabbi Leazar offers the alternative picture of "misgivings" about Abraham on the part of some members of the heavenly court, he bases this possibility on the occurrence of the conjunction "and" (one Hebrew letter) preceding the word God in that first verse (where it is unnecessary, and usually rendered in English as "that"). For him "*wa-elohim,*" where *Elohim* would suffice, intimates the presence of those with God in the heavenly court who speak of misgivings (55:4). One conjunction, basically one letter, provides an interpretative possibility with ethical and theological significance.

Another feature of this midrash that is both creatively playful and provocatively serious is its use of narrative expansions.[74] In the example just discussed, the interpretive possibilities that Rabbi Leazar finds in a single letter are expressed through the telling of an additional (extra-biblical) story about an exchange between members of the heavenly court and God. In fact, the whole account of Abraham failing to designate a sacrifice to God on the occasion of a celebration is an addition to the biblical story. So, of course, are the wonderful accounts of a dispute between Isaac and Ishmael (in 55:5). In both of these cases, two different versions of the extra-biblical expansions are given: neither is absolute (in that there is "another") but both seem interpretively relevant, even authoritative. They provide ways of understanding Genesis 22 in terms of human concerns and theological ethics. In these imaginative moments of the midrash, God's omniscience and faith in Abraham and Isaac are expressed, the trial is cast in terms of serving Abraham and Isaac in some way (and not a capricious whim of God), and Abraham and Isaac are vested with qualities of humility and willingness to be sacrificed. Through these additional stories, concerns raised by the Genesis text are dealt with (why this trial? why these men?) and the interpretations given, not merely with analysis of the

---

73. See the explanatory notes in Freedman and Simon, 484, n. 3.

74. This term comes from James Kugel, who characterizes the ancient biblical interpreter's view of the text thus: "Any little item in the biblical story — an apparently unnecessary repetition, a logical inconsistency, an unusual grammatical form, a no longer understood word or phrase — could generate a wealth of additions to the narrative, for interpreters tended to regard all such things as opportunities, nay, *invitations,* issued by the Bible itself, to create some new bit of action or dialogue." *In Potiphar's House: The Interpretive Life of Biblical Texts* (Cambridge, MA: Harvard University Press, 1990), 6.

biblical text itself, but through imaginative exploration of the possibilities it leaves open.

The rabbinic interpretation of Genesis 22 takes a different form in 55:3, where, leading up to an explanation of why it is reasonable and just that God prove Abraham even though human beings are commanded not to try God, we are presented with what can be described as a kind of homily. This section, about the teacher and the student, is introduced as Rabbi Abin's "discourse." Beginning with a passage from Ecclesiastes (and following this up with references to Deuteronomy and Leviticus), Rabbi Abin describes the differing situations of teacher and student in order to provide a comparison that will eventually help make sense of the differing situations of God and Abraham. His discourse is apparently intended to teach humility, respect, and the importance of (trained and careful) discernment in the application of the law. It serves both as an ethically based interpretation of the biblical text and a lecture on appropriate behavior and understanding.

It is important to identify here another crucial feature of method and form in the rabbinic treatment of Genesis 22 — the practice of reading the text with other texts. *Genesis Rabbah* 55:2, the passage immediately preceding Rabbi Abin's discourse, begins with a verse from Psalm 11, "The Lord trieth the righteous," which is here identified as alluding to Abraham ("that God did prove Abraham"). But the entire chapter engages in such juxtaposition of biblical texts, from the initial association of Psalm 60:6 ("Thou hast given a banner to them that fear Thee, that it may be displayed because of the Truth") with the commencement of the *akedah* episode in Genesis 22:1. This intertextual use of the Hebrew Bible is a persistent interpretive device throughout the midrash and one of its most prominent characteristics. Using biblical texts to read biblical texts might appear at first glance to be both a constraining and arbitrary form of interpretation, but in the hands of these ancient scholars it is neither. Instead, this method reveals exciting interpretive possibilities and, in the case of a discourse like Rabbis Abin's, illuminates ethical concerns arising from the reading of Genesis 22.

Whether in attention to small details (a conjunction, for example) or examination of relationships between diverse biblical texts, nothing appears too minute or too remote to be relevant to the rabbis' theological and ethical interpretation of Genesis 22. And as this commentary negotiates between the textual minutiae of one chapter and the shape of the whole canon, it still reveals concern for the narrative quality of the *akedah* itself. The pace of the narrative, the timing of events, the phrasing of the elements of God's command speech: all are occasions for discernment of meaning, even ethical meaning. The deliberate three-day journey is understood to show that Abraham is not confused or unreflective in his obedience. The strange manner of God's disclosure of the object of the sacrifice is viewed as God's way of making Isaac even more beloved (55:7). With their many ways of seeing the text, with their different voices joined in conversation, the rabbis of *Genesis Rabbah* contribute a rich and exciting reading of Genesis 22 that, while certainly rational and moral, is not so in any simplistic way. And while certainly understood as á unified and authoritative commentary on the biblical text, *Genesis Rabbah* is not reducible to any one interpretive approach, to any one way of reading, or to any one (human) voice.

The authors and redactors of the midrash interpret the *akedah* (among other biblical texts) to make sense of their own historical situation, which is understood as having continuity with the past and, obviously, with the authority of the Bible itself. The story of Abraham's sacrifice is interpreted in this context and with this confidence in the ultimate relevance and applicability of the narrative. The interpretive interests are clearly ethical, as well as historical and theological, and they are driven by the text itself. In *Genesis Rabbah* (compared to other *Midrash Rabbah*) this is made particularly obvious by the line-by-line address to the chapter in question. But attentive reading takes many forms; it does not simply entail carefully analytical or expository attention. Meaning is also explored and expressed through creative and imaginative means, most obviously with narrative expansions, like the exchanges between Isaac and Ishmael. This attentive and imaginative reading of the texts shapes the discussion, a discussion often presented literally as such — a conversation between the commentators. The nature of the presentation evokes a sense of richness or abundance of meaning that in turn seems to make adherence to the authority of the biblical text more evidently reasonable. All these meanings are there — the text holds them all. And all these voices can make its meaning(s) known, authoritatively and together.

How does this close reading of one chapter from *Genesis Rabbah* supplement the presentation of traditional Judaism in the contemporary work of Ronald Green? Green aims to demonstrate that this tradition reads Genesis 22 as a rational and moral text, and, in some obvious ways, my analysis of *parashiyyoth* 55 confirms this view. However, our analyses differ in important ways, both specific and general. Some of the more interesting specific points of comparisons between the examination of *Genesis Rabbah* 55 presented here and Green's broader look at Jewish sources center around particular interpretive ideas: how the trial was understood as appropriate, how the relationship between father and son was viewed, and the manner of Isaac's participation. (If we were to move beyond 55, I would anticipate differences on the issue of Abraham's [and the ram's] silence and on interpretation of both the rewards and the "costs" of the *akedah*.) Green argues that the trial is justified in the traditional Jewish sources by characterizing its purpose as demonstrating Abraham's righteousness to the world. While this understanding of the trial's purpose is certainly present in *Genesis Rabbah*, it is only one of several ways that the trial is understood as having purpose (as Green rightly implies, it appears fundamental to this rabbinic interpretation that the trial *not* be viewed as cruel, arbitrary, or necessary only for God's benefit or knowledge). Acknowledging the other ways *Genesis Rabbah* sees the trial as appropriate gives its ethical interpretation more depth. The trial becomes not just an occasion to show people how great God's chosen one is, but also an occasion to show this to Abraham himself (as well as to the heavenly court). It has both internal and external, personal and universal purpose.

The reading of *Genesis Rabbah* 55 presented here then basically agrees with Green regarding the commentary's interpretive aims and assumptions — namely, the preservation of the morality and rationality of both God and Abraham as well as of the Genesis 22 narrative itself. But *Genesis Rabbah* does this in ways much more complex and rich than Green's presentation reflects. That the rabbis see the text as rational is clear. However, this interpretive view is expressed not in a univocal or simple reading but in a multiplicity of interpretations, in coexistence of several different "versions," and in a combination of serious textual analysis and playful and imaginative speculation. The differences between the view of *Genesis Rabbah* presented here and of "traditional Judaism" in Green's work owe largely to different intentions in our respective analyses. Green's aims are comparative and his study of interpretive approaches is wide-ranging; his goal is to illuminate patterns and similarities, particularly in the interpretive *ideas* found in these and other texts. The reading of *parashiyyoth* 55 provided here is, by contrast, interested not in identifying an overarching pattern or tendency in these ideas, but in exploring their complexity. The various ways of reading and relating to the biblical text manifest in *Genesis Rabbah* 55 are, for this project, as important as the content of the interpretations. Thus the multi-vocal and discussion-oriented character of the reading, the attentiveness to the biblical text itself, and the creative possibilities of relating to it as an interpretive community in a different historical situation are here viewed as relevant to its ethical role in ways not considered in Green's work.

We have said that the interpretive aims of the rabbis in reading Genesis 22 are moral, as well as rational. Again, however, it is important to stress that these "moral" readings are neither simple nor easy. For Green, religious reasoning eventually leads to interpretation that "affirms that present suffering is not the ultimate fate of the just," a view that is certainly supported by *Genesis Rabbah*. But the understanding of "present suffering" in the ancient rabbinic interpretation of Genesis 22 is far from simplistic. Consider their discussion of God's phrasing of the command, given to Abraham in such a way as to make Isaac more beloved — an ethically complex way of relating the trial and reward. Or what of the connection drawn by the rabbis between these events and Sarah's death? The trial, as they see it, is not without negative effect, without cost, though Isaac himself is spared. And it seems that *Genesis Rabbah* does not read the *akedah* simply as "a narrative about the forgiveness of sin" as Green puts it, even though the events at Moriah are tied to other actions, counteracting and combining with them in the social history of God's people (past and future). The cost, the suffering, the rewards, the strengthening of belovedness, the interrelationship of historical events, are inseparable. Certainly this text can be read as a story in which God "makes possible moral renewal" (Green again) but not merely through stopping the sacrifice (or resurrecting Isaac) or by the rewards of future blessings. The trial itself is the occasion for possible renewal within the participants themselves, and, as I will argue in Chapter Five, for its readers as well.

One of our purposes of this study of the ancient midrash has been to supplement Green's treatment of Genesis 22 in "traditional Judaism." But it is worth pausing also over connections between the rabbinic reading found in *parashiyyoth* 55 and the other two contemporary treatments of the sacrifice of Isaac, in the work of Timothy Jackson and Philip Quinn. Jackson's interpretation of Abraham is very different from the one found in *Genesis Rabbah*. Jackson's Abraham has to be schooled out of an imperfect way of justice, justice without love, through the *akedah*. For the rabbis, not only does Abraham's moral righteousness antecede his being chosen for this trial; he becomes even more faithful (through his actions) than he realizes. Yet both of these very different readings of the text see the purpose of the trial as something that transforms Abraham in some ethically important way. Jackson's Abraham is moved to a new way of understanding and participating in God's justice, while the rabbis cast the trial as showing Abraham to himself and making Isaac more beloved to his father. Attention is given in both accounts, contemporary and ancient, to the trial itself and not just to its outcome and later rewards and blessings. The events of Genesis 22 affect Abraham, his self-understanding, and his love of Isaac.

It is possible also to draw connections between the playful and imaginative elements of the reading found in *parashiyyoth* 55 and Philip Quinn's insistence that if we are to read Genesis 22 well, we must read "carefully and imaginatively." It is certainly careful and yet imaginative reading that produces both a narrative expansion out of a single conjunction and six voices comparing possible meanings of the one name, Moriah. It is not as clear in the rabbinic text that such careful and imaginative reading leads inexorably to the "plumbing of the tragic depths" of Genesis 22, though it is this kind of attentiveness to the narrative and to the texts around it that makes possible the picture of an Abraham to whom Isaac is made more beloved merely by the form of God's speech or the connection of these events to Sarah's death.

Attentive and imaginative reading is also, of course, a hallmark of Kierkegaard's *Fear* and *Trembling*. Obviously, Green's contrast of his reading of Kierkegaard and that of "traditional Judaism" would apply to this more narrowly focused reading from rabbinic tradition: there is nothing anti-rational or anti-moral in the interpretive ideas of *parashiyyoth* 55. Nonetheless, there are significant points of comparison between Kierkegaard's text and that of the ancient midrash. Along with a shared sense of the ultimate authority of the text,[75] it is possible to identify some similar interpretive concerns. For example, Kierkegaard's de Silentio draws attention to the length of the trial, the journey to Moriah, the deliberation with which Abraham must have undertaken his obedience. He does this in order to criticize those around him who reduce the trial to a moment, a decision made and done with. Rabbi Akiba likewise focuses on the unequivocally slow and deliberate character of the trial, which he sees as preventing misinterpretation of Abraham's actions (the rabbinic concern being that it might be suggested that Abraham was confused or perplexed). Both readings also share the essential conviction of Abraham's uniqueness: "Can you do what Abraham did?" It might even be argued that the four

---

75. Though for Kierkegaard this was an authority above and other than ethical while for the rabbis such separation of the theological and the ethical would be foreign.

versions of the story offered early in *Fear and Trembling* function as "midrashic" narrative expansions. Through the imaginative interpretation of the possibilities left open by the narrative of Genesis 22, Kierkegaard, like the rabbis, gives attention to the subjectivity (and possible experiential reality) of the characters involved. One ought not to take these comparisons too far. The rabbis tell their stories in a manner very similar to the ways biblical stories are told; they do not dwell on the internal thoughts and motivations of the characters. We learn what Abraham, Isaac, and Ishmael are thinking through their speech and God's speech about them. The four versions in *Fear and Trembling,* on the other hand, directly express the internal concerns, struggles, and motives of Abraham and Isaac. My point is that these two very different treatments of the text, not without their connections, can be put into conversation with each other, and can both contribute to our understanding of Genesis 22.

What points of contact might be adduced between *Genesis Rabbah* and the medieval reading of Philip the Chancellor? Certainly there is a common interest in reason and justice. Both of these pre-modern sources deeply assume the rationality and morality of God and Abraham. But perhaps more interestingly, both Philip and the rabbis express their understanding of the authority of Genesis 22 through the importance they place on clarifying the relevance of the text for themselves and their "contemporary" readers. For Philip, the biblical text is the most authoritative source for the scholastic task of working out the system of natural law. His philosophical and ethical ideas must be refined and nuanced in terms of his reading of Genesis 22. The rabbis, while uninterested in such systematizing, also stress continuity between their own and biblical times. The past of the biblical texts is their source of knowledge about their present world. The *akedah* is not read as a narrative about a remote world: Abraham, Isaac, Ishmael, and God still speak through the narrative; their speech is even amplified in this fourth-century text. (Such immediacy is also, of course, part of the force of Kierkegaard's treatment. The awfulness of the trial for Abraham is felt so strongly by the man spoken of in the "Attunement" that he is "virtually annihilated.")

Like the rabbis of *Genesis Rabbah,* Philip uses other biblical texts in interpreting Genesis 22. For Philip, this practice is largely focused on demonstrating the absence of contradictions and in drawing connections between and among apparently related narratives and ideas. Though anxiety about possible textual contradiction is unimportant (read, impossible) in *Genesis Rabbah,* unexpected connections between texts occasion new insights. Instead of concentrating on "harmonizing" apparently contradictory texts (or, as seen in Jackson's contemporary treatment, reading one text, Genesis 22, *through* another, the Christian New Testament), *Genesis Rabbah* appears to regard the relationship between biblical texts (all of which share in the unity and perfection of the whole) as generating fruitful interpretive possibilities.

Further, Philip shares with the writers and editors of *Genesis Rabbah* a view of interpretation as a communal endeavor. As we have seen, a medieval theologian like Philip sees his work as part of a common task, the (re)accumulation and refinement of human knowledge. He also writes as if in conversation with others; the very form of the *quaestio,* with its objections and replies, suggests alternating voices and perspectives, all of which are led through the writer's argument toward a common understanding. The idea of community and communal interpretation is even more pronounced and important in *Genesis Rabbah*. It is heard in the multiple voices, in the connections between its contemporary community and the communities of the past, and even in the assumed relevance of actions taken on a mountain top to actions and communities that are lands and generations away. In this ancient midrash, many voices are necessary to interpret the biblical text, an indication of its richness and complexity; the reading of Genesis 22 is and must be a collective activity. While the particular readings compiled in *Genesis Rabbah* are presented as authoritative, they are not presented as univocal or static. The dialogue between readers (rabbis, students, and teachers) evokes a sense of a community actively and continuously engaged in reading Genesis 22.

This feature of ongoing and shared interpretation is reflected in part in the incorporation, in both of these sources, of authoritative interpretations from the past. Philip the Chancellor, in his reading of Genesis 22, speaks of the earlier interpretation of Bernard of Clairvaux. *Genesis Rabbah* is itself a compilation of earlier materials, which in turn draw from still more ancient writings. The religious tradition founded by the ancient "Rabbi" (of which *Genesis Rabbah* is only a small part) is unique, in Kugel's words, "because it was a dynamic one, engendering new generations of teacher-interpreters . . . stretching even to the present day."[76] For these different sets of readers, Christian medieval or ancient Jewish, an authoritative text and an inheritance of authoritative interpretations do not end the

---

76. James Kugel and Rowan A. Greer, *Early Biblical Interpretation* (Philadelphia: Westminster, 1986), 72.

conversation about meaning and application; they participate in it, encourage it, even engender it.

In different ways, Philip the Chancellor and the ancient rabbis demonstrate a connection to and a confidence in their communities that is missing in Kierkegaard's *Fear and Trembling,* where the appeal is to the individual, and against the "paucity" of reading in "our times." The interpretive community challenged by de Silentio consists of precisely those who claim to understand Abraham, and thus are done (quickly) with reading the story. How unlike the communities evoked by Philip's *quaestio* (the students and theologians who are the assumed audience of the *Summa de Bono*) and by the *Genesis Rabbah,* who are presented as collectively involved in the reading of the narrative. This ongoing, shared involvement in the text recalls Yvonne Sherwood's observation that "ancient interpreters sometimes seem *more* able to live with and through the paradox of *binding-unbinding* than some of their co-religionist contemporaries."[77] She argues that the pre-modern ways of being religious "before all choice" allow ancient interpreters to engage reading the text more actively and complexly. Whereas the modern tendency is to demonstrate complete, intentional acceptance of the authority of the biblical text through claims about what it says (and thus being "done" with interpreting it), the pre-modern reader granted authority to the biblical text not by claiming mastery of it but rather through complex and active engagement. Such engaged, ongoing, and active reading of Genesis 22 can, in this way, be understood as an act of granting the text authority, the means by which it transforms its readers and thus the world.

In saying that all three of the readings of Genesis 22 represented in this chapter find ways of engaging the text as authoritative in dynamic ways, it is crucial to recognize that all do so differently and that all avoid treating the story in the prevalent "pious" or "traditional" ways described by Jackson. Kierkegaard's *Fear and Trembling* considers Genesis 22 through the deeply personal and powerful "dialectical lyric" of Johannes de Silentio, for whom the ongoing experience (of reading) of Abraham's sacrifice calls into question all of contemporary philosophy. Philip's engagement of Genesis 22 in his *quaestio* offers a present refinement of past ideas about natural law. And *Genesis Rabbah* presents all of its ideas (historical, ethical, theological) in the context of a verse-by-verse discussion of the biblical text. Recognizing the power of these forms does not imply that

77. Sherwood, "Binding-Unbinding," 855.

contemporary ethics must (or could) mimic them in order to engage the Hebrew Bible in a vital way. Nonetheless, it is important that we find new and authentic forms of engagement with the biblical text in our ethical reflections.

The role of the interpreter's ethical and theological commitments in shaping a response to Genesis 22 is most obvious in Philip's treatment (though it is also a significant facet of the others). In addition to his (assumed) engagement of the Bible as authoritative, Philip reads Genesis 22 in relation to a particular understanding of ethics (natural law), human reason, and the (textual and logical) perfection and unity of the biblical text. While allowing the biblical text to compel the refinement of ideas about moral theology, Philip simultaneously accords an important status to those very ideas. Not only are the moral and theological ideas he brings to the biblical text important; they are the very locus of its influence in Philip's world and the means by which it is able to transform his ethics. Similarly, the rabbis bring certain ideas (even limits) to their interpretations. Assumptions about God's relationship to God's people, to (God's) law, to justice and reason, are presented from the very outset of the commentary on Genesis 22. And while this does not (contrary to Green's view) generate a simple pattern of interpretive ideas about the text, it does shape the possibilities presented in the midrash. Interpretive energy is directed towards demonstrating the justice and reasonableness of the text. *Genesis Rabbah* explores the *akedah* as a response to human needs, a transformative experience for Abraham and Isaac, and a part of a people's complex social history. The means used to do this — textual analysis (ranging from smallest detail to the breadth of the canon) and imaginative expansions — are themselves possible because of the views held by these ancient interpreters about the multivalent meaning of the Torah and their own God-given relationship to it. Important status is given to (the philosopher's/interpreter's) theological and ethical formation in Kierkegaard's treatment of Genesis 22 as well. Obviously, part of the impetus behind *Fear and Trembling* is the concern that the systems/philosophies of his contemporaries are impeding their ability to read the Bible well. Thus Johannes de Silentio envisions a choice (strangely a "choice" belied by the treatment itself) between philosophical ethics (that demands only an application of reason) and religious faith (which involves an absurd "leap"). Again, connections to Sherwood's characterization of the modern situation are apparent in that here we see (good) interpretation of the Bible equated with what she calls the modern "macro choice" between being religious or not.

Through this either/or Kierkegaard shows his own reading to be shaped by his assumptions about reason, about religious faith, and about ethics. The exploration of Genesis 22 through the personal, life-long interest of a particular (if fictitious) reader is another characteristically modern feature of *Fear and Trembling,* demonstrating nicely the turn to the subject.[78] Interestingly, the power of *Fear and Trembling* as a reading of Genesis 22 lies not in the characterization of the "choice" de Silentio argues for between ethical reason and faith (though the influence of this characterization is far-reaching), but in its careful attention to (the experience of reading) the biblical story with the skills of a trained, thoughtful, and imaginative reader — in this case a philosopher/poet, whose ethical sensitivities prompt special attentiveness to the awfulness of the story.

All three of these readings from the history of interpretation of Genesis 22 grant simultaneous attention and importance to the interpreter's ideas and experiences and to the biblical text itself. All three find ways to hold these (sometimes competing) sources together, productively and transformatively, in their ethical reflections. All find ways to engage Scripture in ongoing ways, giving it authority to challenge the world. All use the best methods of interpretation, study, reflection available to them, even if these do not *easily* reveal the text as answering to their preconceptions. All treat the variety of possible responses to the *akedah* with utmost seriousness. Reflection on these three examples of past approaches to the *akedah* prompts a range of questions for contemporary ethics: How do we view the biblical text? What are our tools for studying it? What are our possibilities for imagining it? Who are our conversation partners (past and present) and how do we relate to them and each other? What are our ethical concerns in light of Genesis 22? How can we hold together, *now,* our Scriptures, our theologies, our histories, and our ethics in creative, productive, and (trans)formative relationship?

78. The interest in the personal is also identifiable in the occasion of this reading of Genesis 22, his broken engagement to Regine Olsen.

CHAPTER FIVE

Demands of the Text, Demands of the Other: Why (and How) the *Akedah* Matters for Christian Ethics

Even this brief examination of six readings of Genesis 22 — three from contemporary scholars with ethical proposals and three from the past — has yielded insights about how to negotiate the relationship between doing ethics and reading the Hebrew Bible. But our analysis of these readings and their various contributions has highlighted a more general and problematic issue. The challenging and seemingly inexhaustible power of the text as experienced and communicated in the three readings from the past appears diminished, ignored, even rejected in the contemporary treatments. Kierkegaard, Philip the Chancellor, and the ancient rabbis all assume and/or insist on the authoritative status of the biblical text with respect to their own interpretive projects. But they do so in ways that preserve the significance, even authority, of those very projects (and thus avoid the trap of simplistic or fundamentalist readings). Moreover, all three exhibit the importance of a particular historical situation for interpretation. *Genesis Rabbah,* produced during the Christianization of Rome, presents a deep sense of the interconnectedness of events and relationships, the relevance of actions in the (biblical) past to present and future identity. Philip the Chancellor's treatment participates in the medieval project of (re)accumulating human knowledge and understanding, knowledge that may not be identical to the content of Scripture but must be in accord with it. And Kierkegaard's work reflects the context of both his personal situation (his broken engagement to Regine Olsen) and his intellectual one (his dissatisfaction with contemporary philosophy). In their very different interpretive situations, all three of these historical responses to the *akedah* maintain in their own way an ongoing engagement with the text without dismissing their own concerns and sensitivities *and* without absorbing the text itself into some formulation of the overall significance of Scripture or into any other overarching moral or theological theory. It is precisely this engagement without domestication that seems to elude the three contemporary treatments, in which theoretical proposals and/or the assumed norms of moral theology allow the scholar to avoid any real, ongoing encounter with the biblical text and ultimately allow a given theory or interpretation to supersede the text.

Even though there are many readings of the *akedah* that continue to merit our attention, we are still left with the challenge of performing our own readings. While responses to Genesis 22 like those explored in Chapter Four continue to be important interpretive resources, we cannot really imitate them and their ways of maintaining ongoing and challenging engagement with Scripture without ignoring and rejecting our critical perspectives on the Bible (and our own interpretive positions). Our contemporary situation as readers is vastly different. Our views of the biblical text and our interpretations of it are shaped by modern and postmodern ideas — ideas that are important in all the disciplines relevant to this project, including biblical studies, ethics, and literary theory.

Historical-critical study of the Bible has radically changed ideas about the simple harmony and unity of the biblical text. We work now with a text understood to have been written and compiled over a very long period of time and containing diverse and evolving (theological, anthropological, and ethical) perspectives. Not only does this present us with a more complex view of the creation and the content of the biblical canon, it also presents a more complicated view of our relationship to that text. Approaching the biblical text and traditions of interpretation with a hermeneutics of suspicion is ethically important. Being open to the possibility that the biblical text and/or interpretations of it may contain real and dangerous distortions is part of taking seriously its history and complexity. Thus, like earlier assumptions of the Bible's harmony and unity, simplistic ideas regarding its moral "perfection" and universality are no longer unquestionably accepted.

Another consideration that shapes contemporary interpretation is self-consciousness about the act of reading. Recognition that the Bible is a text is an important element in engagement of Scripture in contemporary scholarship. This recognition demands attention to the biblical text's literary characteristics and to the process of reading (how and what happens when we read). Beyond the appreciation of the biblical text as text (and its interpreters as readers), there is the further crucial identification of the text as sacred, as Scripture, as Text — a genre identification that significantly affects its role and status in ethical reflections of a biblical religious tradition like Christianity. The Bible's special status is not only externally determined, something assigned to it (though it certainly owes to a historical process and the ongoing relationships between readers/communities and the text). It may also reside in the stories themselves: in literary scholar Erich Auerbach's words, biblical stories "seek to subject us."[1] As contemporary interpreters of this text (as of other texts) we cannot escape a historical consciousness of ourselves as interpreters. While desiring to engage the text, to be readers of the text, we recognize ourselves as situated selves who have preconceptions and prejudgments prior to and entering into such engaged reading. Not only are we aware of the historicity of the biblical text; we are also aware of the limited character of our own categories. Just as we lack an easy or simple confidence in the text as unified and perfect, we also lack an easy or simple confidence in our own reasoning. We cannot see the biblical text of Genesis 22 with the pre-critical eyes of the ancient rabbis or Philip the Chancellor, nor can we, as Christian ethicists, be satisfied in finally distancing ourselves from the challenges of the biblical text by seeing interpretation of it merely as gathering data about patterns of human moral reasoning (Green), as an illustration of theological impossibility (Quinn), or as a story containing theological irony ethically understandable only through events of the New Testament (Jackson).

I am saying nothing new here. In an introduction to current biblical interpretation, David Tracy (adapting Gadamerian idea of conversation) proposes a "model of correlation" which

> alerts theological interpreters that they must attend to three realities: first, the inevitable presence of the interpreter's own preunderstanding (situation); second, the claim to attention of the text itself; third, the conversation as some form of correlation (identity, similarity, or confrontation).[2]

Many modern and postmodern religious ethicists and theorists have been and are struggling explicitly with the implications of the first of these realities. It is the second, the claim to attention of the text itself, and the implications of this claim for the third reality, the possibilities of an (in)formative engagement, that are of special concern in this volume.

---

1. Erich Auerbach, *Mimesis: The Representation of Reality in Western Literature,* trans. Willard R. Trask (Princeton: Princeton University Press, 1953), 15.

2. Robert M. Grant, with David Tracy, *A Short History of the Interpretation of the Bible,* second edition (Minneapolis: Augsburg Fortress, 1984), 171.

I have also suggested that these differences in the ways we understand and study the biblical text now have particular ramifications for religious *ethics.* Yet there seems to be very little interest in or pertinent understanding of the role of the Hebrew Bible as central and powerful in contemporary Christian ethical scholarship. An articulation of this role, a willingness to assert ways in which the biblical text claims us and how these claims might work in a (post-)critical world, is almost entirely missing (or perhaps amiss) in contemporary Christian ethical scholarship. Neglecting to examine the demands incurred by engaging the Hebrew Bible in contemporary ethics, and thus avoiding the struggle to meet them, leads not only to the kinds of problems diagnosed in Chapters Two and Three, but also to the prevalence of an oversimplified "pious/traditional view" of Genesis 22 as described by Jackson. (Re)finding ways of seeing the Hebrew Bible as ethically authoritative would require us, then, as Christians, to be better readers of it (seeking neither to domesticate or simplify it, nor to evade its interpretive and ethical challenges through neglect or fundamentalism).

Can we then realize a significant and authentic role for the biblical text in our ethical scholarship and in our moral lives? The possibilities of doing so, however paradoxically, are held in the very historical, literary, and philosophical perspectives that are our critical means of scrutiny (and thus profound engagement) of the text. Critical stances demand rigor as they demand attentiveness and self-awareness. In the words of Jon Levenson, contemporary study of the Bible demands "scholars who are prepared to interpret the text against their own preferences and traditions, in the interest of intellectual honesty."[3] In a post-critical world, critical methods themselves become the means by which the text claims our attention and demands our effort, the means by which we find ourselves engaged and our assumptions challenged. Further, critical approaches to the biblical text make the text strange[4] (again), peeling away the familiarity by which we tend to domesticate it, conform it to our own assumptions, and tame it to our own ends. For Christian ethicists (and other readers who believe biblical texts affect their lives) this strangeness does not or should not provide an excuse to avoid engaging the Hebrew Bible. Rather, it creates the possibility that such engagement (putting our ethics and our contemporary selves in relationship to this strange text) will challenge us, disturb

3. Jon Levenson, *Death and Resurrection of the Beloved Son: The Transformation of Child Sacrifice in Judaism and Christianity* (New Haven: Yale University Press, 1993), 3.

4. I owe this way of putting it to Joseph Blenkinsopp.

our moral or theological complacency and, thousands of years and count-less interpretations later, transform the world.

My own reading of Genesis 22 falls in line with these claims about the possibilities created by critical study of the biblical text. In fact, this po-tential role for critical perspectives in describing the relationship between the Hebrew Bible and contemporary Christian ethics was a significant part of the intuition that generated this "case study" of the *akedah*. Nonethe-less, as I will discuss later, the project turned out to involve much more than a reading of Genesis 22 in the light of pre-conceived ethical proposi-tions (though I freely admit, even as I accuse others, that one's ideas often drive the questions and are the occasions for particular readings). My reading supports, though in ways more complex and challenging than I expected, my methodological claims about the vital yet neglected status of the biblical text in Christian ethics. On the other hand, the ethical reflec-tions themselves, the moral concerns I continue to grapple with because of this story, represent the ongoing effect of four years of being bound to the reading and study of Genesis 22. The nature of this interpretive "moment" in an ongoing engagement and the experience of reading itself demand scrutiny; but before I attempt to analyze my own reading, it is obviously necessary to present it, or at least its key points.

Most broadly, critical scholarship on Genesis 22 reveals two paradoxi-cally related characteristics of the narrative: its deep interconnectedness to the rest of the biblical canon and its oddness, that is, its uniqueness within that same canon. The narrative's crucial place in the Hebrew Bible — at-tested to, of course, by the attention the story receives in the history of in-terpretation — is in many ways obvious.[5] Nonetheless, it is worth laying out these connections here because they make clear that any ethicist who claims to be working within a biblical religious tradition *must* grapple with Gene-sis 22. The connection between this episode and larger biblical narratives and concerns begins with its role as the last, ultimate, and defining "trial" of Abraham. Through this narrative Abraham becomes known in biblical tra-ditions as much for his willingness to slaughter Isaac as for his role as ances-tor of the nations. The *akedah* is connected to Abram/Abraham's larger story in its wording, structure, and themes. The command to "go [*lek leka*]

---

5. Though it is interesting that this attention is relatively post-biblical and that the story has an "obscurity within the Hebrew Bible" (amongst the prophets and other authors outside the Pentateuch). See the discussion in Levenson, *Death and Resurrection,* especially ch. 14, "The Rewritten Aqedah of Jewish Tradition," 173-76.

to the land of Moriah and offer him (Isaac) there as a burnt offering on one of the mountains that I will show you" (Genesis 22:2) echoes God's first command to Abram/Abraham in Genesis 12:1 to "go [*lek leka*] from your country and your family and your father's house to the land that I will show you." The wording of these imperatives is strikingly similar. Not only is Abraham commanded to go, but to go to a place God "will show" him. In structure and theme, the sacrifice of Isaac repeats the pattern of Abraham sacrificing another son — expelling his older Ishmael with his mother Hagar, at Sarah's request — in the immediately preceding chapter. In that story Abraham "rose early in the morning" to make preparations just as he does in the *akedah*, placing Ishmael on Hagar's shoulder in a gesture similar to putting the wood on Isaac's. Then at the end of the *akedah*, in the second angelic speech (Genesis 22:15-18), Abraham's actions are identified as the reason for God's fulfillment of the promise of offspring, land, and blessing (Genesis 12:2-3), again tying this story to Abraham's larger story.

These connections — the word-choice, patterns, and theme of the promise in Genesis 22 — also reach beyond the Abraham narrative, integrally linking this episode to an ever-widening complex of stories, of the ancestors, of the nations, and for Christians, of the New Testament. The theme of the covenant, with its interrelated concerns for progeny, land, and blessing, is identified by Gerhard von Rad as the "scaffolding supporting and connecting" the materials woven together into the "history of the patriarchs."[6] The content of the promise, repeated often in these stories, is specifically reiterated in that second angelic speech in Genesis 22:17-18:

> I will indeed bless you, and I will make your offspring as numerous as the stars of heaven and as the sand that is on the seashore. And your offspring shall possess the gate of their enemies, and by your offspring shall all the nations of the earth gain blessing for themselves, because you have listened to my voice.

Possessing the land, surviving and producing male children or heirs, and being blessed by God are the thematic concerns of these stories when read on their own terms.[7]

---

6. Gerhard von Rad, *Old Testament Theology: The Theology of Israel's Historical Traditions*, vol. 1, trans. D. M. G. Stalker (New York: Harper and Brothers, 1962), 167.

7. See the discussion of heirs, land, and blessing in the chapter on the ancestors in Joseph Blenkinsopp's *The Pentateuch: An Introduction to the First Five Books of the Bible* (New York: Doubleday, 1992), 100-111.

Related to the idea of promise is the pattern of its postponed fulfillment. This pattern recurs throughout the stories of the ancestors but is most vividly presented in Genesis 22, where the command of God to Abraham appears to make fulfillment of the promise impossible. Isaac as Abraham's only son (after the banishment of Ishmael) is the only means through which Abraham can become the father of nations and source of the blessing of future generations. God's command to slaughter this only son stands in logical contradiction to the promise of that future. There are many other complications concerning fulfillment of the promise that occur throughout the ancestral stories. Earlier in Genesis, Abram is told to leave his homeland and go to the place the Lord will show him, but then is quickly forced into sojourning in Egypt and is unable to produce an heir. In the next generation, Isaac is able to produce an heir, or in fact twin boys, but complications arise in passing on the birthright and blessing; the younger son Jacob and his mother resort to trickery to usurp Esau, the rightful heir. Then, in the midst of this deceit Isaac and his family are forced by famine to leave the land and settle in Gerar. In Jacob's story, also, there are long periods in which his role as patriarch is suspended and difficulties arise with his heir(s) — including fourteen years of servitude to his uncle Laban early in his adulthood and the escalating tension among his sons which leads to the apparent death and actual exile of his favorite, Joseph. The problematization or postponement of fulfillment of the promise of land, progeny, and blessing continues far beyond these examples from the ancestral stories throughout the biblical narrative. In many ways, Genesis 22 can be seen as a radical intensification of this theme.

Time spent sojourning — journeying to and living in unfamiliar places, where power lies with someone else — plays an important role in this pattern of delay. Though it is not the most prominent feature of the postponement pattern displayed in Genesis 22, it is worth noting. The suspension of the promise (and concurrently the suspense of the story) is present in the journey to Moriah. A three-day journey may seem brief compared, for instance, to the fourteen-year servitude of Jacob, yet it is horrifically long and painful considering what we (and Abraham) know lies at its end. While there is some discussion in biblical studies about the identity of this mountain,[8] the limits in establishing its identity should again redirect our attention to the text, to what we can know about this

---

8. See discussion of the *akedah* as the etiology of a cult-site in Levenson, *Death and Resurrection*, 114-24.

place: it is not disclosed immediately to Abraham; it is a mountain, one of the high-places, a location associated with God's presence and power; it is a place outside of Abraham's knowledge and control.

The manner in which Abraham's departure is narrated immediately following the (non)disclosure of the destination bespeaks careful deliberation:

> So Abraham rose early in the morning, saddled his donkey, and took two of his young men with him, and his son Isaac; he cut the wood for the burnt offering, and set out and went to the place in the distance that God had shown him. (Genesis 22:3)

Clearly there is no hesitation or stalling on the part of Abraham; this verse follows directly on the heels of God's command. And Abraham takes no unnecessary action (unless you count the saddling of the donkey that so distresses the ancient rabbis, who see such work as beneath Abraham's status). But this listing and describing of actions *does* delay the reader, and it is not until all preparations are made and Abraham has set out that we find out that the place has indeed been shown to him (and apparently only to him). The descriptions of the preparations and of the three-day journey do more than convey Abraham's deliberate obedience; they also create suspense in the reader and emphasize the *work* of carrying out such a command. After God tells Abraham what he is to do, we want a report that it is done or not done (a desire increased by the awfulness of the command). Instead, we hear about Abraham getting up in the morning, preparing the donkey, collecting his servants and son, cutting wood, and only then setting out. Abraham is not asked merely to kill Isaac (a command horrific in itself but involving much less labor). He is required to ready himself and others for a journey, prepare to perform a ritual, and travel for three days. The event that will apparently suspend the fulfillment of the promise (the death of Isaac) is itself performed in a kind of suspended animation.

The lengthy preparations and journey to an unknown place at the beginning of Genesis 22 signal the pattern of postponement or interruption of the promise in its most dramatic form: a command to destroy the only son and heir of the promise. Before the *akedah*, all of Abraham's other heirs have been disqualified (his nephew Lot and son Ishmael), but he has now (against all odds of barrenness and old age) a son with his beloved wife Sarah. The supernatural conception of Isaac and the expulsion of Hagar and Ishmael (prompted by Sarah but authorized by God) combine with the promise that Abraham will father nations to identify Isaac as the one means of the realization of God's promise; he embodies the potential of continuance of the covenant between Abraham and God. God's command to Abraham to take this son and offer him as a burnt sacrifice is thus shocking in ways other than those most obvious to us (the very idea of child-sacrifice). It is shocking that God appears to renege on the promise by commanding the destruction of the only heir left to Abraham and the son whose conception God orchestrated by supernatural means. The story contains the possibility of the divinely commanded undoing of the special relationship between this man and the God who singled him out. Abraham was called, was chosen to receive a promise and "to charge his children and household after him to keep the ways of the Lord by doing righteousness and justice" (Gen. 18:19a), but now the means of fulfilling this charge and the promise are to be removed, to be given back to God. Many, like Kierkegaard's de Silentio, have argued that Abraham's obedience to this command of God was a leap of faith, that, somehow, Abraham believed in the absurd, that he could sacrifice Isaac and yet *have* Isaac, that his son would be returned or resurrected. As Gerhard von Rad puts it, Abraham's obedience proves his ultimate faith in the promise, his belief in God's ability to make him a father of nations even if his only son is sacrificed:

> [This] . . . story goes beyond all the previous trials of Abraham and pushes forward into the realm of faith's extremist experience where God himself rises up as the enemy of his own work with men and hides himself so deeply that for the recipient of the promise only the way of utter forsakenness by God seems to stand open. . . . In no case may interpretation of Genesis XXII be divorced from the matter of promise.[9]

Von Rad argues, using the Hebrew sense of "making oneself secure in Yahweh," that Abraham's faith is faith in God's plan for history, its reality, and his security. It is a faith in the fulfillment of the promise no matter what. The experience of apparent contradiction or of forsakenness by God is, in this reading, the testing of this faith. Such a view is supported both by the beginning and ending of the story — "God tested Abraham" and "because you have done this and have not withheld your son, your

9. von Rad, *Old Testament Theology,* 174.

only son, I will bless you." Passing the test becomes a necessary condition of receiving (however delayed) the content of the promise: progeny, land, and blessing.

In *The Death and Resurrection of the Beloved Son: The Transformation of Child Sacrifice in Judaism and Christianity,* which contains one of the most important discussions of Genesis 22 in contemporary biblical scholarship, Jon Levenson agrees that one of the great paradoxes of this narrative is that "Abraham's willingness to give up Isaac . . . insures the fulfillment of the promise that depends on Isaac."[10]   But Levenson moves beyond the pattern of promise and paradox and identifies a more complex connection between the *akedah* and the concerns of the biblical canon and its subsequent traditions — the role and status of beloved sons. Through this important designation that encompasses familial and theological ideas of favor and chosenness, Levenson traces a pattern of humiliation and exaltation of beloved sons in biblical traditions spanning from Abel and Seth in the early chapters of Genesis to Jesus in the Christian Gospels and into the interpretive traditions of post-biblical Judaism and Christianity. In both his historical-critical study of child sacrifice and his explication of the theme of belovedness, Genesis 22 plays a significant role. As Levenson sees it, because the *akedah* is so important and cherished in biblical traditions and because it so challenges our assumptions within those traditions, its study requires "the brutal honesty of the historical-critical method," particularly concerning the issue of child-sacrifice, the starting place of his investigation.[11] From a broad historical study of ritual sacrifice of children and a critical examination of Genesis 22, Levenson draws several interpretively important conclusions: that the firstborn son is valued as the most precious offering; that the *akedah* does not present child-sacrifice as a strange pagan ritual or as a punishment for disobedience but rather as a "test of devotion";[12] and that there is a broader interpretive importance to child-sacrifice — that the people of Israel themselves are viewed in the biblical texts and subsequent traditions as "not only YHWH's son, but as his first-born son."[13] Against the influential idea that the *akedah* is an etiological narrative explaining the abolishment of human sacrifice and its replacement with animal sacrifice, found, for example, in

---

10. Levenson, *Death and Resurrection,* 142.
11. Levenson, *Death and Resurrection,* 111.
12. Levenson, *Death and Resurrection,* 12.
13. Levenson, *Death and Resurrection,* 37.

the influential *The Last Trial* by Shalom Spiegel (as well as the interpretations of William Blake and subsequently Timothy Jackson), Levenson convincingly argues that this *is* a story of child-sacrifice: Abraham is not commanded to offer an animal, nor is this story ever referred to in other biblical texts or early commentary to encourage or explain animal sacrifice; the ram in this story is offered as a *substitute* for Isaac and not a replacement, and besides, Abraham is rewarded precisely for his willingness to sacrifice Isaac.[14] There is another etiological explanation sometimes offered for Genesis 22: the story explains the name and place of an important cultic site, the eventual location of Solomon's temple. Levenson offers a good review of the various arguments, demonstrating how inadequate are our means of (re)solving them.[15] The limits of historical-critical investigations lead us away from these dismissive etiological explanations and back to the challenges of the story. Levenson appreciates that his rejection of these kinds of interpretations of the *akedah* is frightening; it forces us to interpret the story as paradigmatic; what is experienced by Abraham becomes possible for us.[16] And what is "experienced" through this narrative is, for Levenson, divinely required child-sacrifice.

The experience of child-sacrifice explicitly connects this story to others in the Hebrew Bible. As we have seen, there are interesting semantic and structural connections between the story of the sacrifice of Isaac and the story of the expulsion of Ishmael. Levenson sees the story of Isaac as repeating and intensifying a general pattern of sacrifice in Genesis 16 and 21, both of which involve Ishmael. Taken together these are linked by familial and chronological relationships to a larger narrative pattern in the biblical text. With the "sacrifice" of Ishmael, Isaac, the second son and child of the beloved wife, is, using Levenson's designation, "exalted." Though Isaac is not actually or even legally the firstborn (despite Ishmael's birth to a surrogate), he becomes so once Ishmael is exiled. Isaac then becomes Abraham's only son.

Levenson's study reveals that "only" son in biblical narrative is a complicated and symbolically powerful designation. The term "only" (*yahid*) is uncommon, occurring twelve times in the Bible; three of these twelve instances are in Genesis 22. Levenson demonstrates that in biblical tradition *yahid* is associated with the even rarer term *yadid*, or "beloved

14. Levenson, *Death and Resurrection*, 12, 13, 22.
15. Levenson, *Death and Resurrection*, 115-24.
16. Levenson, *Death and Resurrection*, 16.

one." This terminology recalls for biblical audiences a "dark side": to be loved/favored by father/God "included symbolic death at the hands of the father."[17] The connection between "only" and "loved" is explicit in the command of Genesis 22:3, and this association in the designation of Isaac foreshadows the action content of the command before it is put into words. To be a "beloved son" in the Bible means to be "marked for both exaltation and for humiliation."[18] By this identity a son is placed over any/all others, and, yet, must experience complete (logical) loss of this powerful status, usually by extreme means — exile, servitude, or even death. Isaac's story repeats Ishmael's, but it also completes it as the second son becomes the "only" and "beloved" son, exalted over his brother even as he experiences the complete forfeiture of his life by the father who loves him.

> The exaltation of the chosen brother . . . [here] Isaac over Ishmael . . . has its costs: it entails the chosen's experience of the bitter reality of the unchosen's life. Such is the humiliation that attends the exaltation of the beloved son.[19]

In becoming the "beloved" and "only," Isaac is elevated and yet must experience in intensified degree the life (or perhaps more accurately the almost-death) of those over whom he is elevated. Genesis 22, then, is part of a broad pattern of concerns regarding the meaning of being chosen/unchosen, being simultaneously placed in position over and under others.

In addition to the expulsion of Hagar and Ishmael, there are two other stories, more explicitly stories of child-sacrifice, which can be compared with Genesis 22: the story of Jephthah's daughter (Judges 11:29-40) and the story of the son of Mesha, the king of Moab (2 Kings 3:27). The story from Judges entails a hasty vow made by the Israelites' warrior-leader, Jephthah, to sacrifice as a "burnt-offering" the first thing coming out of his house when he returns from battle if God will grant a particular military victory. Horrifically, it is his daughter and "his only child," joyfully celebrating her father's return home, who first emerges and thus is designated the object of sacrifice. In 2 Kings, when losing a battle against the Israelites, the Moabite king, Mesha, takes his firstborn son, who is to succeed him, and offers him as a burnt offering, and, by doing so, apparently secures victory. The connections between these three stories, particularly in

17. Levenson, *Death and Resurrection*, 28-30.
18. Levenson, *Death and Resurrection*, 59.
19. Levenson, *Death and Resurrection*, 96.

the context of Levenson's focus, are in many ways obvious. In Genesis 22, Judges 11, and 2 Kings 3, leaders, who are also fathers, perform ritual sacrifices in the form of "burnt-offerings" of children with special status (only, firstborn, beloved) and the ritual performance seems in some way validated by supernatural authority. In the Genesis story and the Judges story, the patriarchs are leaders of the (future) Israelites, and the God who commands Abraham and to whom Jephthah directs his vow and credits his victory is Yahweh. While Mesha of 2 Kings fights against the Israelites, his offering is nonetheless described in similar terms and seems connected in the narrative to the "great wrath" that comes upon the Israelites and causes them to withdraw from the fight and retreat home. Critically comparing Genesis 22 with other instances of child-sacrifice shifts in many ways the interpretive understanding of the emphasis and challenge of this story. The story is not uniquely challenging simply because it presents a (near) experience of child-sacrifice. It appears to be part of much larger patterns — the explicit stories of such offerings and of the greater and more complex one surrounding the status of beloved sons (and daughters).

The interconnectedness of Genesis 22 and other stories, patterns, and concerns of the Hebrew Bible revealed through biblical scholarship provides a means to a new way of grappling with the Bible as a whole, as a canon, and has definite ramifications for contemporary Christian ethics. Moral theologians must engage the story of the binding/sacrifice of Isaac because it forms an integral part or manifestation of a larger whole and a complex series of concerns. Even if some interpretations of the binding/ sacrifice of Isaac have a legacy of justifying ways of being in the world that need to be challenged, this is a story that cannot be ignored or de-privileged without neglecting (and thus distorting) a crucial voice in the biblical canon. The interconnectedness of this story with surrounding biblical ideas and patterns is not accounted for in the narrowly focused reading(s) of Genesis 22 in *Fear and Trembling* (and consequently in much contemporary ethical scholarship).[20] Nor is this interconnectedness given its due in pre-critical methods of harmonization of the texts or in supersessionist readings. By contrast, the historical-critical view of the complexity of the authorship, composition, and canonization of Scripture makes assumptions about its logical consistency and perfect harmony un-

---

20. See Jung Lee, "Abraham in a Different Voice," in *Religious Studies* 36 (2000): 377-400. The author follows Kierkegaard, yet connects what Abraham does with an ongoing relationship with God reaching beyond Genesis 22, and thus explains it in light of an "ethics of care."

necessary. At the same time it takes seriously and regards as interpretively important the relationship of Genesis 22 to its biblical contexts. Attempting to read the story in relationship to larger and more complex canons and traditions provides an attentive alternative to harmonization or supersessionism. Instead of forcing the text to harmonize simplistically with other texts and theological doctrines, and, thus, at the very least, missing its complexity and, possibly, significantly misconstruing its concerns, critical biblical scholarship demands we be open to, even look for, the concerns of the text as they are revealed through study, even if these concerns "go against our preferences and traditions." In this way, critical stances do not rob the biblical text of its claims on us but recast them in ways that encourage an engagement of the text through discovering its own concerns. In the case of Genesis 22, critical study compels us to confront theological and ethical challenges in new ways. The complexity of the covenant and its connected concerns of heirs, land, and blessing illuminate the complexities between action and result, promise and fulfillment. Ideas about the status and role of the "beloved son" bring to the forefront concerns about favor, religious/ethic identity and responsibility, and the theology of chosenness. This does not mean our own, perhaps different, concerns are unimportant, ethically or even interpretatively, but it does mean that we need to attend to those raised by the story in the text's own terms.

Critical study of the *akedah,* while revealing its connections with other biblical narratives, also uncovers its uniqueness among these texts. The story of the binding/sacrifice of Isaac is, in fact, odd in many ways. For example, in Levenson's comparison of the three explicit stories of child-sacrifice discussed above, only Genesis 22 provides vivid clarity about the source or sanction of the sacrifice. In the Judges story, Jephthah makes a vow of his own accord that may not have been necessary for military victory (he was apparently doing pretty well), and the intended object of the sacrifice lacks what Levenson calls the "lucidity" found in Genesis 22.[21] The story in 2 Kings shares similar terminology and the sacrifice seems to achieve its purpose, but unlike Genesis 22, it is a spontaneous and desperate action and one distanced from Yahweh as Mesha is a Moabite king fighting against Yahweh's people. My own study of these texts uncovers other differences. First, the lack of clarity regarding Jephthah's sacrifice starkly contrasts with the "lucidity" of Genesis 22 through the striking difference in the disclosures between father and only child. Jephthah tells his

---

21. Levenson, *Death and Resurrection,* 14.

daughter about his vow and she encourages him to do to her "what has gone out of your mouth," clearly indicating consent to the sacrifice. Jephthah's distress about the sacrifice is painfully apparent when he (however unfairly) admonishes his daughter for being the first to come out to meet him: "Alas, my daughter, you have brought me very low" (Judges 11:35). In Genesis 22, no speech of Abraham's indicates his feelings, nor is Isaac's understanding or participation made explicit. The only exchange between father and son in Genesis 22 (vv. 7-8) is remarkably equivocal:

> Isaac said to his father Abraham, "Father," and he said, "Here I am, my son." He said, "the fire and the wood are here but where is the lamb for a burnt offering?" Abraham said, "God himself will provide the lamb for a burnt offering, my son." And the two of them walked on as one.

The ambiguity of this text with regards to the issues of both Abraham's subjectivity and Isaac's comprehension will be discussed later in this chapter. Here it is sufficient to see the difference between the participants in these sacrifices.

Another key difference that emerges through a comparison of these stories, one that again characterizes Genesis 22 as particularly odd and challenging even within a series of odd and challenging narratives, is that Abraham's ritual sacrifice is not demanded by a great and immediate national need. Even if Jephthah's vow was rash and unnecessary (in that he seemed to be steadily victorious) or even abhorrent, it seems that Jephthah believed that he was vowing to make a burnt sacrifice to Yahweh in order to secure an important victory for the people he had been chosen to lead and protect. Similarly, Mesha saw his people making a last stand behind the walls of Kir-hareseth (the Israelites having overturned everything else as they followed the enemies back into the land of Moab), and, after an unsuccessful military effort (involving seven hundred swordsmen), he made a burnt-offering of his son and heir. If it is unclear whether or not Jephthah's vow guaranteed his victory, it seems as if Mesha's sacrifice brings a supernatural force (the "wrath") and protects him (and one assumes the people under his kingship) from defeat. These two stories of child-sacrifice take place in the midst of desperate, violent, and difficult situations. The leader/father sacrifices the only/oldest child in order to get the supernatural backing he believes necessary to achieve a military victory.[22] The sacrifice of Isaac by

22. They are in many ways much more like Agamemnon than is Abraham.

Abraham differs in many important ways. It is cast amidst a *domestic* drama (with interruptions like the horror at Sodom and Gomorrah), involving the establishment of an lineage. Unlike Jephthah or Mesha, Abraham does not himself conceive the idea of the sacrifice and has no reason to perform it (in terms of the logical good of those in his care and protection) beyond its being God's command. It is important, of course, that God does reward him for his willingness to sacrifice, to "not withhold his son," by renewing the blessing of offspring and their possession of the land. However, prior to the command we (and Abraham) have no reason to suspect that this promise *needs* renewing, nor does the narrative make any reference to this outcome until the dramatic/ritual action has already taken place. In no way does the story seem to indicate that Abraham believes he must kill Isaac in order to receive a blessing that was already bestowed upon him. In fact, critical scholarship tends to reveal just the opposite: he is willing to kill Isaac even though Isaac is the only apparent means of his receiving the blessing. Unlike the other fathers, Jephthah and Mesha, Abraham's motives are not military and are, in fact, left undisclosed. No "motive" is put forward — only divine command and active obedience to it.

The description of the act of obeying the command and thus carrying out child-sacrifice also distinguishes Genesis 22. It is, as Levenson puts it, our only biblical account of the "procedure" of child-sacrifice. Abraham's actions are laboriously recounted throughout, particularly weighed against the overall brevity of the story. Verse 3 has already been mentioned with regard to the delay and journey. In addition to this long verse, there are verses 6 and 9-10. Each of these describes in oddly "observant" detail Abraham's actions:

> Abraham took the wood of the burnt offering and laid it on his son Isaac, and he himself carried the fire and the knife. So the two of them walked on together. . . . When they came to the place that God had shown him, Abraham built an altar there and laid the wood in order. He bound his son Isaac and laid him on the altar, on top of the wood. Then Abraham reached out his hand and took the knife to slaughter his son.

This detailed description is striking for at least two reasons: it occurs in a narrative that is only nineteen verses long, and it is the only narrative of the stories of child-sacrifice that recounts the "how." As a literary device, this description achieves many things: it creates suspense, demonstrates the deliberate character of Abraham's actions, describes the work and time entailed in performing such a ritual, and draws attention to the horrifying nature of this sacrifice; having the child carry the wood which will eventually provide the fire that will consume him, binding him, placing him on an altar on top of the firewood, and finally picking up the knife. This is not a simple moment of assent, but a lived experience. It is not a point in the plot to be skimmed over but rather an experience that the reader must painfully negotiate.

In addition to being the only biblical account of the procedure of child-sacrifice, Genesis 22 is odd even among accounts of ancient sacrifice generally. First, there is the ambiguity of the binding — the strange act from which the story gets its Jewish name, the *akedah*. This binding has been interpreted in many (sometimes opposing) ways. For some it signals the need to constrain an unwilling object of sacrifice. In *Genesis Rabbah,* it is the carrying out of Isaac's request, as he is unsure of his own resolve but does not want to jeopardize the sacrifice.[23] Second, there is the strange word for knife: *ma'akeleth,* a word that comes from the root *'akal:* to devour. It is used twice as the word for knife in this short narrative and then appears only twice more in the rest of the Bible — both appearances being of a very disturbing nature. It is the word for knife used in Judges 19 when the Levite husband cuts into twelve pieces the (dead or alive) body of his wife/concubine after she has been raped for an entire night by the men of the city where they were staying. That act is both a warning and indictment to all Israel, but it also (unwittingly) conveys the Levite's own deception regarding his part in the horror of the previous night. The other occurrence of this word is in Proverbs' violent description of the greedy: "those whose teeth are knives to devour the poor from the earth, the needy from among mortals" (30:14). Abraham reaches for a knife that should disturb us — a knife that devours. Again, like the careful description of Abraham's actions, this word choice defeats any easiness or accommodation. The possibility, even the presence, of real horror is there.

The uniqueness of Genesis 22 is apparent not only when it is compared to the other explicit stories of child-sacrifice in the biblical text but also when it is considered within the larger patterns of the promise of the patriarchs and the delay or suspension of that promise. As von Rad puts it, this "story goes beyond all previous trials of Abraham" as "God himself rises up as the enemy of his own work with men."[24] It is only in this story

---

23. *Genesis Rabbah* 56:8.
24. von Rad, *Old Testament Theology,* 174.

that God appears to be the sole and possibly arbitrary force against the fulfillment of the promise God made to Abraham. In my own struggle to read this text, the peculiarity evidenced by this story within the larger narrative complexes of the ancestors and the covenant calls into question the possibility of resolving or even identifying this as just another, albeit extreme, manifestation of that pattern of promise and suspension. While reading the *akedah* completely apart from those concerns is deeply misleading, reading it completely through them also depletes the richness of the story. There is a sense in which this narrative seems to draw attention away from the fulfillment of the promise — by not framing the test within its demands, by concentrating our attention on the acts necessitated by Abraham's obedience, by the very nature of the suspension: God's contradiction of the promise by asking for the destruction of the means of its fulfillment. No sense emerges from the story that Abraham believed he would receive Isaac back or that he would be granted offspring, land, and blessings if he obeyed. There is no carrot dangled in front of his nose. Compare the command to sacrifice Isaac with the earlier and similar command to leave the home of his ancestors in Genesis 12. The earlier command (12:1) is immediately followed by two verses (12:2-3) full of promises, narratively giving the impression that God is telling Abram/Abraham what reward obedience will bring and "so Abram went as Yahweh had told him" (v. 4). In Genesis 22, the command is not followed by any promises until *after* Abraham performs all the action necessary to obey it. In no way do I want to ignore Genesis 22:15-18, where God blesses Abraham with the contents of the promise because the father has offered the son, because he has listened to God's voice. These verses, while probably a later addition, are an integral part of the story as it stands as a biblical text and, as von Rad puts it, connect the story to the promise or even more strongly, as Levenson argues, make Genesis 22 a foundational narrative.[25] On the other hand, it is important to note that these promises are given at the end: that, yes, Abraham is rewarded for his performance in Genesis 22:1-14, but that his actions are not preceded by any mention of the promise. The story does not frame Abraham as obeying God in order to receive (again) the promise he has already been given.

If this notion of reward is removed as the motivation for Abraham,

---

25. Levenson, *Death and Resurrection*, 140. This is done partly through connecting the acts in the story with the promise, but also through the "superabundant allusiveness" of the verses that recall not only Hagar but Adam and Eve.

then what remains? God's command (voice), Abraham's actions, and Isaac's presence (physical and questioning). The relationship between God and Abraham (and Abraham and Isaac) is not one of simple promise, obedience, and reward. This story suggests a deeper complexity in that relationship. Abraham listens to God's voice; he attends to that voice throughout all the painfully drawn-out actions that attention demands. God and Abraham are present to each other. Abraham answers God's call in Genesis 22:1 with *"hinneni,"* a somewhat untranslatable word but with the sense of "here I am, present and ready." It is an answer that indicates active and responding presence to the caller and is confirmed in the difficult actions Abraham performs. God's presence to Abraham is indicated first by God's voice and then by God's (appearing in a) vision: we are told in verse 14 that Abraham calls the place Adonai-yireh (God-vision). This name, which is given before the renewal of the promise, does not survive and cannot be clearly connected to any historical place. Instead, "what survives from Abraham's experience," says Levenson, "is not the name of the mountain, but the vision of YHWH that takes place there."[26] God is present to Abraham in the *akedah*, both speaking to him and appearing to him, as Abraham is present to God in his response and in his actions.

Genesis 22 is also a narrative in which Abraham and Isaac are present to one another. While certainly the object of the command/sacrifice, Isaac is not depicted as a mere object in the story. Instead, he participates in the actions of Abraham, journeying with him and carrying the wood his father has laid on his back. He asks a question about the whereabouts of the sheep for the sacrifice. While not settling the ambiguity regarding his age, understanding, or consenting participation, asking this question dramatically indicates his real presence as subject, not merely object. And Abraham answers his son's call with the same word he uses to answer God's, *"hinneni,"* showing that the father's attentive response to his son is like his response to his God. Twice the narrative tells us that Isaac and Abraham went on together, literally, "went as one." These relationships in Genesis 22 are depicted in terms that indicate deep presence, detached from reward, demanding response, action, and trust. Part of the power of this story lies not in the fact that Abraham's obedience in the face of a horrific command gets him a reward, but that Abraham's response in the face of a horrific demand draws him closer to God and to Isaac.

The uniqueness of Genesis 22 continues to be discernable within the

---

26. Levenson, *Death and Resurrection*, 122.

pattern, identified by Levenson, of the exaltation and humiliation of the beloved son. Its distinctiveness within this pattern lies in the story's clarity and direct engagement. Of the stories of favored children in the first book of the Pentateuch, only this story tells of the symbolic death of the son, the humiliation of the son, directly and knowingly at the hands (literally) of the father. "For among the[se] tales of the beloved sons in Genesis [Abel/ Seth, Ishmael, Jacob, Joseph] the aqedah is unique in that in it alone the father directly and deliberately brings about the symbolic death of this favored offspring."[27] And of the explicit stories of child-sacrifice, this is the only one in which God's direct command is clearly the source of the need to carry out the sacrifice, and the only one in which the sacrifice appears to be the means of destroying the father's patriarchal role and promise rather than a means of insuring them. Abraham's direct action in the (symbolic) slaughter of his son and God's direct command for him to take this action give us perhaps the most concrete and evocative example of the pattern of the sacrifice/restoration of the beloved son but also an example that transcends rather than merely repeating that pattern. Unlike the problem of chosenness emphasized in the narrative of Joseph, the story of father and son in Genesis 22 in no way shows that "human nature . . . is not constituted so as to facilitate the acceptance of chosenness."[28] Instead, Genesis 22 is a story that moves beyond complete acceptance of this role into the subsequent interactions and lived experience that follow from that special relationship between persons and God. Levenson describes Abraham not as a knight of faith but rather as a "knight of observance."[29] This is not the story of the assent to chosenness or of faith in the restoration of Isaac or of fulfillment of promise. Rather we are told the story of a father in relationship, present and responsive, to God and son; showing "faith" is not an assent to a proposition, idea, or position, but rather a way of being and acting in the world. The presence of God in the story through voice, actions, and vision connects ritual observance to presence. The horrifically real consequences of ritual observance connect this presence to action in the world. Levenson argues that the *akedah* is a test of whether Abraham is prepared to give Isaac back to the God who interceded to provide him. If Abraham had not "heeded" the command he would have elected "Isaac his

27. Levenson, *Death and Resurrection*, 225.
28. Levenson, *Death and Resurrection*, 155. Levenson does show that the Joseph narrative, and most of the Genesis beloved son narratives, do "make clear" this conflict between the "fragility of the human ego and the mysterious operation of the choosing Deity."
29. Levenson, *Death and Resurrection*, 141.

own son" over Isaac the "beloved son of the larger Providential drama."[30] By following the command, then, Abraham's actions do not just evoke and accomplish his own real and present relationship to God but also show forth his acceptance of Isaac as real and present, as having his own center of importance and value, in some ways his own subjectivity, theologically understood.

Critical biblical scholarship reveals, among many other important things, that Genesis 22 is an integral part of larger canon(s) and traditions and its own concerns cannot be properly engaged without consideration of these. Simultaneously, such scholarship discloses a story that is strangely unique and challenging. Traditionally, in modern biblical studies, there are two broad ways of studying biblical texts, historical-critical and literary, though the distinctions between these approaches have diminished and the field is certainly not limited to these. Historical-critical scholarship offers some, though not in this case many, insights into the complex and human history of the text or possibilities regarding its composition. By a perhaps happy coincidence, the paradigmatic yet odd character of Genesis 22 can be attested through source criticism (a historical-critical method) — though the identification of the four ancient literary sources of the Pentateuch does not have much to offer to this particular study. Von Rad links the concerns of this chapter with the sources known as J and E through the content of the promise (possession of the land and provision of innumerable progeny), since the promise is evidently at stake in the story and reiterated at its conclusion.[31] While von Rad does not connect Genesis 22 with the concerns of the Priestly source (that God promises to have a special relationship to his people), these concerns are certainly relevant to the reading given above. Joseph Blenkinsopp links the story to concerns about the law (through verses 16-18), and thus to the Deuteronomist contribution to the Genesis narrative.[32] Some scholars assign this narrative to E (see Blenkinsopp and Levenson for reasons this is unsatisfactory),[33] but many identify it as an independent tradition. Even from the perspective of source criticism, this narrative both connects with other biblical texts and their concerns and also eludes identification with any of the major sources believed to make up most of the first five books of the Bible. Source criticism

---

30. Levenson, *Death and Resurrection,* 126.
31. von Rad, *Old Testament Theology,* 168-9.
32. Blenkinsopp, *Pentateuch,* 122.
33. Blenkinsopp, *Pentateuch,* 121; and Levenson, *Death and Resurrection,* 122.

does not, then, add a great deal, at least from the point of view of this volume, to historical-critical study of the *akedah*.

Overall, historical-critical work not only illuminates important ideas such as blessing, covenant, and sacrifice. It also demonstrates the limits of what we can know, something illustrated, for example, by the quest for the historical ancestors like Abraham and Isaac.[34] Such limits, at the very least, remind us that ways of understanding what is important, true, or significant (and the manner in which such things are recorded) were very different in the ancient world, and that our incapacity to historically substantiate Genesis 22 does not undermine (and may even help sustain) its challenging power. Our modern desire to know "what happened" is checked by the unknown historical status of the story itself and forces us back to the text, not the people or places behind it. The story cannot be dismissed as merely a report of something that happened (or didn't happen) in the past; its power to challenge does not lie in its historicity.[35] It is an irreducibly strange, disturbing, and difficult text. And not just in terms of modern sensibilities: even as we attempt to meet the text on its own terms, using such analytical tools as are available to us, the story remains extraordinarily challenging.

In the case of Genesis 22, then, historical-critical approaches contribute to rigorous engagement of the text, but also betray some real limitations. As a probable independent and ancient tradition, this story falls outside the usual insights of source criticism. Many of the "answers" to a variety of historical questions are not accessible to us. These constraints prompt us to turn our attention to the literary character and concerns of the text — to consider the way, *as a text*, the *akedah* reveals meaning. As Blenkinsopp puts it more generally about the stories of the ancestors, "it is still necessary to insist that we cannot even begin to address historical issues until we have come

34. Though some debates regarding this issue continue, Joseph Blenkinsopp, *Pentateuch*, 126-27, describes the present situation in these terms: "in the current state of our knowledge there is no realistic expectation of establishing historicity of the ancestors." By this he means not just that their historical existence cannot be established but that our ability to know anything about the social and political contexts of these figures is also significantly restricted.

35. Auerbach, *Mimesis*, 14-15. This is a different point, but obviously related to Quinn's rejection of its "actuality." A way to see a distinction here is to draw on the characterization given to the story by Erich Auerbach who sees the narrative of Genesis 22 as "not primarily oriented toward 'realism'... [but] oriented towards *truth.*" Believing in Abraham's sacrifice (which is distinguished from identifying it as a historical event) is a necessary perspective if the narrative is to serve the purposes for which it was written.

to terms with the literary problems."[36] The preceding discussion of the inter-connectedness yet uniqueness of this story within the biblical canon and its traditions has already significantly blurred the lines between literary study and historical study. But from a literary-critical perspective there remain three important ideas that need to be made explicit within this project: first, that this biblical text is a narrative; second, that it is a particularly sparse and ambiguous narrative; and third, that these qualities, especially combined with the difficult content of the story, affect one's experience of reading it.

That Genesis 22 is a story, a narrative, with all the basic elements of a story is obvious. There are characters and plot line(s). Things happen. People (inter)act. As obvious as this categorization may be, it is important to acknowledge within the scope of the larger concerns of the project. I intend this to be a case study of the relationship between the Hebrew Bible and Christian ethics. However, the narrative character of Genesis 22, taken together with the distinctive features of *this* narrative, place important limits on the possibilities of my overarching claims. The Hebrew Bible contains a variety of genres, each with different characteristics and functions and each to be read, studied, and engaged in different ways. To argue that all biblical texts will be comparably accessible to the similarly complex study of moral theology would be preposterous. Even to assume that all biblical *narratives* will function similarly for ethical reflection and formation would be misleading. To take this a step further, we need to acknowledge the unique character of any *particular narrative,* such as Genesis 22, and even of any interpretation. So in some sense, this study is (my) study of the *akedah* and only the *akedah.* Nonetheless, the potential of contemporary literary-critical perspectives to provide the means of meaningful engagement with biblical texts can, I think, be seen in even a (limited) case study such as this.

Many of the literary characteristics of the story of the near-sacrifice of Isaac have already played a part in this analysis: structure, repetition (both within the narrative and within the larger biblical canon), pacing, semantic choices, creation of tension, and ambiguity. It is this last characteristic that demands more attention here. Genesis 22 is well known for its sparseness as a narrative. One of the most famous accounts of this quality is that of literary historian and critic Erich Auerbach, *Mimesis: The Representation of Reality in Western Literature,* the first chapter of which compares Homeric narrative to biblical narrative. In an oft-quoted passage, Auerbach describes the narrative of Genesis 22 in the following terms:

36. Blenkinsopp, *Pentateuch,* 126.

the externalization of only so much of the phenomena as is necessary for the purpose of narrative, all else is left in obscurity; the decisive points of the narrative alone are emphasized, what lies between is non-existent; time and place are undefined and call for interpretation; thoughts and feeling remain unexpressed, are only suggested by the silence and the fragmentary speeches; the whole permeated by the most unrelieved suspense and directed towards a single goal, remains mysterious and "fraught with background."[37]

Auerbach's fascination with Genesis 22, which he describes as an epic, lies in just these characteristics — the scarcity of detail and description and the complete lack of subjective expression. In an analysis of "Gaps, Ambiguity, and the Reading Process," biblical scholar Meir Sternberg likewise notes that "biblical narratives are notorious for the sparsity of detail"; in particular he designates the binding of Isaac as an "episode celebrated for leaving details in obscurity."[38] The recognition of this characteristic of biblical narrative does not belong to modern literary and biblical scholars alone. According to James Kugel, "biblical stories were viewed by ancient interpreters as fundamentally elliptical: the narrative was believed to say much in a few words and often to omit essentials, leaving a number of details to be filled in by the interpreter."[39] Genesis 22 stands as a particularly vivid example of such honed and spare story-telling.

The narrative is comprised almost entirely of essential action and speech and very little, however significant, description. These qualities create several interpretive concerns about the inner state and motivations of the characters and the purpose or focus of the narrative. For example, Auerbach draws attention to the question of the location of God and Abraham at the beginning of the story: "Where are the two speakers? We are not told. The reader, however, knows that they are not normally to be found together in one place on earth."[40] Auerbach sees the lack of specific location as theological — that God's (lack of earthly) location is con-

---

37. Auerbach, *Mimesis*, 11-12.

38. Meir Sternberg, *The Poetics of Biblical Narrative: Ideological Literature and the Drama of Reading* (Bloomington: Indiana University Press, 1987), 191-2.

39. James Kugel, *In Potiphar's House: The Interpretive Life of Biblical Texts* (Cambridge, MA: Harvard University Press, 1990), 6.

40. Auerbach, *Mimesis*, 8. The introduction of what the "reader knows" here is part of what Auerbach means when he talks about biblical stories being "fraught with background"; the reading of these stories is caught up in their past and in the reader's connection to that past in her present and future.

nected to a concept of God and a way of representing reality and that Abraham's answer, *"hinenni"* (to which Auerbach gives the sense of "Behold me, here I am, awaiting thy command"), is obviously not a designation of location (which is left unspecified) but of "a moral position in respect to God." Auerbach notes that it is "up to the reader to visualize" this scene, which he goes on to do.[41] Auerbach's handling of the obscurity of the location of God and Abraham in the beginning of Genesis 22 thus illuminates two functions served by this literary feature (the creation of ambiguity): giving the narrative theological and moral potential that details might exclude, and creating the necessity of actively imaginative reading.

Of course, as the studies already considered in this volume show, the ambiguity that draws most interpretive attention, historically and in contemporary thought, is Abraham's inner state — his thoughts, his emotions, his motivations. The story represents Abraham in a variety of ways, though never through his own subjectivity. He answers God's call with the one word, *"hinenni,"* and subsequently answers his son and the angel in the same way. He deliberately and carefully performs the actions necessary in carrying out the command. In addition to answering when called, Abraham speaks three times in this story (to the two young men, in answer to Isaac's question, and in naming the place), and in each case what he says has multiple interpretive possibilities. The ambiguity of his speech (consider his answer to Isaac's question: "God himself will provide the lamb for a burnt offering, my son") is particularly remarkable when compared to the care taken in describing his actions. Even in the midst of ancestral stories that offer "very little authorial comment on the characters or their actions,"[42] this story stands out for its (apparently calculated) omission of any conclusive clues as to its characters' inner states. In other trials, Abraham's concern or distress is evoked through speech and action. When God shares God's plans to destroy Sodom and Gomorrah, Abraham "remained standing before the Lord," even "came nearer" and attempted to talk the Lord out of his plans for the sake of fifty, forty, thirty, twenty, or ten righteous people (Genesis 18:18-32). There is no counterpart in Genesis 22 when he is faced with the destruction of his son (whom we can surely assume to be righteous in this sense) to this bold, perhaps even impudent, speech made on behalf of these cities. In the story of the expulsion of

41. Auerbach, *Mimesis,* 9.
42. Blenkinsopp, *Pentateuch,* 98.

Hagar and Ishmael (which echoes or foreshadows much of the pattern and wording of Genesis 22), Abraham's internal reaction is directly reported. When Sarah asks to have the Egyptian mother and firstborn son sent away, the narrator tells us that "the matter was very distressing to Abraham on account of his son" (21:11). Again, there is no counterpart to this distress reported in the *akedah*.[43] The comparisons serve to demonstrate the particularity of this story as one that is crafted to reveal nothing. As a reader one can scarcely help noticing the difference between the expulsion narrative and the binding episode, since they occur, side by side, between the miraculous conception and birth of Isaac and his commanded destruction. In Genesis 22, speech "does not serve . . . to manifest, to externalize thoughts — on the contrary, it serves to indicate thoughts which remain unexpressed."[44] The *akedah*'s careful veiling of the motivations of the speakers has a purpose beyond merely creating obscurity. As Auerbach points out, it serves to indicate that the characters, the speakers (in this case Abraham) actually have subjectivity (are beings with emotions, thoughts and intentions), even if we cannot know what they are.

Refraining from offering any textual evidence that would close the gap of Abraham's subjectivity is one of the great strengths of this story. For no description or even clue to Abraham's thoughts, feelings, and motivation, could create or allow for the rich and challenging interpretive possibilities present in this story. A report of what Abraham is feeling or thinking would not only close off possibilities; it would also lessen the power of the experience of reading, sparing the reader the need to make her own journey, creating that subjectivity herself. Since we are not told how Abraham felt about all this, we attempt to imagine, by entering through our own personal experiences into Abraham's story. The mystery surrounding Abraham's thoughts or feelings has, perhaps, been one of the most evocative features of this story throughout its history. It is one of the "invitations" of the text, using Kugel's word, so appealing to ancient interpreters like the writers of *Genesis Rabbah*. It is the imaginative hook for *Fear and Trembling* and the inspiration for the narrative fragments in the "Attunement" (which are unbiblical in the way they report internal states). In the contemporary work of Timothy Jackson,

43. There are, of course, important reasons to differentiate these situations. As Levenson points out, the Sodom and Gomorrah episode involves the questioning of a divine plan rather than a divine directive, while in the expulsion of Hagar and Ishmael, Abraham reacts with distress to a wish of Sarah and is seemingly calmed by God, who then authorizes Sarah's request. See *Death and Resurrection*, 129.

44. Auerbach, *Mimesis*, 11.

not only is the inner state of Abraham a central focus, but its transformation is the argued purpose of the trial. Even the carefully legal-minded and logical Philip the Chancellor expresses a concern that Abraham did not wish for Isaac's murder (thus expressing an interest in intention).

Since, as Levenson puts it, Abraham's motivations remain, "and *will always* remain unclear,"[45] narrative focus falls on the *what* and not the *why* of his actions. Kierkegaard's Johannes de Silentio (and thus, many contemporary ethicists) moves from the report of what Abraham does to designating him as a "knight of faith." His actions show his complete assent to a faith-centered (and absurd) proposition — that Isaac will be returned to him. Because of the gaps surrounding his subjectivity, as well as the description of his actions, Levenson prefers to call Abraham a "knight of observance." Meir Sternberg argues that "the focus of interest lies in Abraham's supreme obedience regardless of any possible thought."[46] In his reading, this obedience is highlighted by the lack of information concerning Abraham's state of mind.[47] That the narration focuses on Abraham's actions in accord with God's command is most certainly the case. But that obedience or assent to a proposition of faith is the only concern of the story does not immediately follow. Based on the narrative as we have it, what is important is the nature of Abraham's relationship with God. The story moves beyond a simple report of his obedience (compare, for example, Judges 11 in which we are merely told that Jephthah "did with her according to the vow he had made"). Instead, in showing us Abraham's preparations for and carrying out of the sacrifice of Isaac, it invites us to observe his (inter)actions and to consider their meaning.

This story not only fails to provide access to Abraham's subjectivity; it also refuses to provide unambiguous information about God's intentions. The narrator tells us that God "tested" *(nissah)* Abraham. After Abraham raises the knife to slaughter Isaac, the angel of the Lord tells him that "now I know *(yadaʿ)* that you fear God" and again later, that "because" Abraham has not withheld Isaac, "I will indeed bless you." But what does the "testing" of Abraham mean from an interpretive perspective? Is it an ordeal meant to effect something in him (like beating high quality flax or making a son more beloved)? Is it a trial to prove something about Abra-

---

45. Levenson, *Death and Resurrection*, 131.

46. Sternberg, *Poetics*, 192.

47. He goes so far as to say that "it would doubtless enrich the drama" if his state of mind were indicated (*Poetics*, 192), a proposal I disagree with, instead seeing this gap as increasing the drama (tension and suspense) of the *akedah*.

ham's faith in God or specifically in the divine promise? Is it, in Levenson's words, a test of his devotion? Is it necessary for God's knowledge? The "now I know" of the angel's first speech would seem to indicate so. Walter Brueggemann claims that this story clearly suggests that God wants to know something about Abraham and that "the flow of the narrative accomplishes something in the awareness of God . . . a genuine movement in the history between Yahweh and Abraham."[48] Most traditional interpretations are more comfortable viewing the *akedah* as a test to demonstrate something to the world (or to the heavenly court or to Abraham himself), showing "retroactively" the righteousness of God's choice. For some, the story seems to reverse the test: does Abraham end up testing God? This ancient midrashic tradition, picked up by Elie Wiesel, envisions the second angelic speech and the renewal of the promise as necessary because Abraham does not immediately put down the knife; rather, he demands that God himself rescind the order that God gave, and that God add to the promise future forgiveness to his children's children.[49] It seems, then, that even by providing an explanation for God's command by casting it as a "test," the narrative retains God's inscrutability. Gerhard von Rad tells us that we look in vain in a story like this "for any formulation of the narrator's own theological judgment."[50]

The ambiguities that surround God's intentions in this story are dramatically increased, it seems, by theological ideas regarding God's omniscience, unchangeability, and even rationality. The convincing claims of Levenson's study, that this is a story of child-sacrifice, certainly strain our modern ideas about God. Even interpretations that attempt to clear God of any charges of injustice or of willing child-sacrifice by claiming that this story recounts what was just a test (von Rad) or "ironic schooling" (Jackson) by God do not fit easily into a consistent theology as divinity appar-

48. Walter Brueggemann, *Genesis: A Bible Commentary for Teaching and Preaching,* Interpretation Series (Atlanta: John Knox, 1982), 187.

49. Elie Wiesel, *Messengers of God: Biblical Portraits and Legends,* trans. Marion Wiesel (New York: Summit Books, 1976), 92-93. Another view of the test is an argument (reminiscent of Jackson's interpretation) that Abraham was great because he refused to kill Isaac. In Omri Boehm's "The Binding of Isaac: An Inner-biblical Polemic on the Question of 'Disobeying' a Manifestly Illegal Order" (*Vetus Testamentum* 52 [2002]: 1-12), a historical-critical argument attempts to demonstrate that Abraham refused to sacrifice in the "original" version of the story.

50. von Rad, *Old Testament Theology,* 165. Interestingly, he will go on to claim that in referring to this as a test, the story tells us that the sacrifice won't happen (betraying his discomfort with an idea of a God who might really command child-sacrifice).

ently misrepresents itself through the command. And recall Philip Quinn's rejection of the actuality of this story based on an argument of logic following from such propositions about God. Against this, Brueggemann points out that "this text does not flinch before or pause at the unreasonableness of this story. God is not a logical premise who must perform in rational consistency."[51] The ambiguity surrounding God in Genesis 22 confronts our own theological confidence, adding to the powerful experience of engaged reading.

Sternberg characterizes the gaps or the narrative ambiguities of Genesis 22 as functioning to turn our attention to the complete obedience of Abraham. This allows him to contrast this story with another story in which the gaps create multiple interpretive possibilities, thus furthering the story's purpose (his example of this being the story of David, Bathsheba, and Uriah in 2 Samuel 11). I am not convinced that the purpose of the gaps in Genesis 22 is necessarily as different from their purpose in 2 Samuel as Sternberg characterizes them. While our theological concerns are directed towards Abraham's obedience, the story does not seem to be one-dimensional — a perfect assent to a theological idea, or even faith in the promise. In this story, we do not see God's nature or human nature (even Abraham's) but rather an interaction between the two (and other) characters. As unlikely as this may be, God and Abraham are present to each other, in voice, in vision, in action, and in Levenson's word, observance. And while the content of their subjectivities remains obscure, there is no question that, even though there are these gaps (and in some ways because of them), God and Abraham are experienced by the reader in a round and evocative way. We can't help but wonder about their intentions and concerns throughout the narrative. Precisely because we *don't* know the purpose of God's test, we wonder what it might be. Precisely because we are *not* told what is going through Abraham's head as he prepares for the sacrifice, we imagine what he might be feeling and thinking, especially about God, God's command, and Isaac. The story forces us into an experience of interaction and presence — presence indicated through what must be done and through what is done. God is not Abraham's God here because God is omniscient, unchangeable, or reasonable — or even the source of the promise. God evokes God's relationship to Abraham here by calling him. Abraham evokes his relationship to God by responding to the call and performing the actions in the world demanded by that call.

51. Brueggemann, *Genesis*, 193.

Obviously, any discussion of relationship and presence in the world together must examine Isaac and his place in the story. But, before doing this, it is important to consider those who are not present in this story. The *akedah* evokes the missing presence of Ishmael, the unchosen son, through the wording of the command ("take your son, your only son, whom you love, Isaac") and through the repetition of the patterns in Genesis 21 (where, in obedience to the request to cast out Hagar and Ishmael, Abraham "rose early in the morning" and lay the burdens of exile on Hagar's own back). But we and Abraham already know that the missing Ishmael, while unchosen and thus falling outside the covenant, will still become the father of a nation.[52] The other presence missing from Genesis 22 is, of course, Sarah. And if presence is an important feature of what is evoked by this story, then Sarah's exclusion, already a concern for many readers, ancient and contemporary, becomes even more profoundly troubling. The gap where Sarah should be does not just involve her inner state. She is missing in every sense; she goes unmentioned throughout the entire episode. This is not merely the representation of a patriarchal arrangement in which a father sets out to brutally sacrifice the life of his child to a "greater power" with no reference (by God or father/husband or story) to the mother, which would be disturbing enough as a model of faith. If we are to imagine this as a story of "presence," of relationship with God and with the world, then why is a woman, Isaac's mother, not present, excluded from these relationships? And what is the cost of such exclusion? Reading beyond chapter 22 (and interpretively following the suggestion of the ancient rabbis in *Genesis Rabbah*), perhaps the cost is Sarah herself, for, when next we hear of her, we hear of her death. Interestingly, if seen in this way, Sarah's exclusion recalls the exclusion of Hagar that Sarah caused (though the text indicates Hagar survives that "sacrifice" in Genesis 21:21). While it is perhaps not historically surprising that Sarah is not involved in the journey and performance of a sacrificial ritual, the absence is certainly unusual in a narrative that heretofore has been primarily a domestic drama. Sarah, who had been given her own blessing (17:16), who had cooked for the God who appeared to Abraham as three men (18:6), who had overheard the men's/God's declaration that she would have a son and had laughed at these words, who had been directly chastened by God for doing so (18:9-

---

52. The connections between the stories of Ishmael and of Isaac are more complex than I can describe here. For the best work on this subject, including the way these narratives evoke the experience of chosen/unchosen, see Levenson.

15), and whose wishes (regarding Hagar) God had sanctioned, has no presence in the *akedah* and, afterwards, no presence in the (story-)world except as an object of mourning and burial.

Finally, if this story evokes the relationship between God and Abraham in the world, the object of the actions in the world that are demanded by this relationship (namely, Isaac) requires attention. There are countless ambiguities surrounding Isaac as well. Isaac's very existence is orchestrated by God outside the natural course of events; he is conceived by an old and barren Sarah. Both of his parents laugh in disbelief when his conception is announced to them. He is then named (on God's instruction) "Isaac" ("laughs"). Levenson points out that this name insures that "whenever the second patriarch is mentioned, the miraculous circumstances of his conception will be recalled."[53] His name, recalling his parents' disbelief at the possibility of his conception, constantly reminds us that he belongs to God as well as to his parents — that he is the child of supernatural intervention. In my reading of Genesis 22 this name has further repercussions. The son who is to be slaughtered and offered as a burnt sacrifice on God's command was first greeted by his parents with disbelief and, perhaps, joy. And this reaction, Abraham's and then Sarah's laughter, is significant enough that God demands its recollection in the child's name. In what seems to me a subtle irony, Isaac/laughter (almost) dies through the faithful and obedient relationship his father has with the God that granted his conception and gave him his name. In his name the very surprising and joyous gift of his existence is evoked throughout the story of his commanded destruction. And Sarah's relationship to her son, a relationship that began with laughter, ends in separation and her death.

The way we explore the gaps surrounding the characters in the *akedah* is connected to the way we designate these characters and the role we imagine each is playing. Such designations become particularly relevant when exploring the ethical analogies it is possible to draw from in this story. My own reading tends to focus on Abraham as the main human agent. Isaac, then, while clearly also a subject, is the object of Abraham's actions, the "other." Certainly there is a long tradition, evident in ancient midrash, of viewing the story as a trial for Isaac as much as for Abraham. To read the story from the perspective of Isaac is to adopt a powerful interpretive posture. Elie Wiesel once wrote in his own midrash on the story: "The time has come for the storyteller [Wiesel] to confess that he has always felt much

---

53. Levenson, *Death and Resurrection*, 41.

closer to Isaac than to his father, Abraham."[54] This identification makes sense to me, as do readings of Genesis 22 in which the author identifies with the absent Sarah or even the sacrificed lamb.[55] Nonetheless, I continue to read the story as "primarily an ordeal for Abraham"[56] and, more importantly, in my reading I am most interested in Abraham. I suspect this is because I have lived a rather privileged and empowered life. In ethical and religious reflections I do not find myself concerned with finding my voice, reclaiming my presence, or recovering from horrible victimization. Rather, I am confronted with the implications of responsibility for and power over others. So it is Abraham as agent, as actor in the world, that interests me. Interestingly, this identification with Abraham forces attention on Isaac, for it is Isaac who is Abraham's "other" in the events of Genesis 22. From the power and ambiguities surrounding Isaac in this story, a challenging sense of the other arises. As mentioned previously, Isaac, while clearly the object of God's command and Abraham's actions, is also undoubtedly a subject himself, with his own subjectivity, his own destiny, his own (moral) life. So even if this story is read primarily as the story of Abraham's trial, the participation of Isaac, the role and status of the "other," still strongly claims our attention, often through narrative ambiguities.

The overarching ambiguity of Isaac in the *akedah* is the extent of his comprehension and participation. Just as the text refuses to disclose Abraham's motivations, thoughts, and feelings, it refuses to give clear evidence about whether or not Isaac fully understands and/or knowingly cooperates in what his father intends to do. Smaller gaps are apparent here. First there is the ambiguity of Isaac's age: is he a child or a grown man? In *Genesis Rabbah* 58:5 and 56:7-8 the rabbis calculate his age from what is known about Sarah's death and her age at the time of his conception and argue that he is thirty-seven (or, in an alternative calculation, twenty-six). From this, they argue that he must be a full and willing participant in the events, for how could a very elderly father fool and subdue a man in his prime? The inconsistent calculations, however, illustrate the uncertainty of such reckonings. On the other hand, it is often imagined that Isaac is just a child

54. Wiesel, *Messengers of God*, 90.

55. Here I am thinking of the ancient Syriac stories of Sarah discussed by Sebastian Brock, "Genesis 22: Where Was Sarah?" in *Expository Times* 96 (1984): 16-17; and the modern poem of Yehuda Amichi, "The Real Hero," in *The Selected Poetry of Yehuda Amichi*, ed. and trans. Chana Bloch and Stephen Mitchell (Berkeley: University of California Press, 1986, 1996), 156-7.

56. Levenson, *Death and Resurrection*, 142.

in the story — innocent, unsuspecting, perhaps thinking he is going off to study the Torah with his father. The narrative itself does not settle the issue. Isaac is big enough to carry the wood for the fire, but must have it placed upon his back by his father. Does he carry this burden willingly, helping carry out the sacrifice of his own life, or unknowingly? (This action, as pointed out earlier, echoes the carrying of Ishmael by Hagar, and this in turn, illuminates a similar problem in figuring out Ishmael's age — presumably he is over thirteen, the age he was circumcised, and yet he is small enough for Abraham to lay on his mother's shoulder). The lack of clarity regarding age is significant here because it shows that not only are internal states veiled by this story but external (and ethically relevant) facts as well.

Isaac sounds like a child the one time he speaks in this story, at Genesis 22:7: "The fire and the wood are here, but where is the lamb for a burnt offering?" At first, this question seems to indicate a complete lack of suspicion as well as awareness about the purpose of his journey with his father. And Abraham's answer, "God himself will provide the lamb for a burnt offering, my son," does very little to inform him. And yet it is possible to imagine this exchange taking place with less innocence on Isaac's side and more disclosure on Abraham's; the son, knowing or guessing what his father is planning to do, is seeking confirmation or at least acknowledgment from him. And his father gives it to him: "my son, the child God provided, you are to be the lamb." While the first reading is simpler, neither is ruled out by the text. And, as Auerbach points out, by conveying Isaac's question the story presents him as possessing his own subjectivity. In his response to his son, beginning with *"hinnenni,"* Abraham responds to him as such. The exchange between father and son is framed by the report of the two walking on together, or "as one" (*yahdaw*). Often this togetherness is used to demonstrate Isaac's participation with Abraham in obeying God's command (this seems to be why Levenson, for example, describes the second instance of the term as more powerful than the first). And yet, they are together before Isaac asks his question as well as after. This togetherness leaves open whether the participation of Isaac is conscious or unknowing. What is clear is the relationship between the two, father and son. In this passage, the discourse, as well as the description of their walking as one, expresses the concrete presence of each with and to the other, regardless of age, circumstance, awareness, or understanding.

Another uncertain element of Genesis 22 is the actual binding of Isaac — such a distinct and important component of the story that it became the story's name in Jewish tradition (the *akedah*). It is a strange action in that it is not a usual part of ritual sacrifice (though, of course, as Levenson points out, this is our only account of the "procedure" for human sacrifice in the Bible).[57] The binding seems to indicate an unwillingness on Isaac's part or at least a literal restriction of his actual participation. However, it has been interpreted otherwise. In a narrative expansion in *Genesis Rabbah* 56:8, Isaac asks his father to bind him because, though he is willing, he is unsure he will be able to control his body; he might flinch at the last moment and ruin the sacrifice. In this wonderful expansion a rich picture is painted of Isaac's informed consent to the sacrifice as well as a recognition of his possible (human) weakness. Isaac, as hero/other, appears brave and active, yet also self-reflective and a little unsure of himself. Because of all the ambiguities that surround Isaac, this object, the "other" of Abraham's action, emerges as a complex, yet somewhat impenetrable person in his own right. This is underscored at the end of the story. After the *akedah*, we are presented with an Isaac who "is less his father's son than a patriarch in his own right."[58] This is indicated by Isaac's absence from the report in verse 19 of Abraham's return. Before the ordeal, Isaac and Abraham walked as one and now, it seems, Abraham returns without his son. Then, in the genealogy provided at the end of the chapter, Isaac's future with Rebekah is mentioned for the first time (v. 23), implying that Isaac is no longer primarily someone else's son, but a man ready to take a wife. This is one of the paradoxes of Abraham's relationship to and action towards Isaac. Isaac is transformed by this narrative, by these events. No longer is he primarily his father's (beloved son) — not because he has been sacrificed as a burnt offering, but because Isaac has become an agent himself, a primary actor, in traditional terms, a patriarch in his own right, with his own relationship to God.

The study of Genesis 22 presented here thus far has presented some important and challenging ethical ideas. First, the story can be characterized as paradoxically odd and yet crucial — within the patterns and concerns of the larger biblical canon(s) and within the moral theologies of various biblical traditions (including Christian ethics). The story is extraordinarily challenging when read on its own terms as well as ours. Regardless (and perhaps because of) the terrible possibilities it contains and the often harmful and sometimes frightening legacies of its interpretation,

---

57. Levenson, *Death and Resurrection*, 135.
58. Levenson, *Death and Resurrection*, 142.

this narrative demands our attention. That attention, rigorous and imaginative, reveals to us a story that is remarkable in its sparseness and ambiguity. The *akedah* explicitly tells us very little other than that God called upon Abraham who responded, who traveled in the company of his son to Moriah and set about performing the action commanded of him, only to be stopped by God's angel and have the promise renewed. But in this chapter of Genesis the experience of the characters is powerfully evoked by the very gaps the narrator uses to depict them. Our (un-resolvable) interest in their experience creates a more profound experience for us in reading their story. This experience is our own and, as such, is morally significant.

The gaps surrounding all the characters in Genesis 22 are like the ambiguities we sometimes face in our moral lives in acting towards and with others. Reflecting on Isaac as the "other" who is the object of God's command and Abraham's actions elicits several interesting ethical ideas or challenges. First is the vivid and important insistence that Isaac is much more than an object and heir (like Mesha's son). He walks with his father, he carries the wood, he asks a question, and ultimately he is transformed in this story, by these events. The ambiguity surrounding the extent of his knowledge or his willingness to be sacrificed distinguishes him from Jephthah's daughter who, while demanding time and bewailing her fate, clearly articulates her support for her father's performing the vow he made that demands her destruction. Through the ambiguities of age and understanding, the Isaac of Genesis 22 evocatively represents object and subject at the same time — a condition that is similar to all those toward whom we act. The transformation of Isaac is significant as well — signifying the theological, personal, and social value of the "other." Isaac has his own life, purposes, and value that stretch beyond Abraham's action and relationship to him. Isaac is subject to Abraham's actions and also transcends them. Isaac has the status of the "beloved"; he is both under the ultimate power of another and beyond it. As such he and his father are both the object of others (and their actions) and subjects/agents themselves, acting in ways that affect others. Thus, my own identification with Abraham as one who must act, turns over on itself. I am also Isaac.

The ambiguities and possibilities surrounding Isaac challenge simplistic ideas of agent and other, but even when conceived simplistically the "other" is at least acknowledged. Isaac is named and narrated in Genesis 22. But then there are the gaps created by those not in this story — Ishmael and Sarah. Ishmael is Abraham's son, circumcised to God, presumably valued, as the possibility of his expulsion distresses his father. Excluded from this story and from chosenness, firmly and ritually replaced, he un-becomes. No longer "only" or even "first" as Abraham's son, he is uninvolved in this particular horror (though his own story prefigures it) and simultaneously removed from the opportunity to increase in belovedness. The possible consequences of Sarah's exclusion are less direct in the narrative itself but are more starkly devastating. As husband and son walk as one toward the vision of God, Sarah is (narratively) nowhere. When the trial is over, she is dead. Abraham's and Isaac's acts of being present to each other (and God) alone seem to open the possibility of not being fully present to another (Sarah). Even more disturbing, these exclusions remind us that the reality of being chosen, beloved, and favored only has meaning if others are not. The exclusion of Ishmael and Sarah forces examination of this problematic of human ethics. In no way am I claiming here that such exclusion and its consequences are (presented) as a necessary evil. The very real consequences (Sarah's death) and concerns (Abraham's for Ishmael) in the narrative proscribe such a simplistic interpretation. Rather, these characters, missing from this story of presence but strikingly present in the chapters framing it, afford a narrative recognition and exploration of this problem.

While the "gaps" of Sarah and Ishmael are an important consideration in reading Genesis 22, the most challenging ambiguities remain those concerning the characters actually present in the narrative: God's purpose, Abraham's inner state, and Isaac's participation. The text is irresolvable on these points and the ambiguities work simultaneously in two directions; they guide our attention to what is narrated and they awaken our imagination to what is not. When reflecting on the story's participants — God, Abraham, and Isaac — what is narrated is their presence — through speech and response, through vision, through actions. Purposes and motives, thoughts and feelings, remain veiled. But Abraham is called by God, by son, by angel, and in each case he answers, "Hinnenni." God is present in God's call and command, in God's vision, through God's calling off of the sacrifice, and in the renewal of God's promise. Abraham embodies his presence to God through his actions in carrying out God's command and his presence to his son as they walk together. In this walking as one, in his questioning of his father, and his carrying of the wood, Isaac is also present to his father (and to God). By emphasizing these presences, the content of the story can never be forgotten — the context in which these figures exemplify presence to each other is one of horror. God calls Abraham to offer his beloved son as a burnt offering. Abraham's actions are directed towards fulfilling this command, towards the slaughter of

Isaac. Isaac carries the wood that is necessary to his own destruction. Being present to others is portrayed as neither comforting nor easy nor rational, but it is portrayed as significant, powerful, and transformative. Instead of reading this as a narrative that illustrates faithfulness, or a relationship to God and others as a once-and-for-all act of assent of obedience, attention to the text demonstrates the experience of presence as a crucial way God is involved in the world and a crucial way people transform the world. The experience of being present is an experience of vulnerability. Through the command to destroy Isaac, God makes vulnerable the orderly relationship of the covenant. By responding to that command, Abraham relinquishes the concrete possibility of the fulfillment of the promise made to him. In his presence and participation, either knowingly or practically (as a child), Isaac is vulnerable to his own destruction. Through this vulnerability, God interacts with God's people through voice and vision, and God remains with God's people through changing commands, in Abraham's naming of "that place" — "God-(pro)vision," and through the renewal of promises. By relinquishing Isaac, risking the destruction of what has been given to him (this beloved son) and what is promised to him, Abraham makes possible the renewal of the promise and allows Isaac to become a patriarch, to be transformed toward his own unique theological and social destiny. The demands of presence are full of ambiguity and paradox in ways that traditional notions of power and obedience are not. The risks of vulnerability and exclusion always accompany acts of authentic presence. Just as the *akedah* raises concerns evoked by being beloved, it offers ongoing challenges to ideas about what it means and entails to be authentically present to others.

This reading is, however, only one of two ethically interpretive responses emerging from my own experience of ongoing attention to the *akedah*. The first consists of ideas generated by the story itself. But the text's dynamic ambiguity draws our attention to another level of interpretation relevant to Christian ethics. Walter Brueggemann urges that the "expositor must take care to not explain, for it will not be explained." Abraham is "set in the midst" of the contradictions of testing/providing, of divine and human mystery and ambiguity. This may be problematic for moderns but should not be dismissed or explained away because of our own discomfort.[59] Going further, Jon Levenson writes, after quoting Auerbach's famous description of Genesis 22:

59. Brueggemann, *Genesis*, 188-89, 192-93.

It is to be wished that the narrator's reticence about Abraham's and Isaac's "thoughts and feelings" would be honored by the theologians who interpret the story of the aqedah: not that interpretation should be forgone, but that it should respect "the silence and fragmentary speeches" characteristic of the narrative and recognize that the ambiguity that these enhance is to be upheld rather than resolved.[60]

These scholars urge that readers refrain from solving the story, from resolving ambiguities that they view as an intentional part of the narrative itself. Yet this creates another tension, one discernible in Levenson's words: interpretation cannot be "forgone." In working with Genesis 22 readers are faced with, perhaps, an unresolvable story, but also the call or demand to interpret the story in such a way that this narrative matters in our ethical reflection. Further complicating these tensions is the significance of our own theological and ethical commitments in our interpretation of the narrative. Like the rabbis or Philip the Chancellor, every reader has his or her own (and his or her own communities') assumptions — about God, about our traditions of interpretation, about justice between people. These often push our interpretations beyond the most "simple sense" of the story, creating more ambiguities, encouraging us to solve others in particular ways. Some readers will search for ways to interpret this story that uphold theological ideas about God's justice, reasonableness, or (against Brueggemann) consistency. Some readers will pursue interpretive possibilities that maintain the congruency between God's command and human reason. We may find ourselves searching for possible ways to understand and give voice to Sarah's role and fate and thereby challenge patriarchal structures. We may seek to see differences (or connections) between what Abraham did and instances of "child-sacrifice" (construed broadly) in our own world. Genesis 22 is not only a narrative rich with interpretive possibilities, demanding rigorous attention; it is a text that challenges us on many levels.

The recognition of these disturbing challenges was, as suggested in Chapter Four, one of the foremost contributions of Søren Kierkegaard's *Fear and Trembling.* But this treatment moves beyond a modern recognition of the horror of what Abraham is commanded to do into a realization of how that horror is experienced in the ongoing project of reading Genesis 22. Johannes de Silentio's awareness and critical examination of self and

---

60. Levenson, *Death and Resurrection,* 132.

context, as these affect and are affected by reading Genesis 22, afford a powerful presentation of the tensions of Genesis 22 in a post-critical world. The tense, even fractured, situation is resolved in *Fear and Trembling* by separating and ranking theological obedience and ethical action in the world. And while this interpretive idea is influential (not to mention a counter-suggestion to the central proposal of this volume), it is less powerful than the book's portrayal of the experience of reading itself. This experience is portrayed as ongoing, demanding, devastating. And it occurs in and against the context of "our times." Any neat dialectical exchange between reader and text is called into question. This is signaled in the designation "lyric" as well as in the four partial narratives (in pointed contrast to the three stages of dialectical argument) presented in the "Attunement," none of which correlate to the "teleological suspension of the ethical." One is left with the impression that the man's engagement of the text continues beyond the pages of the book.

Kierkegaard's work does more, however, than represent a modern and post-critical interpretive condition. It illustrates the importance of reflecting on the experience of reading itself. In this it accords with the second part of my own interpretive response to the *akedah,* which is to consider the experience of reading Genesis 22 as a morally formative practice. In this second part of our task, we are no longer looking for models or possibilities embodied in the characters and plot of Genesis 22, but rather asking how the experience of reading Genesis 22 affects our moral lives, influences our decisions and actions in the world, and shapes our relationships with others. These questions become even more important considering that the two prominent features of the story (the disturbing content and the ambiguity of the narrative) come together in a particularly vivid experience — an experience depicted in *Fear and Trembling* — as ongoing, demanding, and terrible. This experience, this obligation, is intensified when we cast our inquiry explicitly in terms of the relationship with this text as Bible, as religiously central (and as foundational for critically urgent interreligious reflections).

In his essay, "The Uncommon Reader," George Steiner writes, "To read well is to answer the text, to be answerable to the text, 'answerability' comprising the crucial elements of response and of responsibility."[61] It seems likely that Christian ethicists, *as* Christians, are called to be uncom-

---

61. George Steiner, "The Uncommon Reader," in *No Passion Spent: Essays 1978-1995* (New Haven: Yale University Press, 1996), 6.

mon readers of the *akedah*, as they are called to an uncommon response to other persons. Engaging Genesis 22 not only kindles considerations of our relationship to others through the relationships it presents us, it also calls for reflection on our relationship to the story of the *akedah* itself. The idea that readers are in relationship with the texts that they read, that readers experience texts, especially narratives, in a relational way, has received significant attention in the fields of literature and philosophy in recent decades. While not wishing to elaborate these theories here, applying them to the question of the reading of Genesis 22 in Christian ethics has interesting implications. About twenty years ago, literary critic Wayne Booth entitled one of his important works about ethics and literature *The Company We Keep* because his work partially developed out of the premise that the narratives we read are like the people with whom we spend time. Texts are our companions and they influence us as such, affecting who we are and how we view the world and what we do in it. Reading is thus a morally relevant activity; it forms us.[62] Literary theorist Adam Zachary Newton sees another implication in an analogy between texts and people: "one faces a text as one might face a person." The encounter with a text is one of immediacy, and the immediacy of this contact is prior to meaning, prior to the interpretive moment.[63] When we are readers, stories are present with us; we encounter them and are affected by that encounter in ways that are not strictly cognitive. In this project then, Genesis 22 is that "other" in whose company we find ourselves. It is present in immediate ways and in ongoing reflective ways — through encounters with the text itself, through the relationships/ interpretations of others, through engagement, research, and study, and

---

62. Wayne Booth, *The Company We Keep: An Ethics of Fiction* (Berkeley: University of California Press, 1988). In this second interpretive layer I draw on the work of Wayne Booth, Martha Nussbaum, Adam Zachary Newton, and J. Hillis Miller. While their contributions do not stand alone in this field and have some limitations, these scholars remain useful in projects such as this that attempt to connect reading to ethics. Booth and Nussbaum are popular with other Hebrew Bible scholars interested in exploring the relationship between biblical narrative and the moral life; both are rigorous and sensitive readers and theorists themselves, and articulate their analyses and intuitions of this process and their relevance to ethics in accessible ways.

63. Adam Zachary Newton, *Narrative Ethics* (Cambridge, MA: Harvard University Press, 1995), 11. I owe my awareness of this work to Carol A. Newsom, who draws on these same scholars (Booth, Nussbaum, and Newton) in her reading of the Book of Job in "Narrative Ethics, Character, and the Prose Tale of Job," *Character and Scripture: Moral Formation, Community, and Biblical Interpretation,* ed. William P. Brown (Grand Rapids: Eerdmans, 2002), 121-34.

through the relevance of all these to our lives in the world. These encounters with the text reveal the *akedah* to be a strange "other" — an ancient, ambiguous, and disturbing story whose concerns may not be our own and whose terms and style certainly are not. But in a religious-ethical tradition that views the *akedah* as sacred, we must be readers of it. We must find ourselves in relationship to it. Genesis 22 is a text with "whom" we struggle to be in vital, responsible, and transformative relation.

Because of such analogies between texts and others, literary critic and secular moral philosopher Martha Nussbaum connects the practices of reading and ethics, claiming that reading stories helps develop skills important in relating to others in ethically responsible ways. She claims that morality centers on seeing oneself as one among others, as a being in relationship to other beings. To be in relationship to others, people must be both "observant and observable"; we have to recognize others but also be present to them ourselves. We do this in part by the telling and reading of stories. Thus, awareness of others can be developed through literary sensitivity and interpretation. This sensitivity is not counter to reasoning about the moral life but is, itself, a kind of rationality, demanding critical thought. Defining ethics as "impartial respect for human dignity," Nussbaum argues that its achievement demands developing the ability to enter "imaginatively into the lives of distant others and have emotions related to" them.[64] (A Christian philosopher might cast the meaning of ethics in more theological or traditional terms, perhaps Timothy Jackson's *agape* or "love of neighbor." If an ethics that requires "impartial respect for human dignity" fails without the ability to relate sensitively to distant others, then an ethics that insists on a loving relationship is unimaginable without such skills.) Kierkegaard's portrayal of de Silentio's experience of reading is valuable when re-envisioning Nussbaum's claim in terms of Genesis 22. Through reading, the man described in the "Attunement" journeyed with Abraham, climbed up Mount Moriah over and over with a man who was certainly distant from him — not only worlds and ages away, but distant to comprehension, unfathomable in his uniqueness. Yet instead of distance, the man experienced closeness through reading this story, even without full comprehension. Abraham and Isaac were his neighbors. He felt the awfulness of the events they experienced with immediacy. And through his attempts to read, to understand, and to interpret the

---

64. Martha Nussbaum, *Poetic Justice: The Literary Imagination and Public Life* (Boston: Beacon Press, 1995), preface.

unmediatable Abraham, he had his own analogous experience of relating to the incomprehensible. This ability to enter into the distant lives of this biblical father and son is powerfully realized in *Fear and Trembling*, with its self-conscious "attunement" to the *experience* of reading. But the close identification of the ancient rabbis with the characters of the *akedah* is a predominant (if implicit) feature of *Genesis Rabbah*. And even Philip the Chancellor's more philosophical treatment evokes a deep sense of connection between his view of human beings in the world (reflected in his conception of natural law) and the events and characters of Genesis 22.

This immediacy is all but lost in the contemporary treatments of Genesis 22. Green's comparative look at interpretations keeps a twice-removed distance, preventing entrance into the lives of Abraham or Isaac. While Quinn encourages imagination and sensitivity in order to "plumb the tragic depths" of Genesis 22, he ultimately allows the tragedy to be set aside as "not an actuality." Jackson's essay comes the closest, though perhaps most strongly in its title: "Is Isaac *Our* Neighbor?" (emphasis mine). But Jackson finally reads the narrative as an event of a past that no longer applies, an ethical etiology, a necessary schooling of a way of being that is finally resolved in the love of/on the Cross. Each contemporary treatment locates itself a safe distance away from the narrative, erecting a barrier between contemporary morality and Genesis 22, thus diminishing the reader's power to enter imaginatively into the events and characters of the text and diminishing the text's power to transform the reader.

Another parallel between reading and ethics is the comparable tension between the need to interpret/act and the ongoing nature of the relationship between the reader and the text/other. Interpretive moments must occur, they are the locus of the act of reading itself. And yet engagement of a text like Genesis 22 is an ongoing process — the work of a lifetime (the man in *Fear and Trembling*), or of several generations of teachers and students (*Midrash Rabbah*), or of the collective discernment and refinement of human understanding (the medieval project). If deep engagement rather than assumed mastery consists in part in an ongoing experience of reading the *akedah*, then any given interpretive act falls short of the text itself and yet is necessary in experiencing this relationship. Similarly, interpretation of another person, and actions consistent with that interpretation, will always fall short of fully comprehending the complexity of that person. Nonetheless, actions are absolutely necessary in the moral life and are the lived reality of any relationship. Reading demands interpretation, ethics demand action.

Nussbaum also draws another analogy between the activity of inter-preting stories and the "public reasoning" necessary in leading an ethical life in relationship to others. Such reasoning demands a movement back and forth between personal relationships and broader, more communal discernment of those relations. Booth argues that assessing what we read in community with other readers is an ethically valuable activity — he calls this communal assessment of stories "co-duction."[65] Acts of reading and interpreting Genesis 22 demand both immersion — very personal im-mersion — and critical conversation, comparing what one has read both with one's unfolding experiences and with responses and arguments formed by others in their reading. Acts of reading this text and responding to the experience are, like the moral life, ongoing and communal activities, as well as activities of individual immersion and interpretation. The prac-tice of moving between the personal and the communal is particularly crucial in reading a text like Genesis 22, whose special status is assigned and affirmed by its relationship to religious communities and an ethics that understands itself as part of religious tradition.

While the term is inelegant, Booth's idea of "co-duction" is useful in signifying the crucial role that our communities and traditions play in the process of interpreting the Bible, and it does so in a way that avoids a strict insider/outsider or sectarian understanding of reading and ethical discern-ment and practice. All the treatments, past or contemporary, examined in this volume demonstrate the importance of communities and traditions in interpretation, though the back-and-forth between the personal and the communal is more dynamic in the readings from the history of interpreta-tion. *Genesis Rabbah* and its multivocal presentation vividly evokes the mutual significance of individuals and community. Philip's *quaestio* ac-counts for opposing positions and assumes it contributes to an ongoing and universal refinement of knowledge. *Fear and Trembling* flows between critiques of contemporary philosophy and deeply personal experience, though it eventually distinguishes ethics as the ground of the first and reli-gion as the ground of the second. The back-and-forth between individual readers and their community(-ies) is startlingly diminished in contempo-rary treatments of Genesis 22. Quinn's treatment of Genesis 22 is certainly shaped by wider and shared ideas — from other scholars of "reading" like Nussbaum and from orthodox Christian theology. But in his essay, the reader, the communities, and the text itself are surrendered to ideas and

65. Booth, *Company,* 70-75.

theory. Unlike Philip, with whom Quinn perhaps has the most in common, he fails to evoke the presence of people, of others also engaged in reading and reflecting, behind the objections. In Jackson's treatment, other interpreters are present — most pointedly Kierkegaard and Blake, along with several biblical scholars. But Jackson reads the story so completely through the lens of the Cross that the others he references do not express a community of interpreters so much as represent a theological premise. (Green, of course, writes for and about widely ranging and different communities in his work but is not interested in engaging the text himself as a reader.)

Yvonne Sherwood describes the interpretive situation of pre-critical interpreters of Genesis 22 in this way:

> Could it be that the pre-Enlightenment condition of being Jewish, being Christian, being Muslim before all choice leads to more active and audacious acts of interpreting, deciding, and choosing in complex relation to the text and vocabularies in which one lives, moves, and has one's being?[66]

Religious communities, with their special relationship to the text, were a given for the ancient rabbis and for Philip. Contemporary ideas about autonomy and the choice to be (or not to be) religious tend to suppress dynamic movement between the individual and the communal. One possible way around the modern impasse diagnosed by Sherwood — choice between being "'religious' or 'non-religious' and identify[ing] with (protect[ing]) that choice thereafter" — could be to engage the text through critical tools and the perspectives of our own age. Again, in Levenson's words, such an approach demands that interpreters of the text "be prepared to interpret the text against their own preferences and traditions, in the interest of intellectual honesty," paying attention not only to the text but also to others whose insights differ, precisely because of the importance and complexity of that task. Booth's and Nussbaum's scholarly focus is on literature, where the advantages of diverse communities of interpretation seem obvious. An interpretive community comprised of people who all read a text in the same way, with the same background, and with the same ends, is the least likely to interpret it richly, carefully, and

---

66. Yvonne Sherwood, "Binding-Unbinding: Divided Responses of Judaism, Christianity, and Islam to the 'Sacrifice' of Abraham's Beloved Son," *Journal of the American Academy of Religion* 72 (2004): 856.

transformatively. All the more should Christian ethicists read Genesis 22 in critical conversation with the insights, scholarship, and perspectives of others; the crucial, complex, and challenging nature of the sacred text itself demands that it be engaged with *at least* the tools and possibilities that would be utilized in the interpretation of another great text. Interpretive movement still occurs between individual immersion and ongoing broader communal reflection, but the challenges of a text like Genesis 22 should compel us to reject any sectarian limitations on our readings.

As illustrated in the back-and-forth practice of reading between personal immersion and communal assessment, or the mutual importance of moments of insight and ongoing process, the interpretation of Genesis 22 involves constant balancing acts. For instance, in the engagement of diverse perspectives, one's own religious tradition (and/or discipline) is one among many and yet necessarily unique — unique in being both the occasion for and locus of one's interpretive practice. A Christian ethicist reads Genesis 22 (at least in part) because she is Christian: her concerns are formed (in part) by her religious ethics, and she reads with an assumption that engaging the story of Abraham's near-sacrifice of Isaac contributes to her life, her world, and her tradition. Ongoing engagement of a text like Genesis 22 entails recognizing this, even valuing it, and yet seeking interpretive possibilities from outside one's own tradition. It also entails appreciating and utilizing the best resources available — the insights of biblical scholarship, literary theory, critical theory, and so forth. But these scholarly insights and perspectives are not the only interpretive resources available. From the pulpit, from the media, from artists and writers, readings of Abraham's near-sacrifice of Isaac come from diverse sources in our culture. While it is beyond the scope of this project to examine examples of these readings here, [67] the diversity in styles or forms of interpretation of the *akedah* seems limitless; the way treatments are presented — as we have seen in the lively rabbinic dialogue of *Genesis Rabbah* or the provocative philosophical meditation of *Fear and Trembling* — reflects the richness of the biblical text and the power of the experience of reading it.

A related tension can be experienced in balancing the concurrent needs of rigor and imagination in engaging the *akedah*. The text itself places limitations on our interpretation of it. Careful study helps identify those limitations and thus interpretations can be scrutinized and criticized in

---

67. Yvonne Sherwood has undertaken the work of examining modern and postmodern readings of Genesis 22, in a forthcoming volume.

terms of their attentiveness to the text — to what it says and what it does not say. On the other hand, Genesis 22 not only leaves room for interpretive play but almost compels readers imaginatively to fill in gaps, consider ambiguities, and resolve apparent contradictions. Nussbaum identifies one of the important skills of reading (and ethics) as the ability to enter imaginatively into the lives of others. It is not surprising that Philip Quinn, in an essay influenced by Nussbaum, advocates both attention and imagination in reading Genesis 22. Jackson's essay ("Is Isaac Our Neighbor?"), likewise, expresses its own creative inclinations and appreciation for those of others, particularly Blake.[68] From its very opening, with four partial retellings of the *akedah*, *Fear and Trembling* is memorably creative and evocative. This imaginative side of interpretation has an ancient pedigree in the rabbis. They read Genesis 22 as full of "invitations" to create narrative expansions. And yet their midrash is painstakingly attentive to the text. Nor do these expansions really serve to "close" the gaps or solve the ambiguities, as they themselves usually consist of several equally plausible versions. These ancient interpreters seem to have struck a powerful balance between imagination and rigor — exploring deeply the ambiguities without resolving them, creatively interpreting the text without replacing it.

Finally, ethical interpretation of the *akedah* incorporates negotiating a difficult balance between the reader's concerns and the concerns of text. Biblical scholarship shows the concerns of Genesis 22 as strange to contemporary Christian readers. The establishment of a male heir, the sacrifice of the beloved son, the possession of a particular land, the tangible passing of a blessing, and ritual observance are not the primary terms now used in Christian ethics to describe the challenges of life in the world. Yet to read Genesis 22 attentively involves discovering and applying such ideas to its interpretation. At the same time, the kinds of ethical concerns raised by contemporary readers of this story have their own interpretative significance: responsibility for the innocent; attention to the voiceless; relations between parent and child; rejection of religiously motivated violence. Authentic and ethically transformative engagement between the reader and this text entails taking seriously the moral significance of both sets of concerns in interpretation. In the modern/postmodern world, critical perspectives are profound tools in attempting this mutual engagement of

68. Since Green's work avoids engaging the biblical text itself these concerns are not applicable, though they might be appropriately applied in considering his treatment of Vâlmîki's Râmâyaòa.

sometimes conflicting concerns. The perspectives and approaches provided by historical criticism, literary theory, and critical theory allow readers to appreciate the complexity of both the text and our own ethical assumptions, while recognizing that our own perspectives and our interpretations of Genesis 22 will always be limited.

All of these balances, all of these competing interpreters, communities, approaches, and concerns in reading Genesis 22 are not unlike the tensions encountered in relating ethically to another person. Just as the concerns of the text and those of the reader, however distinct, are both significant and valuable in authentic engagement, so too the concerns we bring to the "other" with whom we are called to be in relationship. Authentic and transformative relationship with others does not entail impressing absolutely our own concerns upon them or accepting theirs without question but rather engaging in true conversation our distinct sets of concerns. This demands rigor in attending to the lived reality of the other, imagination in understanding and relating to the possibilities open to that reality, and effective expression of our own experiences and concerns. In order to relate to another, one must actually be responsible and responsive to who that other is and what her concerns and desires are. For many reasons, then, the practice and experience of reading and interpreting a text, especially a complex and challenging text like Genesis 22, can form, influence, even improve the practice and experience of relating to other people. Nussbaum certainly assumes this to be the case in secular reading and ethics — that the skills of attentive, sensitive, and critical reading are similar to those needed in ethical discernment and action, and that the one activity can help develop the abilities needed for the other. This kind of mutual reinforcement would seem to be even more likely in a religious ethical tradition that identifies a text (the Bible generally, and Genesis 22 in this particular case) as a necessary and authoritative resource for our lives in the world. The approaches taken by Christian ethicists in engaging that text should matter, should influence who they are and what they propose.

There are other aspects of the ethical importance of reading Genesis 22 worth noting here. Both Nussbaum and Newton observe that narratives are irreducible to propositions or "content." Newton views narrative as having the characteristic of an event: it is something that "happens."[69] The meaning of an event is more than the factual information gleaned from observing it. So too with a narrative text: along with whatever proposi-

---

69. Newton, *Narrative Ethics,* 11.

tional content it might have, it also has a direct relationship to its readers as something they experience or encounter. And because such an encounter has an immediacy prior to any reflection on it, it continues to act on us beyond any conclusions or interpretations we may draw from it. If this is the case, than the significance of Genesis 22 for Christian ethics can never be only the propositions or moral ideas generated from it, its evidentiary value in supporting certain theories or systems, or even its critical role in challenging the claims of such theories. Always, and in addition to these possible contributions, the *akedah* narrative demands encounter and ongoing engagement.

Genesis 22 contributes to ethical reflection in another way, as a powerful story of dilemma. Nussbaum draws attention to the importance of the narrative presentation of dilemmas in a moral philosophy that draws on storytelling in a fundamental way; while she is certainly not discussing Christianity or biblical narratives, this seems a fitting application.[70] In reading a story of a moral dilemma, we can explore our responses to such situations in the world, thereby developing a richer self-understanding and a more complex and empathetic recognition of the situation of others.[71] While the experience of reading a story that presents a moral dilemma is not exactly equivalent to the experience of reading the un-resolvable and richly ambiguous *akedah*, such textual encounters function for readers in similar ways. The reader enters into the disturbing and often challenging moral experience of a dilemma, without the pressing practical need to resolve it. A reader of Genesis 22 can involve herself in the experiences of Abraham and Isaac without having to "do as they do." When reading Genesis 22, we travel up the mountain with Abraham and Isaac over and over, but we do not have to decide whether or not to do what Abraham does. We do not even have to fully comprehend it, but we do have to attend to it, to an action and a story that may not make sense or fit our expectations. According to Nussbaum, this experience contributes to the complexity, sophistication, and sensitivity of moral reasoning. It is also analogous to experiences we may sometimes face when encountering another person who, according to our own logic and assumptions, seems nonsensical, whose life and concerns seem un-resolvable. If we model our relationship to that "other" on

---

70. Martha Nussbaum, *Fragility of Goodness, Luck and Ethics in Greek Tragedy and Philosophy* (Cambridge: Cambridge University Press, 1986), 390.

71. Martha Nussbaum, *Love's Knowledge: Essay on Philosophy and Literature* (New York: Oxford University Press, 1990).

our relationship to Genesis 22, then we find ourselves called into engaged and sensitive interaction, without full comprehension.

Nussbaum remarks on another quality of some narratives that suggests fruitful possibilities for reflecting on the relationship between Genesis 22 and Christian ethics. Stories, she observes, are often "subversive." She describes literature as subversive, as morally controversial in its very form. "Good literature is disturbing because it summons powerful emotions, it disconcerts and puzzles. It inspires distrust of conventional pieties and exacts a frequently painful confrontation with one's own thought and intentions."[72] The story of Abraham's near-sacrifice of Isaac is certainly a story capable of disturbing its readers. And critical study of the story reveals it as stranger still, distant from our own ideas about the world and our actions in it. Engagement of the *akedah* critically confronts the reader — her assumptions, intentions, and roles in interpreting the text and in acting in the world. This critical engagement, this trial, calls for the deepening, refining, even modification of our "thought and intentions."

These various insights from literary theory offer productive ways of discussing ethical possibilities of Genesis 22, or more specifically, of the experience of being readers of Genesis 22 — an experience forcefully represented in contemporary Christian ethics consciously indebted to *Fear and Trembling*. Not only does literary theory contribute to ways of articulating the ethical relevance of the relationship between reader and text in this case; it also emphasizes the importance of this engagement, thus preventing propositions, systems, and theories from overriding or substituting for the text itself. And yet Genesis 22 is not *just* great literature for the Christian ethicist, and an immense challenge lies in understanding ways of genuinely accounting for the role of the story as Scripture, that is, as sacred.

Booth claims that "serious" stories are the most powerful form of moral education; moral being, he argues, is in part formed by the stories we hold as important, those stories we really "listen to." [73] This leads him

72. Nussbaum, *Poetic Justice*, 5. She is specifically discussing modern novels but her ideas can apply to other literature as well.

73. Wayne Booth, "'Of the Standard of Moral Taste': Literary Criticism as Moral Inquiry," in *In Face of the Facts: Moral Inquiry in American Scholarship*, ed. Richard Wightman Fox and Robert B. Westbrook (Cambridge: Cambridge University Press, 1998). One of Booth's larger concerns is evaluating the ethical qualities of a text (how a text forms us). But he rejects doing this in any social-scientific way — as, for example, analyzing how people behave after seeing a movie. Instead he says we must ask "What kind of person was implied as

to consider why we read, why we turn the page. He hypothesizes that we read because "we desire" something the text has to offer and thus what we read reflects our desires, choices, and compulsions. Several problems arise if this kind of explanation for engaging the text is applied to Genesis 22. It seems unlikely that a contemporary Christian ethicist would claim that reading the *akedah* satisfies her desires or that she reads the next verse because she wants to know what will happen. Genesis 22 is not a narrative that readily appeals to contemporary sensitivities, cultural or literary. Nor is this familiar story often read because someone desires to find out what happens. Contemporary ethicists are more likely to identify with the man in *Fear and Trembling* who, as a reader, trudged up Mount Moriah again and again, though it left him exhausted, confused, and even devastated. This text demands our continual attention, has a claim on us, even in its very strangeness.

J. Hillis Miller sees reading literature as "a way of being in the material world." Human beings have a "positive need" to experience the "metaworlds" created in literary works and these works then influence "the 'real world' in the effects, often decisive, they have on the belief and behavior of those who read them."[74] Miller argues that the authority secular literature has in human life is in part modeled on the literary authority of the Bible in Western culture. Nonetheless he writes:

> I would hesitate to speak of the Bible as literature. The authority it has been granted as the word of God has far greater force than the authority accorded to secular literature in our culture, great as the latter has been. The reasons to read (or not to read) the story of Abraham and Isaac in Genesis are quite different from the reasons to read (or not to read) Dickens, Wordsworth, Shakespeare, or even Dante and Milton.[75]

The authority Miller describes is that granted the biblical text by churches and states which view the text as "God's word . . . dictated to various scribes and prophetic mediums."[76] While this is a historically accurate

---

the ideal listener to this story?" And even more basically, who is she, what is she like, while reading the story? This same concern is also described in *Company*.

74. J. Hillis Miller, *On Literature*, Thinking in Action Series (London: Routledge, 2002), 80-81.

75. Miller, *On Literature*, 84.

76. Miller, *On Literature*, 85.

(though limited) description of the relationship many people have formed with the biblical text, it is not one that is particularly conducive to the questions here regarding the relationship of the Hebrew Bible to contemporary Christian ethics. This view of relationship (state- or community-enforced authority) or of text (dictation of God's words) is not compatible with modern and postmodern critical perspectives on either the Bible or ourselves. Oddly, in this project at least, engagement of the *akedah* through its reading has much in common with critical reflection on secular literature. Nonetheless, as Booth and Miller point out, our reasons for reading it are not the same. A Christian ethicist *as* a Christian ethicist is not subject to the obligation to be in real relationship with any (particular) piece of secular literature as she is with the Bible. Its status as canon changes her relationship to the text in that it is an obligatory relation. Unlike Booth's readers of literature, she simply cannot choose to end the conversation. Thus, the analogy between reading a text like the *akedah* and relating to the "other" takes on an additional dimension in Christian ethics.

As Miller indicates, the distinctiveness of the relationship between the Hebrew Bible and contemporary Christian ethics certainly lies partially in the role ascribed to the text by readers, communities, and institutions with authority over readers and communities. But there are other factors. Some lie in the character of the text itself. Erich Auerbach describes the claims of biblical narrative to truth (which he distinguishes from realism) as "tyrannical." "The Scripture stories do not, like Homer's, court our favor, they do not flatter us that they may please or enchant us — they seek to subject us." He sees this quality in the way stories like Genesis 22 are told: they are "fraught with 'background' and mysterious," such that they "require subtle investigation and interpretation, [indeed] they demand them." [77] The biblical representation of reality, to use Auerbach's terminology, sees itself as just that: it was not written (canonized, or interpreted) as an alternative or fictional "metaworld" that meets the reader's desires or needs, creating experiences which the reader then brings back to the "real" world. The biblical text, as Auerbach sees it, "seeks to overcome our reality," a task that in the modern world, so removed from that of the Bible, has become problematic. Thus, in its very claims of truth and authority, the biblical text makes necessary "constant interpretive change in its own content" through the demands of engaged attention by its readers (now modern and postmodern). Paradoxically, for readers like Christian

---

77. Auerbach, *Mimesis*, 14-15.

ethicists the authoritative character of the text itself makes the reader's perspectives and concerns essential, even constituent, for its meaning in her world.

Martha Nussbaum, in reading literary characters ethically, articulates this relationship between the reader and the text in a similar way, though her comments are relevant not to the text but to its readers. The power of stories and characters to affect us lies not in the supposed fact that they are "real" but in the fact that we, as far as our understanding of ourselves and others is concerned, are fictional.[78] Human beings know each other through their stories, how they present themselves, how they "read" and comprehend the stories of others. Thus, authentic relationships between people, relationships that are responsive and ethically responsible, are like the relationships between engaged readers and the characters of stories. This analogy shifts in important ways when it is applied to a text (such as Genesis 22) that is viewed by the reader (in this case, a Christian ethicist) as authoritative. Most obviously, the Christian ethicist has an obligation to "read" the text and to do so in ways that are open to the transformative power of that text. And yet, if Auerbach is right, the authority of biblical text makes the concerns and perspectives of the reader crucial rather than extraneous, as they become the means by which she relates to and interprets the text and the reality it conveys. In the post-critical world of "choice" (as described by Sherwood), the Christian ethicist, in being a Christian ethicist, "chooses" to relate to the biblical text, regardless of its strangeness. And for such a reader, it is not the unquestioned universality, perfection, or simplicity of the biblical text, but rather the recognition that we are, at least in part, constructed selves that makes the relationship between ourselves and the story of Abraham's near-sacrifice of Isaac on God's command so powerful that it can change us, and through us, transform the world.

Critical engagement, while certainly recognizing the particularity of every reading of Genesis 22 (and its relationship with others), does not call for or justify relativism in either interpretation or ethics. In fact, part of the ethical promise of our critical methods is that they do not allow the reduction of the text, the other, to be reduced to "what we make of it." From traditional historical criticism to deconstruction and beyond, the reader attempts to engage the text through genuine attention to the text and its possibilities. Approaching the text in these ways presupposes that there is something there, a text, a person (however "constructed" it is itself) that is

---

78. Nussbaum, *Love's Knowledge*, 354-55.

other than us, prior to and beyond what we make of it.[79] Through critical study and engagement we get a sense of this presence. This allows for the evaluation of some interpretations as better than others in their attention to the text. It also shows that no interpretation is equivalent to the text itself (an idea that should be more rather than less appealing to those who view the Hebrew Bible as sacred). Reading critically also demands reading in community, and with the Hebrew Bible that "community" is comprised (in part) by all those who have this sacred text in common.[80] The relationship between readers and text stretches beyond the purely personal, not unlike the rabbinic interpretation of the relationship between what Abraham did on top of Mount Moriah and the rest of their social history. Reading the text is also a shared responsibility with communal consequences. Thus, while the interpretive situation of contemporary Christian ethicists may problematize some ways of relating to a text like Genesis 22 as "authoritative," it also provides new ways of wrestling with the Bible's authoritative status. Critical study and engagement of the *akedah* is not counter to a relationship where the text is understood as authoritative but, rather, necessary to it. Critical perspectives are our means to do the best reading that we can do.

Critically engaging the biblical text as authoritative and complex seems not unlike relating to the other: in Christian ethical traditions, the "other" has claims on us, has authority in our lives, as does the Bible. And like authentic engagement of the *akedah* in a post-critical world, faithful

79. In making these claims, I clearly agree with the views of critics like J. Hillis Miller in characterizing "methods" like deconstruction as "more or less good reading as such." He goes on to say that those who argue that Derrida or Mann asserts that the reader has freedom to make the text mean whatever she says are misreading these philosophers and that "Each in fact has asserted the reverse." See *The Ethics of Reading* (New York: Columbia University Press, 1987), 10. I find myself differing, here, from Gordon J. Wenham, for though the use of critical methods clearly includes attempting to be responsible to the ethical purposes of the "original" author(s)/redactors and their implied readers, I do not agree that a critical theory that emphasizes the role of the (actual) reader makes the interpretive process "entirely subjective" (*Story as Torah: Reading the Old Testament Ethically* [Grand Rapids: Eerdmans, 2000], 1). Attending to the significance of the concerns of the contemporary reader is particularly important for engagement with the Hebrew Bible because of the nature of biblical canon. A contemporary reader who finds herself in ethical disagreement with the implied original readers of the text still struggles to be in transformative relationship with the text.

80. That biblical canons are "shared" is complicated by the fact that authoritative sacred canons are different for Jews, Catholics, and Protestants; the *akedah* is, however, part of the authoritative literature for all three communities.

and responsible relationship to this other involves not only using the resources available to assist us in understanding, but doing so with critical self-awareness. Encountering rather than dismissing or reducing that which is so wholly other than us, and relating to that "other" (even one who seems terrible, nonsensical, un-resolvable) as having extraordinary claims on us, are practices that can be developed through critical engagement of Genesis 22. Relating authentically and transformatively toward others, loving our neighbors, can be understood as giving them critical and ongoing attention, even when they seem incomprehensible. Considering the formative character of "readerly activity" and Genesis 22, Kierkegaard's recollection of Matthew 11:28 seems apt: we labor and are heavy-laden, laden with the burden (of text, of the other), laden with the knowledge that regardless of our pains and ongoing effort, they will remain un-resolved, imperfectly understood, beyond our comprehension. Nonetheless, the "other" demands our attention, makes claims, great claims, on us. Through the practice of reading a text like Genesis 22, perhaps we can learn to recognize and respond to those claims; perhaps we can form habits of response to the other. For Christians, the biblical text claims us, even during its bloodiest and most incomprehensible moments. For Christians, the neighbor, the other, claims us, even during her bloodiest and most incomprehensible moments.

This reading of the *akedah* as the "other" is, of course, another interpretation — as was the reading of Isaac as the "other" that preceded it. It shifted and developed even as I put it into writing: the interpretive moment itself immediately passes, in some sense. I owe awareness of this to post-critical perspectives and to critical conversations with others.[81] And, yet, this interpretation is (ethically) significant in at least two ways. First, it is at this time my best contribution to conversation about Genesis 22 and about our moral lives, one which attempts to engage authentically the biblical story, the insights and scholarship of other readers, and my own concerns. Second, engaging Genesis 22 through this interpretive work has shaped my ideas about the moral life, about the demands of being in authentic relationship to others and what this entails. My reading of this story simultaneously (and perhaps paradoxically) provides ways of understanding those demands while constantly challenging my assumptions

---

81. I mean this literally — for after a recent lecture at Furman University on this reading of the text as "other," a similar point was made by reader-response critic Edgar McKnight.

about them. In continuing to engage (and be engaged by) the biblical text, the aim is not a perfect interpretation or an articulation of the right "ethic" but rather participation in an ongoing relationship.

In the course of this project, conceived as a "case study" in method in Christian ethics, the object of my attention, the *akedah*, transformed the ways I think about others. Beginning with a sense of the inadequacy of the role given to the Hebrew Bible as a (re)source in contemporary Christian ethics, I set out to try to analyze the problem and explore possibilities for re-envisioning that role. In examining three different contemporary ethical works, as different as they are, certain patterns emerged, indicating a general distance from the text itself and a lack of ongoing or authentic engagement. Close reading/study of great treatments of Genesis 22 from the history of interpretation sheds further light on what was at stake here — the powerful mutual relationship between this ancient sacred text in all its complexity and the reader's real historical situation and important moral/theological ideas. It became apparent that if an ethicist claims to be working in a religious tradition (here Christianity) that views the Bible as important or authoritative, the text must be understood as having a transformative role. But such an insistence cannot be a means either to exclude our ethical ideas and reasoning (through a fundamentalist view of the Bible) or to prohibit our critical perspectives on the text (or of ourselves). In contemporary interpretation, our methods, tools, approaches, and pluralistic community of readers are powerful resources for construing a transformative engagement between the biblical text and our ethical scholarship.

But to the methodological and theoretical purposes of this case study the *akedah* added its own demands, and I find now that my reading of the text has overwhelmed methodological concerns in my own reflections. This is not because the interpretive ideas I formed in the course of this study are "right" but rather because it is in this reading that I can see how the time I have spent with this text has (trans)formed my ethics. Over the last few years the text has changed me, given me new ways of being in the world. I find myself asking who is the incomprehensible "other" in my life, and am I attending to her (him, it) with rigor and sensitivity? Am I relating to her as someone existing prior to my own ideas about her and stretching beyond my grasp? Do I grant her a claim on my own life? Do I in this sense recognize her "authority"? And I expect that as I change and the world changes, the way this story challenges me will change also. How? I cannot tell. But I take it for granted that this will happen. Timothy Jackson saw Genesis 22 as a story of Abraham's ethical transformation; in the course of this study I came to see this story as an integral part of my own.

Both interpretive layers of my ethical reading of Genesis 22 involved my concerns regarding the status of the "other" with whom we are in relationship. Suggestive analogies have been drawn between the other and Isaac, and the other and the text itself. An interesting possibility emerges in connecting these two "others," connecting the status of the beloved son, Isaac, with the status of the biblical text. Loving it, favoring it, recognizing it as "sacred" (a text loved by us and belonging to God) carries with it the willingness to "sacrifice" it, "humiliate" it. Subjecting it to our methods and critical perspectives is the counterpart of allowing the text to emerge in our world with its own value and power. These approaches are our means of traveling to the place that God will show, are our means of performing actions necessary to be in relationship to God and others; they are our donkey, our servants, our knife. Often they are frightening; biblical scholarship and critical theory threaten the very ideas, traditions, or faith that bring us to read the text in the first place. Nonetheless, it is through these means, through who we are in our time, place, and scholarship that the *akedah* can be OUR sacred text. It is precisely through these perspectives and the language they provide that the contemporary reader can respond to the call of the *akedah*: "*hinneni*."

References

Amichai, Yehuda. *The Selected Poetry of Yehuda Amichai*. Newly revised and expanded edition. Translated by Chana Bloch and Stephen Mitchell. Berkeley: University of California Press, 1986, 1996.

Auerbach, Erich. *Mimesis: The Representation of Reality in Western Literature*. Translated by Willard R. Trask. Princeton: Princeton University Press, 1953.

Barton, John. *Ethics and the Old Testament*. The 1997 Diocese of British Columbia John Albert Hall Lectures. Harrisburg: Trinity Press International, 1998.

———. *Understanding Old Testament Ethics: Approaches and Explorations*. Louisville: Westminster John Knox Press, 2003.

Birch, Bruce C., and Larry L. Rasmussen. *Bible and Ethics in the Christian Life*. Revised and expanded edition. Minneapolis: Augsburg Press, 1989.

Blenkinsopp, Joseph. *The Pentateuch: An Introduction to the First Five Books of the Bible*. New York: Doubleday, 1992.

Boehm, Omri. "The Binding of Isaac: An Inner-Biblical Polemic on the Question of 'Disobeying' a Manifestly Illegal Order." *Vetus Testamentum* 52 (2002): 1-12.

Booth, Wayne. *The Company We Keep: An Ethics of Fiction*. Berkeley: University of California Press, 1988.

———. "'Of the Standard of Moral Taste': Literary Criticism as Moral Inquiry." In *Face of the Facts: Moral Inquiry in American Scholarship*. Edited by Richard Wightman Fox and Robert B. Westbrook. Woodrow Wilson Series. Cambridge: Cambridge University Press, 1998.

Brock, Sebastian P. "Genesis 22: Where Was Sarah?" *Expository Times* 96 (October 1984): 14-17.

Brown, Alison Leigh. "God, Anxiety, and Female Divinity." *Kierkegaard in Post/Modernity*. Edited by Martin J. Matustik and Merold Westphal. Studies in Continental Thought Series. Bloomington: Indiana University Press, 1995. 66-75.

Brown, William P., ed. *Character and Scripture: Moral Formation, Community, and Biblical Interpretation*. Grand Rapids: Eerdmans, 2002.

Brueggemann, Walter. *Genesis: A Bible Commentary for Teaching and Preaching*. Interpretation Series. Atlanta: John Knox, 1982.

Chenu, M. D. *Toward an Understanding of Saint Thomas*. Chicago: Henry Regnery, 1964.

Dahan, Gilbert. "Genres, Forms and Various Methods in Christian Exegesis of the Middle Ages." *Hebrew Bible / Old Testament: The History of Its Interpretations*. Volume 1: *From the Beginnings to the Middle Ages (Until 1300)*. Edited by Magne Sæbø. Göttingen: Vandenhoeck and Ruprecht, 2000. 196-236.

Freedman, David Noel, ed. *Anchor Bible Dictionary*. New York: Doubleday, 1992.

Grant, Robert M., with David Tracy. *A Short History of the Interpretation of the Bible*. Second edition. Minneapolis: Augsburg Fortress Press, 1984.

Green, Ronald. "Abraham, Isaac, and the Jewish Tradition: An Ethical Reappraisal." *Journal of Religious Ethics* 10 (1982): 1-21.

———. "Christian Ethics: A Jewish Perspective." *The Cambridge Companion to Christian Ethics*. Edited by Robin Gill. Cambridge: Cambridge University Press, 2001. 138-53.

———. "Deciphering *Fear and Trembling*'s Secret Message." *Religious Studies* 22 (1986): 95-111.

———. "Enough Is Enough! *Fear and Trembling* Is Not About Ethics." *Journal of Religious Ethics* 21 (1993): 191-209.

———. *Religion and Moral Reason: A New Method for Comparative Study*. New York: Oxford University Press, 1988.

Genesis Rabbah. Translated by H. Freedman and Maurice Simon. New York: Soncino Press, 1983.

Hall, Amy Laura. "Self-deception, Confusion, and Salvation in *Fear and Trembling* with *Works of Love*." *Journal of Religious Ethics* 28 (2000): 37-61.

Hays, Richard B. *The Moral Vision of the New Testament*. Edinburgh: T&T Clark, 1997.

Jackson, Timothy. "Is Isaac Kierkegaard's Neighbor: Fear and Trembling in Light of William Blake and *Works of Love*." *Annual of the Society of Christian Ethics* 17 (1997): 97-119.

———. *Love Disconsoled: Meditations on Christian Charity*. Cambridge Studies in Religious and Critical Thought Series. Cambridge: Cambridge University Press, 1999.

Kierkegaard, Søren. *Fear and Trembling: A Dialectical Lyric by Johannes de Silentio*. Translated by Alastair Hannay. London: Penguin, 1985.

Kugel, James. *In Potiphar's House: The Interpretive Life of Biblical Texts*. Cambridge: Harvard University Press, 1990.

———, and Rowan A. Greer. *Early Biblical Interpretation*. Philadelphia: Westminster, 1986.

Lee, Jung. "Abraham in a Different Voice: Rereading *Fear and Trembling* with Care." *Religious Studies* 36 (2000): 377-400.

Levenson, Jon. *Death and Resurrection of the Beloved Son: The Transformation of Child Sacrifice in Judaism and Christianity.* New Haven: Yale University Press, 1993.

Mackey, Louis. *Kierkegaard: A Kind of Poet.* Philadelphia: University of Pennsylvania Press, 1971.

Matustik, Martin J., and Merold Westphal, eds. *Kierkegaard in Post/Modernity.* Studies in Continental Thought Series. Bloomington: Indiana University Press, 1995.

Miller, J. Hillis. *The Ethics of Reading.* New York: Columbia University Press, 1987.

―――. *On Literature.* Thinking in Action Series. London: Routledge, 2002.

Mooney, Edward F. "Art, Deed, and System: The Prefaces to *Fear and Trembling.*" *The International Kierkegaard Commentary* 6: *Fear and Trembling and Repetition.* Edited by Robert L. Perkins. Macon: Mercer University Press, 1993. 67-100.

Neusner, Jacob. *Genesis Rabbah, The Judaic Commentary to the Book of Genesis, A New Translation.* Volume 2. Brown University Judaic Studies 104. Atlanta: Scholar's Press, 1985.

Newmark, Kevin. "Between Hegel and Kierkegaard." *Søren Kierkegaard.* Edited by Harold Bloom. New York: Chelsea House, 1989. 219-31.

Newsom, Carol A. "Narrative Ethics, Character, and the Prose Tale of Job." *Character and Scripture: Moral Formation, Community, and Biblical Interpretation.* Edited by William P. Brown. Grand Rapids: Eerdmans, 2002. 121-34.

Newton, Adam Zachary. *Narrative Ethics.* Cambridge, MA: Harvard University Press, 1995.

Nussbaum, Martha. *Fragility of Goodness, Luck and Ethics in Greek Tragedy and Philosophy.* Cambridge: Cambridge University Press, 1986.

―――. *Love's Knowledge: Essays on Philosophy and Literature.* New York: Oxford University Press, 1990.

―――. *Poetic Justice: The Literary Imagination and Public Life.* Boston: Beacon, 1995.

Otto, Eckart. *Theologische Ethik des Alten Testaments.* Stuttgart: Kohlhammer, 1994.

Philip the Chancellor. *Summa de bono.* Excerpted by Odon Lottin. *Le Droit Naturel chez Saint Thomas d'Aquin et ses prédécesseurs.* Translated by Jean Porter. Second edition. Brussels: Bayaert, 1931, 111-114.

Preminger, Alex, and T. V. F. Brogan, eds. *The New Princeton Encyclopedia of Poetry and Poetics.* Princeton: Princeton University Press, 1993.

Quinn, Philip. "Agamemnon and Abraham: The Tragic Dilemma of Kierkegaard's Knight of Faith." *The Journal of Literature and Theology* 41 (July 1990): 182-93.

―――. "Moral Obligation, Religious Demand, and Practical Conflict." *Rational-*

ity, Religious Belief, and Moral Commitment. Edited by Robert Audi and William J. Wainwright. Ithaca and London: Cornell University Press, 1986.

Ricoeur, Paul. "Kierkegaard and Evil." *Søren Kierkegaard.* Edited by Harold Bloom. Modern Critical Views Series. New York: Chelsea House, 1989. 40-58.

Rodd, Cyril. *Glimpses of a Strange Land: Studies in Old Testament Ethics.* Edinburgh: T&T Clark, 2001.

Rogerson, John. *Theory and Practice in Old Testament Ethics.* Edited by Daniel Carroll. London: T&T Clark, 2004.

Sherwood, Yvonne. "Binding-Unbinding: Divided Responses of Judaism, Christianity, and Islam to the 'Sacrifice' of Abraham's Beloved Son." *Journal of the American Academy of Religion* 72 (2004): 821-61.

————, ed. *Derrida's Bible (Reading a Page of Scripture with a Little Help from Derrida).* New York: Palgrave Macmillan, 2004.

Sinnott-Armstrong, Walter. *Moral Dilemmas.* Oxford: Basil Blackwell, 1988.

Spiegel, Shalom. *The Last Trial: On the Legends and Lore of the Command to Abraham to Offer Isaac as a Sacrifice: The Akedah.* Translated by Judah Goldin. New York: Pantheon, 1967.

Southern, R. W. *Scholastic Humanism and the Unification of Europe.* Volume 1: *Foundations.* Oxford: Blackwell, 1995.

Steiner, George. "The Uncommon Reader." *No Passion Spent: Essays 1978-1995.* New Haven: Yale University Press, 1996.

Stern, David. *Midrash and Theory: Ancient Jewish Exegesis and Contemporary Literary Theory.* Rethinking Theory Series. Evanston: Northwestern University Press, 1996.

Sternberg, Meir. *The Poetics of Biblical Narrative: Ideological Literature and the Drama of Reading.* Bloomington: Indiana University Press, 1987.

Taylor, Mark C. *Kierkegaard's Pseudonymous Authorship: A Study of Time and the Self.* Princeton: Princeton University Press, 1975.

von Rad, Gerhard. *Old Testament Theology: The Theology of Israel's Historical Traditions.* Volume 1. Translated by D. M. G. Stalker. New York: Harper and Brothers, 1962.

Wenham, Gordon. "The Akedah: A Paradigm of Sacrifice." *Pomegranates and Golden Bells: Studies in Honor of Jacob Milgrom.* Edited by David P. Wright, David N. Freedman, and Avi Hurvitz. Winona Lake: Eisenbrauns, 1995. 93-102.

————. "The Gap Between Law and Ethics." *Journal of Jewish Studies* 48 (1997): 17-29.

————. *Story as Torah: Reading the Old Testament Ethically.* Grand Rapids: Baker Academic, 2000.

Wiesel, Elie. *Messengers of God: Biblical Portraits and Legends.* Translated by Marion Wiesel. New York: Summit Books, 1976.

Wilson, Robert R. "Sources and Methods in the Study of Ancient Israelite Ethics." *Semeia* 66 (1994): 55-63.

Index

Abraham's dilemma, 23, 48-56, 65, 72-73, 182

Agamemnon, 50-55, 74, 149

Agape, 24, 56-59, 62, 69-71, 175. *See also* Love

Aquinas. *See* Thomas Aquinas

Auerbach, Erich, 4-5, 137, 156-60, 167, 171, 185-86

Augustine, 39

Authority, 13-16, 27, 93-97, 101-2, 104-5, 107-12, 184-89; of Bible for ethics, 7, 11-19, 36-37, 72-73, 104-17, 133-34, 138, 181, 184-89; of biblical text, 11, 14-16, 19, 27, 36-37, 45, 72-73, 92, 97-99, 104-5, 107, 109, 111-15, 126, 129-34, 138, 181, 184-89; of God, 30, 66, 93-97, 101-2, 104-5, 117, 147; of interpretations/commentaries, 13, 32, 36-37, 45, 72-73, 98, 104-5, 108, 111, 114-15, 123-26, 129-32, 135; of law, 93-97, 101-4

Barr, James, 16

Barton, John, 7-12

Bernard of Clairvaux, 95, 104-5, 108-9, 131

Biblical criticism, 7, 10; historical criticism, 10-13, 16, 21, 28-29, 63-64, 144-47, 155-57, 181, 186; literary criticism, 11-13, 28, 88-89, 136-38, 155-59; rhetorical criticism, 11

Birch, Bruce, 15-18

Blake, William, 58-66, 71, 74, 108, 145, 178, 180

Blenkinsopp, Joseph, 155-56

Booth, Wayne, 12, 18, 174, 177-78, 183, 185

Brueggemann, Walter, 162-63, 171-72

Calvin, John, 41

Canon, 13-17, 133, 136-39, 144, 147-48, 157, 185

Christian ethics, 5-7, 14-22, 23-25, 43, 55-58, 62-63, 80-81; challenges for, 5-7, 12-15, 17, 19-21, 23-24, 43-44, 48, 55-57, 68-69, 71-74, 112, 135-39, 147-48, 168-69, 171-74, 178-89; role of Hebrew Bible in, 5-7, 11, 14-24, 30, 55-58, 63, 68-69, 71-74, 80-81, 91-92, 107-13, 147, 157, 178-89

Community, 15, 17-18, 177-78, 187; character and community formation, 15-16, 18, 21; interpretive, 128, 131-32, 178; reading in community, 177-78, 187-89

Conflicting requirements, 20-21, 26, 30-32, 40-42, 48-58, 62-64, 73, 95-96, 98-107, 110-11, 141-43, 152, 171, 180-81

Contradictions in biblical texts, 8, 14, 33, 130-31; between God's command and God's promises, 73, 141, 143-44, 152

Derrida's Bible (Sherwood), 3-4, 19, 21

De Silentio, Johannes, 58, 61-66, 80-91, 109-10, 129, 132-34, 143, 161, 172-73, 175-76. *See also* Kierkegaard, Søren

Detachment/distance from text, 6, 20, 23-24, 30, 45, 48, 72, 137, 176, 183, 189

Divine command, 27, 30-41, 49-54, 57-58, 73, 91-96, 102-4, 147, 150, 162; to Abraham, 20, 30-33, 35, 37-38, 40-42, 49-54, 58, 61-65, 83-85, 95-99, 101, 119-20, 125-26, 128, 139-43, 150, 152-55, 159-72, 186; ethics, 30, 40, 43, 97; and human reason, 30, 35, 94-103, 105-7, 109-10, 172; moral content and nature of, 31, 35, 37-38, 42, 52-54, 61-63, 67-70, 73, 93, 97, 100-102, 104-5, 112, 116; and natural law, 8, 99-103, 106-7; reasonableness of, 35, 39-41, 93-97, 100-103, 105, 109, 119; tradition(s), 27, 30, 35-36

Engagement of text, 6-7, 11, 18-19, 23-25, 67, 72-73, 79-80, 87, 90-91, 103-4, 109, 131-39, 147-48, 154-57, 173-89; ongoing relationship, 91, 109, 131-37, 172-79, 182, 189. *See also* Experience of reading

Ethical ideals, 12-14

Experience of reading, 4-7, 10-17, 44-45, 55-56, 81-82, 84-87, 90-91, 109-10, 113, 132-34, 139, 157, 160-61, 163, 171-90; as morally relevant, 7, 10-19, 56, 73-75, 79, 109, 113, 132-34, 169, 171-77, 182-85, 188-90; power of, 4-5, 11, 19, 90, 132-35, 138, 153; rereading and retelling, 7, 24, 44, 46, 71, 74-75, 79-80, 91, 109; as transformative, 89-90, 132-34, 139, 170-71, 174-81, 186-90. *See also* Power, Transformation, and Engagement of text

Faith, 17, 30, 35, 38-42, 54, 62-65, 69, 81-91, 103, 118, 121-24, 133-34, 154, 161-64, 190; of Abraham, 30, 38-39, 41, 43, 62, 65, 69, 81-91, 118, 123-24, 143, 161-66; biblical, 29-30, 39-40, 46, 97; and morality, 39-42, 45; and reason, 30, 35, 40-42, 88, 134

Faithfulness, 41, 118-19, 123-24, 128, 165, 171, 187-88. *See also* Faith: of Abraham

Genesis Rabbah 55, 22, 36, 45, 113-34, 151, 160, 164, 166, 168, 176-79

Green, Ronald, 23-48, 55, 57-60, 65, 72-74, 79, 92-98, 106-8, 111-14, 119, 122, 126-29, 133, 137, 176, 178

Hall, Amy Laura, 84-85, 89-90

Hannay, Alistair, 85, 88

Hays, Richard, 13

Jackson, Timothy, 23, 48, 56-74, 79, 92-94, 99, 103, 105-8, 111-12, 128-29, 131-32, 137-38, 145, 160-62, 175-76, 178, 180

Justice, 60-62, 66-72, 93, 96-98, 101-2, 109, 116-17, 122, 128-30, 133, 143, 172; of God, 41, 43, 93-94, 96, 98, 102, 105, 116-17, 119, 121-22, 125, 129, 162, 172

Kant, Immanuel, 43

Kierkegaard, Søren, 21, 28, 31, 33, 38-39, 42-43, 45, 49-52, 54-55, 58, 61-65, 70-71, 74, 79-92, 99, 107, 111, 113-15, 129-30, 132-35, 143, 161, 172, 175, 178, 188. *See also* de Silentio, Johannes

Kugel, James, 44, 131, 158, 160

Levenson, Jon, 138-55, 161-68, 171-72, 178

Literary theory, 12-13, 88-89, 136-38, 155-59, 179-86

Love, 56-73, 81-82, 94, 103, 111-12, 128-29, 175-76, 188

Luther, Martin, 41-42

Mackey, Louis, 89

Midrash, 22, 31, 34, 36-37, 44, 60, 79, 114-15, 119-20, 122, 124-26, 128-31, 133, 162, 165, 176, 180

Miller, J. Hillis, 184-85

Mooney, Edward, 85

Moral order, 35, 38, 41, 60-61

Moral reasoning, 25-27, 30-32, 35, 41-43, 45-47, 54, 92, 95, 109, 111-13, 137, 175, 182, 189; deep structure of, 25-27, 30-31, 34-35, 37-38, 40, 42-43, 45, 72-73

Narrative ethics, 14, 18, 21
Natural law, 8-9, 40, 94-96, 98-103, 105-7, 109, 130, 132-33, 176
Newmark, Kevin, 86
Newsom, Carol A., 18, 66-67
Norms, 8-12, 14, 30, 57, 136
Nussbaum, Martha, 10, 12, 18, 49, 51, 54, 174-75, 177-78, 180-83, 186

Obedience, 8-9, 42, 57-58, 93, 101, 120-21, 144, 150, 171-73; of Abraham, 33, 38, 41-42, 49-51, 68-69, 99, 101-2, 105, 120-21, 126, 129, 142-43, 150-53, 161, 163-67
Old Testament ethics, 8-13
Origen, 39
Outka, Gene, 57

Philip the Chancellor, 21, 79, 91-96, 98-115, 130-33, 135, 137, 161, 172, 176-78
Philo of Alexandria, 33
Poole, Roger, 89
Power, 58, 60-63, 68, 141, 146, 156, 160-67, 172-76, 179-80, 186-90; of God, 40, 93-96, 141-42

Quinn, Philip, 23, 48-58, 69, 71-74, 107, 111-12, 128-29, 137, 156, 163, 176-78, 180

Rabbi Eleazar, 122
Rabbi Jose ben Rabbi Hanina, 122
Rabbi Leazar, 124
Ramsey, Paul, 57
Rasmussen, Larry, 15-18
Reason, 8, 25, 30-31, 37, 40, 42-43, 62, 94-101, 103-10, 130, 133-34, 172; and faith, 40-42, 45-46, 62, 88, 133-34; moral reason, 26, 37, 39-40, 46, 97, 109. *See also* Revelation

Religious ethics, 25-26, 37, 43, 73, 113-14, 138, 179
Religious reasoning, 23, 25-27, 30-31, 34, 36, 45, 72, 79, 128
Resurrection, 33-34, 38, 41, 64-65, 68-69, 95, 103, 128, 143
Revelation, 27-31; and moral reason, 31, 35-37, 39-41, 43, 94-95, 97-98, 112
Ricoeur, Paul, 90
Righteousness, 31, 33, 42, 46, 93, 116, 143, 159; of Abraham, 33, 39, 93, 117-18, 122, 125, 127-29; God's, 37-38, 42-43, 69-70, 162
Role of characters, 9-10, 54, 74, 84-85, 90, 130, 156-60, 163, 165, 169-73, 176, 186

Scotus, John Duns, 40-41
Sherwood, Yvonne, 3-5, 19, 114, 132-33, 178-79, 186
Sin, 14, 34-35, 40-43, 57, 83-84, 93, 96-97, 128
Speiser, E. A., 70
Spiegel, Shalom, 145
Status of Bible. *See* Authority
Steiner, George, 173
Sternberg, Meir, 158, 161, 163
Supersessionism, 13-14, 69-71, 103, 148

Thomas Aquinas, 39-40, 57, 92-98, 103, 106
Transformation, 60-61, 63-64, 66, 68-72, 128-34, 160-61, 168-71, 181-90

Vâlmîki's *Râmâyaòa*, 46-47, 180
Von Rad, Gerhard, 140, 143, 151-52, 155, 162

Wenham, Gordon, 11-14, 21
Wiesel, Elie, 162, 165
Wilson, Robert R., 21
Wright, David P., 61